William Lempriere

A Tour from Gibraltar to Tangier, Sallee, Mogodore, Santa Cruz, and Tarudant

And thence over Mount Atlas to Morocco; including a particular account of the royal harem

William Lempriere

A Tour from Gibraltar to Tangier, Sallee, Mogodore, Santa Cruz, and Tarudant
And thence over Mount Atlas to Morocco; including a particular account of the royal harem

ISBN/EAN: 9783337318543

Printed in Europe, USA, Canada, Australia, Japan

Cover: Foto ©Andreas Hilbeck / pixelio.de

More available books at **www.hansebooks.com**

TOUR

FROM

GIBRAL[TAR]

TO

TANGIER,
SALLEE,
MOGODORE,

AND T[HE]

OVER MOUNT ATL[AS]

INCLU[DING]

A PARTICULA[R]

OF TH[E]

ROYAL HA[REM]

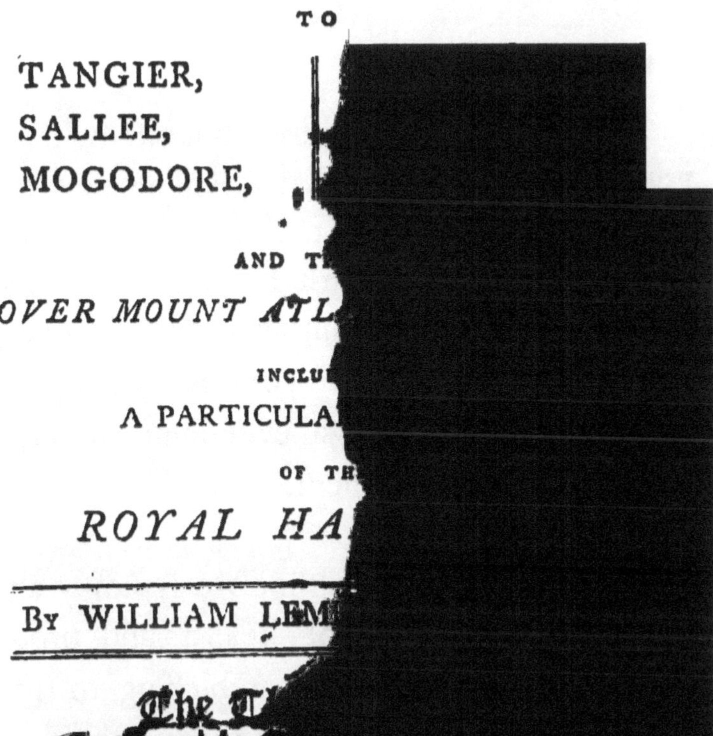

By WILLIAM LEM[PRIERE]

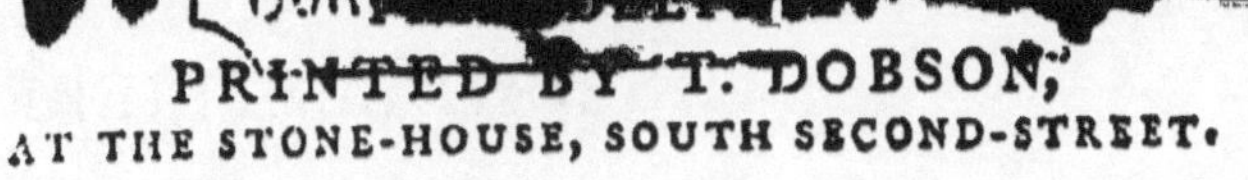

PRINTED BY T. DOBSON,
AT THE STONE-HOUSE, SOUTH SECOND-STREET.

TO

His Royal Highnefs Prince Edward.

━━━━━━

SIR,

THE diftinguifhed honour which your Royal Highnefs has been pleafed to confer upon me, by taking under your auguft protection the firft Effay of a young Author, is a fingular inftance of the benevolence and liberality of your Royal Highnefs's difpofition, and will ever command my warmeft acknowledgments.

That your Royal Highnefs may enjoy an uninterrupted courfe of health and profperity, and long continue a bleffing to the Britifh Nation, and an honour to the fervice, is the fincere wifh of

Your Royal Highnefs's

Moft grateful fervant,

WILLIAM LEMPRIERE.

ADVERTISEMENT.

THE Author cannot help feeling himſelf under an obligation of apologiſing for the frequent egotiſms, which appear in the courſe of the following narrative, and for the ſhare of it which his adventures neceſſarily occupy. The reader will only have the goodneſs to bear in mind, that theſe tranſactions are detailed merely with a view of throwing light upon the character of the people, and the court, which he has undertaken to deſcribe; and in this view, he humbly conceives that they ſerve better to illuſtrate the manners and diſpoſitions of the Moors, than the moſt laboured diſquiſitions.

CONTENTS.

CONTENTS.

CHAP. I.

CHAP. II.

CHAP. III.

CHAP. VII.

CHAP. VIII.

CHAP. IX.

CHAP XIII.

CHAP. XIV.

A

TOUR, &c.

CHAP. I.

Motives of the Author for undertaking this Tour.—Sails from Gibraltar.—Arrival at TANGIER.*—Description of that Place.—Departure for* TARUDANT.*—Instance of Tyranny exercised upon a Jew.—State of the Country and Roads.—Mode of living on these Journies.—Description of* ARZILLA.*—Moorish Luxury.—Application from a Variety of Patients.—Arrival at* LARACHE.

IN the month of September 1789 a request was forwarded through Mr. Matra, the British consul general at TANGIER, to his excellency General O'Hara at Gibraltar, from Muley Absulem, the late emperor of Morocco's favourite son, the purport of which was, to intreat his excellency to send a medical gentleman from the garrison to attend the prince, whose health was at that time in a dangerous and declining state.

As the term MULEY will frequently occur in the succeeding pages, it may not be improper to state in this place, that it is a title of honour, which is confined to the *royal family* of Morocco, and is equivalent to that of lord, or rather *prince*, in our language.

B

The

The promifes of Muley Abfulem to the conful were fplendid and encouraging. The perfon who was to be fent on this expedition was to be protected from every indignity, and to be treated with the utmoft refpect. He was to receive a liberal reward for his profeffional exertions; his expences during his journey, and while he ftaid in the country were to be punctually defrayed; and he was to be fent back without delay, whenever his prefence fhould be required at the garrifon. But the moft flattering circumftance which attended this requifition of the Moorifh prince was, the releafe of certain Chriftian captives who were at that period detained in flavery. Thefe unfortunate perfons confifted of the mafter of an Englifh veffel trading to Africa, and nine feamen, who had been wrecked upon that part of the coaft which is inhabited by the wild Arabs, and were carried into flavery by that favage and mercilefs people.

How far thefe brilliant affurances were fulfilled, will appear in the courfe of the following narrative. It is fufficient for the prefent to obferve, that, influenced by the faith which the inhabitants of Europe are accuftomed to place in the profeffions of perfons of rank and dignity, and ftill more impelled by that impetuous curiofity which is natural to youth, I was eafily perfuaded to embrace the opportunity of vifiting a region fo little known to European travellers, and to undertake this fingular, and (as it was generally regarded) extremely hazardous fervice.

However difappointed I may have been in my hopes of pecuniary advantage and emolument, ftill

I can-

I cannot at this moment regret my rafhnefs, as it was confidered by many. In the courfe of my vifit I had opportunities which no European had ever enjoyed of becoming acquainted with the manners, policy, cuftoms, and character of this fingular people. The fanctity of the royal harem itfelf was laid open to my infpection. Even the dangers which I encountered, and the anxious apprehenfions which I occafionally experienced, I can now reflect upon with a degree of emotion which is not unpleafant. The notes which I made upon the fpot I had the pleafure to find proved interefting and entertaining to a number of my friends. By their perfuafions I have been encouraged to lay them before the public; and my only and earneft wifh is, that the reader may not find his curiofity difappointed, his attention wearied, or his judgment difgufted, by the adventures and obfervations, which, with the moft perfect confcioufnefs of my own inability as a writer, I fubmit to his infpection.

The neceffary preliminaries being fettled, and the baggage of a foldier requiring no great preparation, I embarked at Gibraltar the 14th September 1789, on board a fmall veffel, and in fix hours arrived at Tangier, where I immediately waited on Mr. Matra, whofe polite reception and kind offices during the fix months that I fpent in Barbary, claim, and ever will command, my warmeft acknowledgements.

I foon learned that my intended patient was, by his father's command, at the time of my arrival, at the head of an army in the mountains between Morocco and Tarudant, which obliged me to remain at Tangier, till we received certain intelligence of the prince's return to Tarudant, his ufual place of refidence.

It would be difficult to determine whether furprize or regret was moft predominant in my mind upon my arrival in this country. The diftance is fo trifling, and the tranfition fo fudden, that I at firft could fcarcely perfuade myfelf that I was out of Europe, till I was convinced to the contrary by the wonderful difference of people and manners which immediately prefented itfelf on my entering Tangier. Civilization in moft other countries owes its origin to a commercial intercourfe with foreign nations; and there are few parts of the world, however diftant or uninformed, whofe inhabitants have not, in fome way or other, fallen into the manners of thofe foreigners by whom they are vifited. But here this circumftance feems to have had not the fmalleft effect; for though fituated only eight leagues from Europe, in the habit of a conftant communication with its inhabitants, and enjoying the advantage of a number of foreigners refiding in the place, yet the people of Tangier ftill retain the fame uncultivated manners, the fame averfion to every kind of mental improvement by which the Moors have for ages paft been fo juftly characterized.

It is well known that the the town and fortrefs of TANGIER formerly conftituted a part of the foreign dominions of Great Britain. While in the poffeffion of the Englifh it was a place of confiderable ftrength, but when it was evacuated by the orders of Charles II. the fortifications were demolifhed, and only the veftiges of them are now

vifible

viſible.　There is at preſent only a ſmall fort in tolerable repair, which is ſituated at the northern extremity of the town, and a battery of a few guns which fronts the bay.　From theſe circumſtances it is evident that it could make only a very weak reſiſtance againſt any powerful attack.

The town, which occupies a very ſmall ſpace of ground, and affords nothing remarkable, is built upon an eminence which appears to riſe out of the ſea, and is ſurrounded with a wall.　The land for a ſmall diſtance round it is laid out into vineyards, orchards, and corn-fields, beyond which are tracts of ſand, with lofty and barren hills.　The ſituation is therefore far from beautiful or agreeable. The houſes are in general mean and ill furniſhed, the roofs are quite flat, and both theſe and the walls are entirely whitened over; the apartments are all on the ground floor, as there is no ſecond ſtory.

Contrary to the uſual cuſtom in Barbary, the Moors and Jews live intermixed at TANGIER, and maintain a more friendly intercourſe than elſewhere in this quarter of the globe.　The Jews alſo, inſtead of going bare-footed by compulſion, as at Morocco, Tarudant, and many other places, are only required to do it when paſſing a ſtreet where there is a moſque or a ſanctuary.

The foreign conſuls (except the French who has a houſe at Sallee) reſide at Tangier.　Before the reign of the late emperor Sidi Mahomet, they were allowed to live at Tetuan, a town greatly preferable to Tangier, as well on account of the inhabitants being more civiziled, as of the beauty of the adjacent country.　A ſingular cir-

　　　　　　　　cumſtance

cumſtance occaſioned the expulſion of the Chriſtians from that pleaſant retreat:—An European
gentleman was amuſing himſelf with ſhooting at
ſome birds in the vicinity of the town, and accidentally wounded an old Mooriſh woman, who
unfortunately happened to be within reach of the
ſhot. Upon this accident the late emperor ſwore
by his beard that no Chriſtian ſhould ever again
enter the town of Tetuan. It may be neceſſary
to inform the reader that this oath (by the beard)
is held by the Moors in ſuch ſolemn eſtimation,
that they are rarely obſerved to violate it, nor was
the late emperor ever known to diſregard it in a
ſingle inſtance.

The ſituation of conſuls, indeed, in this diſtant
and uncivilized country, is by no means to be en-
vied; and the recompence which ſhould induce
men of liberal education to ſacrifice their native
comforts and advantages to ſuch a ſyſtem of life as
is required here, ought not to be trifling. They can
form no ſociety but among themſelves; and even
the univerſally allowed law of nations is frequent-
inſufficient to protect their perſons from inſult.
Subject to the caprice of an emperor whoſe conduct
is regulated by no law, and whoſe mind is governed by no fixed principle, they are often ordered up
to court, and after experiencing a very tedious,
fatiguing and expenſive journey, they are frequently ſent back again without having effected the
ſmalleſt point to the advantage of their own country, ſometimes indeed without even being informed
of the purpoſe of their journey.

As an alleviation to ſo unſociable a life, the
Engliſh, Swediſh, and Daniſh conſuls have erected
country

country houses at a small distance from Tangier, where they occasionally retire, and enjoy those amusements which the country affords. These are chiefly gardening, fishing, and hunting. From the plenty of game of every kind with which the country abounds, and and a total freedom from any restriction with respect to it (for there are no game laws in this empire) they give a full scope to the pleasures of the field, and endeavour by those means to procure a substitute for the want of friendly and cheerful society.

On the northern side of Tangier is the castle, which though very extensive, lies half in ruins. It has a royal treasury, and is the residence of the governor. Near the water-side are storehouses for the refitting of vessels, and at this port many of the emperor's row-gallies are built. A number of them also are generally laid up here, when not engaged in actual service. Indeed, from its convenient situation with respect to the Straits, this is the best sea-port that he has for employing to advantage these small vessels.

The bay is sufficiently spacious, but it is dangerous for shipping in a strong easterly wind. The most secure place for anchorage is on the eastern part of the bay, about half a mile from shore, in a line with the round tower and the Spanish consul's house, which makes a very conspicuous appearance from the bay.

On the southern side of the bay is the river, where, before it was choaked up with sand-banks, the emperor used to winter his large ships, which he is now obliged to send to Larache. Most of the rivers in the emperor's dominions, which were

B 4

formerly

formerly navigable, and well calculated for the the fitting out of veſſels, and for the laying of them up in ſafety, have now their mouths ſo continually filling with ſand, that in a courſe of years ſmall fiſhing boats only will be able to enter them. It has often occurred to me, that an enquiry into the ſtate of the emperor's navy, and in particular into the inconvenience of his harbours, might be an objeçt of ſome conſequence to the different European powers, who now condeſcend to pay a moſt diſgraceful tribute to this ſhadow of imperial dignity.

Over the river of Tangier are the ruins of an ancient bridge, ſuppoſed to have been erected by the Romans. The centre of it only is deſtroyed, and that does not ſeem to be the effeçt of time. It more probably was pulled down by the Moors, for the purpoſe of permitting their veſſels to enter the river. The remainder of it is entire, and by its thickneſs and ſolidity it evinces the excellence of the ancient architeçts, and ſhews that ſtrength, as well as beauty, made a conſiderable part of their ſtudy.

As I propoſe in a future part of this Narrative to deſcribe very particularly the architeçture, houſes, furniture, &c. in this country, I ſhall conclude my account of Tangier by obſerving, that in time of peace it carries on a ſmall trade with Gibraltar and the neighbouring coaſt of Spain, by ſupplying thoſe places with proviſions, and receiving in return European commodities of almoſt every kind.

In a fortnight after my arrival at Tangier the conſul received a letter from the prince, informing him of his return to Tarudant, and of his

wiſh

wish that the English surgeon might be dispatched to him immediately. Previous to my departure, however, it became neceſſary to conſider what was required for the journey.

Two horſemen of the Black or Negro cavalry, armed with long muſkets and ſabres, were diſpatched by the prince to eſcort me, and had been waiting for that purpoſe for ſome time. The governor of the town had orders to ſupply me with a tent, mules, and an interpreter. But it was not without much difficulty that a perſon could be found in Tangier who could ſpeak the English and Arabic languages ſufficiently well to perform that office; and it was owing to an accident that I at length was enabled to obtain one.

After ſearching the whole town in vain, the governor ordered, during the Jewiſh hour of prayer, that enquiries ſhould be made among all the ſynagogues for a perſon who underſtood both languages. An unfortunate Jew, whoſe occupation was that of ſelling fruit about the ſtreets at Gibraltar, and who had come to Tangier merely to ſpend a few days with his wife and family during a Jewiſh feſtival, being unacquainted with the intent of the enquiry, unguardedly anſwered in the affirmative. Without further ceremony the poor man was dragged away from his friends and home, and conſtrained by force to accompany me.

Of the mode in this deſpotic government of ſeizing perſons at the arbitrary pleaſure of a governor, an Engliſhman can ſcarcely form an idea. Three or four luſty Moors, with large clubs in their hands, graſp the wretched and defenceleſs

B 5.   victim

victim with as much energy as if he were an
Hercules, from whom they expected the moft formidable refiftance, and half fhake him to death
before they deliver him up to the fuperior power.—Such was exactly the fituation of my unfortunate interpreter.

From the fudden and abrupt manner in which he
was hurried away, in the midft of his devotions,
the women immediately took the alarm, flew in
a body to the houfe of the conful, and with fhrieks
and lamentations endeavoured to prevail on him
to get the man excufed from his journey. The
immenfe diftance, and the ill treatment which they
knew was offered to Jews by the Moors, when
not under fome civilized controul, were certainly
fufficient motives for this alarm on the part of the
women. Upon the conful's affuring them, however, that the wife fhould be taken care of, and
the hufband fent back without any expence to him
on our arrival at Mogodore, where I was to be
furnifhed with another interpreter, and upon my
promifing to protect the Jew from infult, and, if
he behaved well, to reward him for his trouble,
the women immediately difperfed, and returned
home apparently fatisfied.

When this bufinefs was completed, the conful
furnifhed me with a proper quantity of liquors,
two days provifions, a beadftead formed by three
folding ftools, for the conveniency of packing
it on the mules, with proper cooking utenfils, and
an oil-fkin cafe to carry my bedding. The whole
of my equipage, therefore, confifted of two Negro
foldiers, a Jewifh interpreter, one faddle-mule

for

for myfelf, and another for him, two baggage-mules, and a Moorifh muleteer on foot to take care of them.

On the 30th of September, at three in the afternoon, we fet out on our journey; and at fix the fame evening arrived at a fmall village about eight miles from Tangier, named Hyn Dalia, where we flept that night. The country through which we paffed, after quitting the neighbourhood of Tangier, was barren and mountainous, with fcarcely any inhabitants; and it countinued fo the whole way to Larache, only a few miferable hamlets prefenting themfelves occafionally to our view. The villages throughout this empire confift of huts rudely conftructed of ftones, earth, and canes, covered with thatch, and enclofed with thick and high hedges. This defcription exactly applies to that which received us on the firft evening of our expedition.

So careful had the governor of Tangier been in executing his commiffion, and fo attentive to the accommodation of the perfon who was to reftore health to his royal mafter's favourite fon, that upon examining my tent, it was found fo full of holes, and in every refpect fo out of order, that I was obliged to place my bed under a hedge, and make ufe of my tattered tent as a fide covering.

After fpending the night in this fingular fituation, we proceeded on our journey at half paft feven in the morning, and in an hour after croffed the river Marha, which was nearly dry; though I was informed that after the heavy rains it is deep and dangerous to be forded. In a wet feafon,

when

the rivers are fwelled, travellers are frequently detained for feveral days upon their banks. There are in fact but very few bridges in this country, fo that, except at the fea-ports, where they have boats, there is no method of paffing ftreams which are too deep to be forded, except by fwimming, or by the ufe of rafts.

At ten we entered a thick and extenfive foreft, named Rabe a Clow. From its fituation on a high mountain, from the rocky and difficult afcent, and from the diftant view of the ocean through the openings of the trees, this foreft prefented to us an uncommonly wild, romantic, and, I may with truth fay, a fublime appearance. From this profpect, however, our attention was in a great meafure diverted by the miferable road over which we now found we were to pafs, extending for the moft part over fteep mountains and craggy rocks. On this account we were obliged to ride very flow, and with the greateft caution.

At eleven we croffed another river, called Machira la chef, running at the bottom of this elevated foreft, which, though the feafon was dry, was rather deep. Here the eye was agreeably refrefhed, by a fine champaigne country, and a good road before us. On this we continued until we arrived at a rivulet with fome trees growing at a fmall diftance from its margin. At noon I fixed upon the moft fhady fpot I could find, and, agreeably to the Moorifh fafhion, fat down crofs-legged on the grafs and dined.

As the dreffing of victuals would have retarded us too much on our journey, I always made a point of having fomething prepared the night before

fore to eat cold the following day.   Such repasts in fresco were agreeable enough, when wholesome and palatable water could be procured; but very frequently that was far from being the case.   In many places it was so muddy and offensive, that, though extremely thirsty, I could not drink it unless corrected with wine.

Except in the large towns, no provisions could be procured but fowls and eggs; with these, which I had been before accustomed to esteem as delicacies, I now began to be satiated and disgusted.   My usual supper upon my rout was a cup of strong coffee and a toast, which I found much more refreshing than animal food.   Every morning I breakfasted upon the same, and experienced the invigorating effects of this beverage, by its enabling me to support the fatigues of the day.

After pursuing our course for about two hours, we arrived at the river Lorifa, where we were detained an hour by the height of the tide.   The uncertainty and unevenness of the bottom, and the number of large stones which lie in the channel of this river, render it at all times unsafe to be passed.   This circumstance we very sensibly experienced; for when the tide permitted us to make the attempt, though we had men on foot for the purpose of guiding our beasts, still by their striking against the stones, and by their sudden plunges into deep holes, we were continually thrown forward upon their necks.

Hardiness and dexterity are, perhaps, the first among the few advantages which uncivilized nations enjoy.   It was amusing in this place to observe a number of Moors, who were travelling on foot, pull off their cloaths, place them commodioufly on their heads, and immediately fwim acrofs the ftream.

In the evening we reached Arzilla, where, in confequence of the fervice in which I was engaged, application was made by the foldiers to the Alcaide, or governor of the town, to procure me a lodging. Arzilla is eleven hours journey, or about thirty miles diftant from Tangier: for the Moors compute diftances by hours; and as the pace of their mules is at the rate of three miles an hour, the length of a journey is generally calculated in this way with fufficient accuracy.

The apartment affigned me was a miferable room in the caftle, without any windows, and receiving light from a door-way (for there was no door) and from three holes in the wall about fix inches fquare. This caftle covers a large fpace of ground; and though it is now in a very ruinous condition, appears to have been a building erected formerly in a fuperior ftile of Moorifh grandeur.

The town is a fmall fea-port upon the Atlantic ocean. It was once in the poffeffion of the Portugueze, and was at that time a place of ftrength; but through the indolence and caprice of the Moorifh princes its fortifications have been fince neglected, and its walls are rapidly decaying in almoft every part. The houfes have a miferable appearance, and the inhabitants, who confift of a few Moors and Jews, live in a ftate of the moft perfect poverty.

The reader may form fome idea of the manners of this country, by imagining me and my interpreter

ter at one end of the room, as above defcribed, drinking coffee; and at the other, the muleteer and the foldiers enjoying themfelves over a large bowl of Cufcafou, which they were devouring with all the fervour of an excellent appetite, and in the primitive fafhion, that is with their fingers. This fpecies of food is very common among the Moors, who have a tradition that it was invented by their prophet Mahomet, at a time when he could obtain neither fleep nor fubfiftence. It is their principal treat to all foreign minifters, and travellers of diftinction who vifit the country. It confifts of bits of pafte about the fize of rice, crumbled into an earthen colander, and cooked by the fteam of boiled meat and vegetables. The whole is then put into an earthen difh, and butter and fpices added to it. The difh is ferved up in a wooden tray, with a cover of palmetto leaves plaited together.

About an hour after my arrival the governor, and feveral of the principal Moors, paid me a vifit, and brought me, in compliment to my royal patient, a prefent of fruit, eggs, and fowls. After a converfation of about half an hour, during which many compliments paffed on both fides, my vifitors took their leave, and we all retired to reft.

As the report was rapidly and extenfively circulated that a Chriftian furgeon was arrived in the town, I found myfelf vifited very early in the morning by a number of patients, whofe cafes were in general truly deplorable. Many of thefe objects were afflicted with total blindnefs, white fwellings, inveterate chronical rheumatifms, and
dropfies.

dropfies. It was in vain to affure thefe unfortunate and ignorant people that their complaints
were beyond the reach of medicine. All I could
allege gained not the fmalleft credit; a Chriftian
doctor, they afferted, could cure every malady,
and repeatedly offered me their hands to feel their
pulfe; for difeafes of every kind in this country,
it feems, are to be difcovered merely by an application to the pulfe.

From the urgent importunities of my patients,
who all wifhed to be attended to at the fame time,
I was at firft at a lofs how to proceed; however,
I found myfelf under the neceffity of ordering my
guards to keep off the crowd, and permit one only
to confult me at a time. It was truly diftreffing
to obferve fo many objects of real mifery before me,
without having it in my power to adminifter that
relief for which they appeared fo anxious, and
which they were fo confident of obtaining. Though
moft of their complaints appeared to be incurable,
yet had my time permitted I fhould have experienced the moft heart-felt pleafure in exerting
every means in my power to alleviate their fuffer-
ings. Circumftanced as I was, I could only recommend them medicines which could have but a
temporary effect, and which ferved rather to
fend them away fatisfied than to afford a permanent relief.

In the mean time the governor had been paying
attention to the bad condition of my tent, and by
ordering the worft parts to be cut out, and the
reft to be patched, had reduced it fo much in
fize that he had fcarcely left room for myfelf and
interpreter with difficulty to creep into it.

At

At eight o'clock the same morning, October 2d, we began our route for the city of Larache, about twenty-two miles from Arzilla, and arrived there the same day about four in the afternoon. Our journey thither was principally on the beach, so that but little occurred which was worthy of observation. Before we could enter the town, we were ferried over the river Luccos, which in this part is about half a mile in breadth, and after many beautiful meanders falls into the ocean at Larache.

CHAP.

CHAP. II.

Description of LARACHE.——*Application from a Number of Patients.*——*Diseases of the Country.*——*State of Medical Science in* MOROCCO.——*Curious Ruin.*——*Beautiful Country.*——*Encampments of the Arabs.*——*Manners and Customs of this singular People.*——*Oppression of the People.*——*Instances*——*Mode of fishing in the Lakes.*——*Sanctuaries.*——*Moorish Saints.*——*Anecdotes illustrative of this Subject.*——*Journey from* MAMORA *to* SALLEE.

IMMEDIATELY on my arrival at Larache I was introduced to the Alcaide or governor, whom I found to be a very handsome black. He shewed me great attention, and placed me in a very decent apartment in the castle, which is in a state totally different from that of Arzilla.

Larache formerly belonged to the Spaniards; it has tolerably neat buildings, and is of a moderate extent. This city is situated at the mouth of the river Luccos, upon an easy descent to the sea. The agreeable windings of the river, the clusters of date and various other trees irregularly disposed, and the gentle risings of the ground, have a most picturesque effect; which, aided by the reflection that your are contemplating the pure works of nature, unassisted or undeformed by art, cannot fail to inspire the most pleasing sensations.

The town, though not regularly fortified, possesses one fort and two batteries in good repair. The streets are paved, and there is a decent market-place with stone piazzas. This city indeed on the whole exhibits a much cleaner and neater appear-

ance

ance than any town which I visited in Barbary, Mogodore excepted.

At the port vessels are refitted and supplied with stores, though there are no docks nor conveniencies for building large ships. From the depth and security of the river the emperor is induced to lay up his large vessels at Larache during the winter season. It indeed is the only port which he possesses that can answer that purpose. It is however probable, that this river in process of time will be subject to the same inconvenience as that of Tangier, owing to the accumulation of sand, which already has produced a bar at its entrance, of which the annual increase is very perceptible.

As one of my mules had fallen lame, I continued the whole of the following day at LARACHE, with a view of exchanging him; but to my great mortification was not able to succeed in the attempt. During a great part of the day my room was so filled with patients that it might with great propriety be compared to an infirmary, and that not one of the least considerable.

The diseases that I observed to be most prevalent, were the hydrocele; violent inflammmations in the eyes, very frequently terminating in blindness; the itch, combined with inveterate leprous affections; dropsies, and white swellings. I also observed a few intermittent and billious fevers, and frequently complaints of the stomach, arising from indigestion. Though this country has in a few instances been visited by the plague, yet that disease by no means is so prevalent here as in the Eastern parts of Barbary, which are more contiguous

tiguous to Turkey, whence it is fuppofed ufually to proceed.

The caufe of the hydrocele fo frequently occurring in this country feems to be in a great meafure the loofe drefs of the Moors, and the great relaxation which is induced by the warmth of the climate*. The ophthalmy, or inflammation of the eyes, is evidently occafioned by their being expofed to the reflection of the fun from the houfes, which are univerfally whitened over. To this inconvenience the Moors are more particularly fubject, from their drefs not being calculated to keep off the rays of the fun, and from no perfon being allowed the ufe of an umbrella except the emperor.

The leprous affection appears to be hereditary, for I was informed that it has been frequently traced back from one family to another for feveral generations, and it has all the appearance of being the true leprofy of the antients. It breaks out in great blotches over the whole body, in fome few forming one continual fore, which frequently heals up, and at ftated times breaks out afrefh, but is never thoroughly cured. During my refidence at Morocco, I had frequent opportunities of trying a variety of remedies for this complaint, but I never fucceeded further than a temporary cure, for upon difcontinuing the medicines the difeafe was certain to return. The white fwellings and dropfies probably arife from poor living; three

* The medical reader will probably fee a further caufe for the frequency of this complaint, in the great indulgence which the Moors allow themfelves in certain pleafures, and the application of the warm bath immediately after.

parts

parts of the people feldom having any other kind of provifion than coarfe bread, fruit, and vegetables.

With refpect to the ftate of medical and chirurgical knowledge in this country, it is very limited indeed. They have, however, their practitioners in phyfic, both Moors and Jews, who have gone through the form of fitting themfelves for the profeffion, which chiefly confifts in felecting from the antient Arabic manufcripts that remain in the country fome fimple remedies, which they afterwards apply, as well as they are able, to various diftempers.

Their methods of treating diforders are, bleeding, cupping, fcarifying, fomentations, and giving internally decoctions of herbs. Some are bold enough in the hydrocele to let out the water with a lancet ; and there are thofe who even couch for the cataract. I never had an opportunity of feeing the operation of couching performed in Barbary, but I was introduced to a Moor at the city of Morocco, who told me that he had performed it, and fhewed me the inftrument which he ufed for the purpofe. This was a piece of thick brafs wire, terminating gradually at one end in a point not very fharp.

The Moors chiefly depend upon topical remedies, and feldom make ufe of internal medicines. Being ftrangers to the manner in which they are to operate, they feem to entertain no favourable opinion of their efficacy. It is indeed almoft impoffible to perfuade them that a medicine received into the ftomach can relieve complaints in the head or extremities. It is but juftice, however, to add,

that

that I never knew them object to any thing that I adminiftered, provided I clearly explained to them the manner in which they were to be benefited by it. From thefe obfervations, and from the frequent recourfe which the Mahometans have to charms and amulets, it appears that, notwith-ftanding their belief in predeftination, they are not averfe to the ufe of means for the removal of diforders.

Of the number who applied to me for relief at Larache, none appeared to exhibit the leaft fenfe of gratitude except one; the reft behaved as if they thought they did me a greater favour by afking my advice, than I conferred on them by giving it. The perfon to whom I allude, as being fo different in his conduct from the reft, was an old Moor of fome diftinction in the place, who defired me to come to his houfe and vifit a fick friend, with which requeft I immediately complied. The man for this trifling attention was fo uncommonly grate-ful, that reflecting on the place where I was, and on the treatment I had already experienced, I was aftonifhed and gratified beyound expreffion. After fending to my apartment a large fupply of poultry and fruit, the ufual prefent of the country, he waited on me himfelf, and affured me, that while he lived he fhould never forget the favour which I had done him; at the fame time infifting upon my making ufe of his houfe as my own upon my return. As this was the principal inftance of this very fingular virtue among the Moors, which I expe-rienced during my whole tour in Barbary, I have thought it my duty to be particular in mentioning the circumftance.

On

On the 4th of October, at fix in the morning, we left Larache, and at ten paffed the river Clough, a fmall ftream. At four in the afternoon we came to the ruins of a large caftle, faid to have been built fome hundred years ago, by a Moor of diftinction, named Dar Corefy, who was put to death by the then reigning emperor, and his caftle deftroyed. Moft of the caftles and other public buildings indeed, which I faw in this empire, afforded ftrong marks of having fuffered more from the hands of the tyrant, than from the injuries of time.

I have already mentioned the beautiful profpects in the country adjacent to Larache: thofe in the road from that city to Mamora were not lefs delightful. We travelled among trees of various kinds, fo agreeably arranged that the place had more the appearance of a park than of an uncultivated country. We croffed over plains which, without the aid of the hufbandman, were rich in verdure; and we had a view of lakes which extended many miles in length, the fides of which were lined with Arab encampments, and their furfaces covered with innumerable water-fowl. The finenefs of the day greatly added to the pleafure I received from thefe variegated fcenes, which are not unworthy the pencil of the ableft artift.

At half paft four in the aftenoon we arrived at the firft of thefe lakes, and pitched our tent in the centre of one of the encampments.

Thefe encampments are generally at a very confiderable diftance from the cities and towns; the villages, on the other hand, are commonly quite in the vicinity of fome town. The encampment confifts of broad tents, conftructed either of the

leaves

leaves of the palmetto, or of camels hair. Some of them are supported by canes, and others are fixed by pegs. The form of an Arab tent is in some degree similar to a tomb, or the keel of a ship reversed. They are dyed black, are broad, and very low. The tent of the Shaik or governor is considerably larger than any of the others, and is placed in a conspicuous part of the camp. These camps are named by the Arabs Douhars, and the number of tents in them vary according to the proportion of people in the tribe or family. Some of the Douhars contain only four or five, while others consist of near a hundred. The camp forms either a complete circle or an oblong square, but the first is more common. The cattle, which are left to graze at large in the day, are carefully secured within the boundaries at night.

In all the camps the tents are closed on the North side, and are quite open on the South, by which means they escape the cold Northerly winds, so prevalent in this country during the winter season.

The Arabs who inhabit these encampments are in many respects a very different race of people from the Moors who inhabit the towns. The latter, from being in general more affluent, from their intercourse with Europeans, and from their different education, have introduced luxuries, and imbibed ideas, of which the others are entirely ignorant. From their strong family attachments indeed, as well as from their inveterate prejudices in favour of antient customs, these tribes of Arabs appear to be at a vast distance from a state of civilization. As this singular people associate con-

tinually

tinually in tribes, their marriages are confined to their own family; and so strict are they in the observance of this attachment, that they will not permit a person who is not in some degree related to them to inhabit the same camp with themselves.

The husband, wife, and children all sleep in the same tent, commonly on a pallet of sheep-skins, but sometimes on the bare ground. The children remain with their parents till they marry, when the friends of each party are obliged to provide them with a tent, a stone hand-mill to grind their corn, a basket, a wooden bowl, and two earthen dishes, which constitute the whole of their furniture. Besides these they have, however, a marriage portion, which consists of a certain number of camels, horses, cows, sheep, and goats, with a proportionable quantity of wheat and barley: and by grazing and cultivating the neighbouring ground they gradually increase their stock. The Arabs have seldom more than one wife. Their women, who are in general the very opposite to every idea of beauty, do not, like those who inhabit the towns, conceal their faces in the presence of strangers.

Each camp is under the direction of a SHAIK, to whom the rest apply for redress whenever they feel themselves aggrieved. This governor is invested with the power of inflicting any punishment which he may think proper, short of death. He is appointed by the emperor, and is in general the Arab who possesses the greatest property.

As they are generally at a distance from any mosque where they can exercise their religion, an empty tent is allotted for the purposes of worship,

C

which

which is placed in the centre of the camp, and which at the same time serves for the nightly abode of any traveller who may pass that way; and those who take shelter in it are provided with a good supper, at the expence of the whole association. Within this tent all the children assemble every morning an hour before day-break, before a large wood fire, which is made on the outside, and learn their prayers, which are written in Arabic characters on boards, and are always hanging up in the tent. The learning to read the few prayers which are on these boards, and to commit them to memory, is the only education to which the Arabs in general ever attain.

The unsettled turn of these people has conferred upon them the appellation of wandering Arabs. As soon as the land which surrounds them becomes less productive, and their cattle have devoured all the pasture, they strike their tents, and move on to some more fertile spot, till necessity again compels them to retire. I met one of these tribes upon their march, and observed that not only their camels, horses, and mules, but also their bulls and cows, were laden with their tents, implements of agriculture, wives and children, &c.

In the empire of Morocco all landed property, except what is immediately connected with towns, belongs to the emperor. The Arabs, therefore, when they wish to change their situation, are obliged to procure a licence from him, or at least from the bashaw of the province, allowing them to take possession of any particular spot of ground; and in consideration of this indulgence they pay the emperor a proportion of its produce.

The

The treatment which I experienced from thefe people was kind and hofpitable, betraying no figns of that inclination to impofe upon ftrangers, which fo ftrongly mark the character of the inhabitants of the towns.. As foon as my tent was pitched, numbers flocked round it, but apparently more from curiofity than from any intention of offending. On the contrary, they appeared exceedingly defirous to do every thing in their power for my accommodation.

The drefs of the men confifts of a long coarfe frock, made of undyed wool, which is girt about the waift, and is called a Cafhove. In addition to this they wear the Haick, which is a piece of ftuff feveral yards in length, made either of wool, or wool and cotton. This, when they go abroad, they ufe as a cloak, throwing it over the whole of the under-drefs in a carelefs manner, the upper part ferving to cover their head. They wear their hair cut quite clofe, ufe no turban, cap, nor ftockings, and feldom even wear flippers.

The drefs of the women is nearly the fame, differing only in the mode of putting on the Cafhove, which is fo contrived as to form a bag on their backs, for the purpofe of carrying their children; and this they are able to do, and perform all the drudgery of the family at the fame time. Their hair, which is black, is worn in different plaits, and is covered with a handkerchief tied clofe to their head. They are very fond of gold and filver trinkets when they can obtain them, and none of them are without a number of bead necklaces. Their children go quite naked till the age of nine or ten, when they are initiated in the drudgery of their parents.

The mode of living amongſt theſe people is much the ſame as that of the Moors in towns, cuſcoſou being their principal diet. Beſides this, however, they eat camels and foxes fleſh, and ſometimes even cats have fallen victims to their voracity. They uſe barley bread, which is prepared without yeaſt or leaven, and baken in an earthen diſh in the ſhape of a cake.

The complexion of the Arabs is a dark brown, or rather olive-colour. Their features, from their more active life, have ſtronger expreſſion and fewer marks of effeminacy than thoſe of the Moors in towns. Their eyes are black, and their teeth in general white and regular.

The ill effects of ſtrong family prejudices, and of that narrow and excluſive diſpoſition which accompanies them, is ſtrongly marked in theſe little ſocieties. Every camp beholds its neighbour with deteſtation or contempt. Perpetual feuds ariſe between the inhabitants of each, and too commonly are productive of bloodſhed, and the moſt extravagant outrages. When one of theſe unfortunate conteſts proceeds to open acts of violence, it ſeldom terminates till the emperor has taken a ſhare in the diſpute. Whoever is the author, he at leaſt generally derives advantage from theſe diſſenſions; for, independent of the corporal puniſhment which he inflicts, he alſo impoſes heavy fines upon the contending tribes, which proves the moſt effectual mode of pacifying the combatants.

Beſides what the emperor gains in this way, which is frequently conſiderable, he likewiſe receives

ceives annually the tenth of every article of confumption which is the produce of the country; he alfo fometimes exacts an extraordinary impoft, anfwering in value to about the fortieth part of every article they poffefs, which is levied for the purpofe of fupporting his troops. Befides thefe levies, thefe unfortunate people are liable to any other exaction which his caprice may direct him to impofe upon them, from a plea of pretended or real neceffity. The firft tax (the tenth) is paid either in corn and cattle, or in money. The other is always paid in corn and cattle.

The mode practifed by the emperor for extorting money from his fubjects is very fimple and expeditious. He fends orders to the bafhaw or governor of the province to pay him the fum he wants within a limited time. The bafhaw immediately collects it, and fometimes double the fum, as a reward to his own induftry, from the Alcaides of the towns and Shaiks of the encampments in the province which he commands. The example of the bafhaw is not loft upon thefe officers, who take care to compenfate their own trouble with equal liberality from the pockets of the fubjects; fo that by means of this chain of defpotifm, which defcends from the emperor to the meaneft officer, the wretched people generally pay about four times the taxes which the emperor receives—fo little gainers are arbitrary monarchs by the oppreffion of the public! The exactions indeed have been fometimes fo fevere, that the Arabs have pofitively refufed to fatisfy the emperor's demands, and have obliged him to fend a party of foldiers to enforce them. Whenever he is forced to this extremity,

the

the foldiers never fail to give full fcope to their love of plunder.

When a ftranger fleeps in one of thefe camps, he refts in the moft perfect fafety; for if he lofes the leaft article, or is in any refpect injured, all the Arabs of the camp become anfwerable for it. So that a foreigner travels with much greater fecurity under the protection of government in this empire, than among the nations of Europe which are more civilized.

The lakes in this part of the world furnifh great plenty of water-fowl and eels. The manner of catching the latter being in fome degree curious, I fhall trefpafs upon the reader's patience while I endeavour to give fome account of it.

A fort of fkiff, about fix feet long and two broad, is formed of bundles of reeds and rufhes, rudely joined together, leaving only fufficient room to contain one man. The fkiff gradually narrows off towards the head, where it terminates in a point, which is bent upwards in a manner fimilar to the turn of a fcate. It is guided and managed entirely by one long pole, and from its lightnefs is capable of very quick motion. For the immediate purpofe of taking the eels, a number of ftrong canes are fixed together, with a barbed iron in each, and with this inftrument, as foon as the eels are obferved in the water, the man immediately ftrikes at them with great dexterity, and generally with fuccefs.

Almoft the whole employment of the Arabs confifts in the tillage of the ground adjacent to their camps, and in the grazing of their cattle. The grounds at a diftance from the lakes, by the burning

ing

ing of the stubble in the autumn, and a slight turning up of the earth with a wooden plough-share,
produce good crops of barley and wheat; and by
these means the Arabs procure not only sufficient
for their consumption, but are even enabled to
bring a part for sale to the neighbouring markets.
Near the marshes and lakes their flocks and herds
find a very rich pasture, which from the number
of every species which I observed, added in no
small degree to the beauty of the romantic scene.

With respect to their markets, they have spots
of ground fixed upon for that purpose within a
few hours ride of their habitations, where once
a week all the neighbouring Arabs transport their
cattle, poultry, fruit, and corn, to be disposed of,
and sometimes meet with a good sale from the
Moorish merchants, who come from the town to
purchase cattle and grain.

Were the emperor to allow a free exportation
of corn, with moderate duties, and to permit the
people to enjoy what they earn, exacting only the
tax allowed him by the Koran, of a tenth on each
article, his subjects would soon become very rich,
and his own revenue would be trebly increased.
The soil is so fertile, that every grain is computed
to produce an hundred fold; but, owing to the
want of a greater demand for this article, the
Arabs sow little more than is necessary for their
own use.

The only guards of these rude habitations, both
against thieves and wild beasts, are dogs of a very
large and fierce species. If these animals perceive a
stranger approach the camp, they furiously issue in a
body against him, and probably would tear him to
C 4   pieces,

pieces, were they not reſtrained, and called off by
their owners. Through the whole of the night
they keep up an inceſſant and melancholy barking
and howling, which, though doubtleſs very uſe-
ful, in keeping their maſters upon the watch, and
frightening away wild beaſts, yet, when united to
the lowing of the herds and neighing of the horſes
which occupy the vacant ſpaces of the camp, certainly tends to depreſs the ſpirits, and impede that
reſt which the fatigue attending thoſe journeys
naturally requires.

On the 5th of October, between five and ſix in
the morning, we quitted the habitations of theſe
hoſpitable Arabs, and travelled on to Mamora,
where we arrived about ſix the ſame evening. The
greater part of this day's journey afforded us a
continuation of nearly the ſame appearances with
that of the preceding day.

As we approached the town, we obſerved on
each ſide of the lakes ſeveral ſanctuaries of Mooriſh ſaints. Theſe ſanctuaries are ſtone buildings
of about ten yards ſquare, whitened over, with a
cupola at the top, containing in them the body of
the ſaint.

A veneration for perſons of eminent ſanctity has
pervaded all nations and all religions of the world.
The Mahometan religion appears as little favourable to this ſpecies of ſuperſtition as moſt with
which we are acquainted, as it ſo tenaciouſly in-
ſiſts on the unity of God, and ſo ſtrictly inhibits
all creatures whatever from participating in the
honours which are due only to the Deity. Some
degree of idolatry, however, will prevail in every
rude nation. When, therefore, a Mahometan
ſaint

faint dies, he is buried with the utmost folemnity, and a chapel is erected over his grave, which place afterwards becomes more facred than even the mofques themfelves.

If the moft atrocious criminal takes refuge in one of thefe chapels, or fanctuaries, his perfon is fecure. The emperor himfelf, who rarely fcruples to employ any means whatever that may ferve to accomplifh his purpofe, feldom violates the privilege of thefe places. When a Moor is oppreffed by any mental or bodily affliction, he applies to the neareft fanctuary, and afterwards returns home with his mind calm and comforted, expecting to derive fome confiderable benefit from the prayers which he has offered there: and in all defperate cafes the fanctuary is the laft refort.

Saints in Barbary are of two kinds. The firft are thofe who by frequent ablutions, prayers, and other acts of devotion, have acquired an extraordinary reputation for piety. Too many of thefe are artful hypocrites, who under the mafk of religion practife the moft flagrant immoralities. There are, however, inftances of fome among them, whofe practices accord in general with their profeffion, and who make it their bufinefs to attend upon the fick, and affift the neceffitous and unhappy. From fuch as thefe the fevere fpirit of philofophy itfelf will fcarcely withhold refpect and veneration.

Idiots and madmen form the fecond clafs of faints. In every ftate of fociety, indeed, an opinion has been prevalent, that perfons afflicted with thefe mental complaints were under the influence of fuperior powers. The oracles and pro-

                    phets

phets of the heathen world derived their celebrity from this circumftance; and even among the lower claffes in our own country we frequently have to encounter a fimilar prejudice. In conformity, therefore, with thefe notions, fo natural to uncultivated man, the Moors confider thefe unhappy perfons as being under the fpecial protection of Heaven, and divinely infpired. Superftition here, as perhaps in fome other inftances, becomes admirably fubfervient to humanity and charity. In confequence of this prejudice, the moft friendlefs and unprotected race of mortals find friends and protectors in the populace themfelves. They are fed and cloathed gratis wherever they wander, and are fometimes loaded with prefents. A Moor might with as much fafety offer an infult to the emperor himfelf, as attempt by any feverity to reftrain even the irregularities of thefe reputed prophets.

It muft not, however, be diffembled, that opinions which have not their bafis in reafon and philofophy are feldom found to operate uniformly for the advantage of fociety. Independent of the wide fcope which thefe fuperftitious notions afford to hypocrify, numberlefs are the evils with which they are attended, fince whatever mifchief thefe fuppofed minifters of heaven may perpetrate, their perfons are always facred. It is not long fince there was a faint at Morocco, whofe conftant amufement was to wound and kill whatever perfons unfortunately fell his in way; yet, in fpite of the many fatal confequences from his infanity, he was ftill fuffered to go at large. Such was the malignity of his difpofition, that while he was in the

very

very act of prayer he would watch for an opportunity to throw his rofary round the neck of fome perfon within his reach, with an intent to ftrangle him. While I refided at Morocco, I fenfibly experienced the inconvenience of coming within the vicinity of thefe faints, as they feemed to take a particular pleafure in infulting and annoying Chriftians.

Befides thefe, I may mention under the head of faints or prophets, the Marabouts, a clafs of impoftors who pretend to fkill in magic, and are highly efteemed by the natives. They lead an indolent life, are the venders of fpells and charms, and live by the credulity of the populace.

There is alfo among thefe people a fet of itinerant mountaineers, who pretend to be the favourites of the prophet Mahomet, and that no kind of venomous creatures can hurt them. But the moft fingular of this clafs are the Sidi Nafir, or fnake-eaters, who exhibit in public upon market-days, and entertain the crowd by eating live fnakes, and performing juggling deceptions. I was once prefent at this ftrange fpecies of amufement, and faw a man, in the courfe of two hours, eat a living ferpent of four feet in length. He danced to the found of wild mufic, vocal and inftrumental, with a variety of odd geftures and contortions, feveral times round the circle formed by the fpectators. He then began his attack upon the tail, after he had recited a fhort prayer, in which he was joined by the multitude. This ceremony was repeated at intervals, till he had entirely devoured the fnake.

Thus

Thus far by way of digreffion; I now return to the courfe of my narrative. Early in the evening of the fifth, we arrived at Mamora, which is diftant about fixty-four miles from Larache. It is fituated upon a hill near the mouth of the river Saboe, the waters of which, gradually widening in their courfe, fall into the Atlantic at this place, and form a harbour for fmall veffels.

. Mamora, like the generality of the Moorifh towns through which I paffed, contains little worthy of obfervation. While it was in the poffeffion of the Portugueze it was encompaffed by a double wall, which ftill remains; it had alfo other fortifications which are deftroyed. At prefent, it poffeffes only a fmall fort on the fea-fide.

The fertile paftures, the extenfive waters and plantations, which we paffed on our way hither, have already been remarked. The vicinity of Mamora is equally enchanting. What a delightful refidence would it be, if the country had not the misfortune to groan under an arbitrary government!

In the morning, between eight and nine, we mounted our mules, leaving Mamora, and directing our courfe towards Sallee; where we arrived between one and two at noon, after having travelled over a fpace of about fifteen miles. The road between Mamora and Sallee, is in excellent order, and tolerably pleafant. It extends along a vale, towards which the hills gently flope on each fide.

Within a quarter of a mile of Sallee, we arrived at an aqueduct, which the natives affert to

have

have been built many years ago by the Moors; but from its ſtyle, and ſtriking marks of antiquity, it bears more the reſemblance of a piece of Roman architecture. Its walls, which are remarkably thick and high, extend in length for about half a mile, and have three ſtupendous arch-ways opening to the road, through one of which we paſſed on our way to Sallee. Although time has laid its deſtructive hand in ſome degree on this ancient piece of architecture, yet it ſtill ſerves the purpoſe of ſupplying the town of Sallee with excellent water.

C H A P.

C H A P. III.

Defcription of SALLEE.—*Piracies.*—*Curious Letter of* MULEY ZIDAN *to King* CHARLES I.—*Brutal Conduct of a Muleteer.*—*Handfome Behaviour of the French Conful.*—*Defcription of* RABAT.—*Journey from* RABAT *to* MOGODORE.—*Violent Storm.*—*Ruins of* FADALA.—*DAR* BEYDA.—AZAMORE.—*Melancholy Anecdote of an Englifh Surgeon.*—MAZAGAN.—DYN MEDINA RABÆA.—SAFFI.—*General State of the Country.*—*Defcription of* MOGODORE.

THE name of Sallee is famous in hiftory, and has decorated many a well-told tale. Thofe piratical veffels which were fitted out from this port, and which were known by the name of Sallee-rovers, were long the terror of the mercantile world. Equally dreaded for their valour and their cruelty, the adventurers who navigated thefe fwift and formidable veffels, depopulated the ocean, and even dared fometimes to extend their devaftations to the Chriftian coafts. As plunder was their fole aim, in the acquifition of it nothing impeded their career. Human life was of no value in their eftimation, or if it was fometimes fpared, it was not through any fentiment of juftice or compaffion, but only that it might be protracted in the moft wretched of fituations, as the hopelefs flave to the luxury and caprice of a fellow mortal. The town of Sallee in its prefent ftate, though large, prefents nothing worthy the obfervation of the traveller, except a battery of twenty-four pieces of cannon fronting the fea, and a redoubt at the entrance

trance of the river, which is about a quarter of a mile broad, and penetrates feveral miles into the interior country.

On the fide oppofite to Sallee is fituated the town of Rabat, which formerly partook equally with Sallee in its piratical depredations, and was generally confounded with it. While Sallee and Rabat were thus formidable, they were what might be termed independent ftates, paying only a very fmall tribute to the emperor, and barely acknowledging him for their fovereign. This ftate of independence undoubtedly gave uncommon vigour to their piratical exertions. Few will take much pains, or encounter great rifks for the acquifition of wealth, without the certainty of enjoying it unmolefted. Sidi Mahomet, however, when prince, fubdued thefe towns, and annexed them to the empire. This was a mortal blow to their piracies; for when thofe defperate mariners felt the uncertainty of poffeffing any length of time their captures, they no longer became folicitous to acquire them; and at length, when the man who had deprived them of their privileges became emperor, he put a total ftop to their depredations, by declaring himfelf at peace with all Europe. Since that period the entrance of the river has been fo gradually filling up with fand wafhed in by the fea, that was it poffible for thefe people to recover their independence, it would incapacitate them for carrying on their piracies to their former ex tent .

Having

* In perufing the manufcripts of a gentleman lately de-ceafed, who formerly refided a number of years in this Empire,

Having a letter of recommendation to Mr. De Rocher, the French conful-general, I was ferried over the river to Rabat, where he refides, and met with a very polite reception.   Upon landing my

Empire, it appears that Sallee was, fo far back as the year 1648, eminent for its piracies and independence, and that it became an object of conqueft to the monarch of that time.   He expreffes himfelf in thefe words :—

" Sallee is a city in the province of Fez, and derives its name from the river Sala, on which it is fituated, near its influx into the Atlantic Ocean.   It was a place of good commerce, till addicting itfelf entirely to piracy, and re-volting from its allegiance to its fovereign Muley Zidan, that prince, in the year 1648, difpatched an embaffy to King Charles I. of England, requefting him to fend a fquadron of men of war to lie before the town, while he at-tacked it by land.   This requeft being confented to, the city was foon reduced, the fortifications demolifhed, and the leaders of the rebellion put to death.   The year fol-lowing the Emperor fent another ambaffador to England, with a prefent of Barbary horfes and three hundred Chrif-tian flaves, accompanied with the following letter. I infert it as a fpecimen of the loftinefs of the Moorifh ftyle, and becaufe it leads me to think, that Muley Zidan was a more enlightened prince than moft of his predeceffors.   Neither the addrefs, fignature, nor reception it met with at our court, is expreffed in the manufcript.   It appears to be a modern tranflation, and is as follows :

" The King of Morocco's Letter to King Charles the Frift of England, 1649.   Muley Zidan.

" WHEN thefe our letters fhall be fo happy as to come to your Majefty's fight, I wifh the fpirit of the righteous God may fo direct your mind, that you may joyfully em-brace the meffage I fend.   The regal power allotted to us, makes us common fervants to our Creator, then of thofe people whom we govern ; fo obferving the duties we owe to God, we deliver bleffings to the world in providing for the public good of our eftates ; we magnify the honour of God, like the celeftial bodies, which, though they have
                                                            much

baggage a very warm difpute arofe between the muleteer and my interpreter, concerning the method of packing it on the mules again, for the purpofe of carrying it to the conful's houfe.

much veneration, yet ferve only to the benefit of the world: It is the excellency of our office to be inftruments, whereby happinefs is delivered unto the nations. Pardon me, Sir! This is not to inftruct, for I know I fpeak to one of a more clear and quick fight than myfelf; but I fpeak this, becaufe God hath pleafed to grant me a happy victory over fome part of thofe rebellious pirates, that fo long have molefted the peaceable trade of Europe; and hath prefented further occafion to root out the generation of thofe, who have been fo pernicious to the good of our nations: I mean, fince it hath pleafed God to be fo aufpicious in our beginnings, in the conqueft of Sallee, that we might join and proceed in hope of like fuccefs in the war of Tunis, Algiers, and other places; dens and receptacles for the inhuman villanies of thofe who abhor rule and government. Herein while we interupt the corruption of malignant fpirits of the world, we fhall glorify the great God, and perform a duty that will fhine as glorious as the fun and moon, which all the earth may fee and reverence: a work that fhall afcend as fweet as the perfume of the moft precious odours, in the noftrils of the Lord: a work whofe memory fhall be reverenced fo long as there fhall be any remaning among men: a work grateful and happy to men who love and honour the piety and virtue of noble minds. This action I here willingly prefent to you, whofe piety and virtues equal the greatnefs of your power; that we, who are vicegerents to the great and mighty God, may hand in hand triumph in the glory which the action prefents unto us.—Now, becaufe the iflands which you govern, have been ever famous for the unconquered ftrength of their fhipping, I have fent this my trufty fervant and ambaffador, to know whether, in your princely wifdom, you fhall think fit to affift me with fuch forces by fea, as fhall be anfwerable to thofe I provide by land; which if you pleafe to grant, I doubt not but the Lord of Hofts will protect and affift thofe that fight in fo glorious a caufe. Nor ought you to think
this

Both parties appeared fo very ftrenuous in their caufe, that neither of them paid any attention to my interference; and it was at length carried to fuch excefs, that the muleteer ftruck my interpreter. Upon feeing this, I could no longer remain a filent fpectator, and I have reafon to fear my warmth was almoft as intemperate as that of the difputants. The blow was given in fo brutal a manner, that I could with difficulty reftrain myfelf from immediately returning it. It was fortunate, however, that I ftill poffeffed fufficient coolnefs to reflect on the impropriety of fuch a proceeding, and I directed one of my Moorifh foldiers to punifh the muleteer. By means of long leather ftraps which he always carried about him, my Negro deputy performed his part fo well on the back of the delinquent, that he was foon glad to fall on his knees, and intreat a pardon both from myfelf and the interpreter. I was more defirous of punifhing this infult for the fake of eftablifhing my authority and confequence with the foldiers, than

this ftrange, that I, who fo much reverenced the peace and accord of nations, fhould exhort to war. Your great prophet, Chrift Jefus, was the lion of the tribe of Judah, as well as the Lord and giver of peace; which may fignify unto you, that he who is a lover and maintainer of peace, muft always appear with the terror of his fword, and, wading through feas of blood, muft arrive at tranquillity. This made James your father, of glorious memory, fo happily renowned among nations.—It was the noble fame of your princely virtues, which refounds to the utmoft corners of the earth, that perfuaded me to invite you to partake of that bleffing, wherein I boaft myfelf moft happy. I wifh God may heap the riches of his bleffings on you, increafe your happinefs with your days, and hereafter perpetuate the greatnefs of your name in all ages."

from

from an intention of revenging the caufe of the Jew, for I could not find out which of the difputants was in the wrong; but as my attendants had on two or three former occafions fhewn a difpofition to be troublefome, and as fo glaring an indignity was offered to the perfon who looked up to me for protection, I was determined to avail myfelf of this opportunity of convincing them that it was their duty to pay me every attention.

Mr. De Rocher, who refides in an excellent houfe built at the expence of his court, and who is the only European in the place, has happily blended original Englifh hofpitality with that eafy politenefs which characterizes his own nation. He gave me fo preffing an invitation to fpend another day with him, that though anxious to make an end of my journey, I could not refift his urgent folicitations.

The town of Rabat, whofe walls enclofe a large fpace of ground, is defended on the fea-fide by three forts tolerably well finifhed, which were erected fome little time ago by an Englifh renegado, and furnifhed with guns from Gibraltar. The houfes in general are good, and many of the inhabitants are wealthy. The Jews, who are very numerous in this place, are generally in better circumftances than thofe of Larache or Tangier, and their women are by far more beautiful than at any other town which I faw in this empire. I was introduced to one family in particular, where, out of eight fifters, nature had been fo lavifh to them all, that I felt myfelf at a lofs to determine which was the handfomeft. A combination of regular features, clearnefs of complexion, and expreffive

black

black eyes, gave them a diftinguifhed pre-eminence over their nation in general; and their perfons, though not improved by the advantages which the European ladies derive from drefs, were ftill replete with grace and elegance.

The caftle, which is very extenfive, contains a ftrong building, formerly ufed by the late empe- ror as his principal treafury, and a noble terrace, which commands an extenfive profpect of the town of Sallee, the ocean, and all the neighbour- ing country. There are alfo the ruins of another caftle, which is faid to have been built by Jacob Almonzor, one of their former emperors, and of which at prefent very little remains but its walls, containing within them fome very ftrong maga- zines for powder and naval ftores. On the out- fide of thefe walls is a very high and fquare tower, handfomely built of cut ftone, and called the tower of Haffen. From the workmanfhip of this tower, contrafted with the other buildings, a very accu- rate idea may be formed how greatly the Moors have degenerated from their former fplendour and tafte for architecture.

In the evening the conful introduced me to Sidi Mahomet Effendi, the emperor's prime minifter, who was at Rabat, on his way to Tangier. I found him a well-bred man, and he received me very gracioufly. After fome converfation on the purpofe of my journey, he defired I would feel his pulfe, and acquaint him whether or not he was in health. Upon affuring him that he was perfectly well, he expreffed in ftrong terms the obligation I had conferred on him by fuch agree- able information; and having wifhed me fuccefs

in

in my journey and enterprize, we mutually took our leave.

I availed myfelf of my delay at Rabat to get the lame mule changed, and directed my Negro foldiers to arrange our affairs in fuch a manner that we might leave the place early the next morning. Mr De Rocher, in addition to the kindnefs I had already experienced, ordered a quantity of bread, which at this place is remarkably good, to be packed up for my ufe, as well as a proportionable fhare of cold meat, and as much wine as we could conveniently carry with us. This feafonable fupply lafted me three days, and gave me time to recover in fome degree my former relifh for fowls and eggs.

Though I muft acknowledge that the attention and comforts which I experienced during my fhort ftay at Rabat proved a great relief, after the inconveniences I had undergone in travelling thither, yet on the whole, I perhaps fuffered more from the idea of having fimilar inconveniences to thofe I had already experienced ftill to encounter, without a profpect of a fimilar alleviation, than if I had continued the whole journey in an uninterrupted ftate. The confideration that I was to pafs day after day through a country where there is little to amufe the eye; that I had no companion with whom I could converfe, or to whom I could communicate my fentiments ; and that I was to travel the whole day at the tedious pace of three miles an hour, and at a feafon of the year when the coldnefs of the mornings and evenings were a very indifferent preparation for the heats which fucceeded in the middle of the day, altogether

preffed

preffed fo ftrongly upon my mind, that I muft confefs I could not help experiencing a confiderable dejection of fpirits at the idea of leaving Rabat*.

* The Abbe Poiret's remarks on travelling in Barbary are fo appofite and fo juft, that I truft I fhall be excufed for introducing a quotation from that author.—In one of his letters he fays, " I have never known fo well how to appreciate the advantages of living in a polifhed nation, as fince I have refided among a barbarous people. Never has the convenience of our highways ftruck me fo much, as when I have been obliged to travel through thick woods and deep marfhes. How much would a peregrination of eight days, in the manner I have travelled for fome time paft, change the ideas of thofe delicate Europeans who are continually complaining of bad inns, and of the fatigues they endure in their journeys! In this country there are neither inns, poft-chaifes, nor obliging and attentive land-lords. One muft not expect to find here broad highways, beaten and fhady paths, or places for repofing and refrefh-ing one's-felf; too happy, if, at the end of a fatiguing jour-ney, one can meet with a fmall hut, or a wretched couch! But this is feldom to be expected."

Again, in another letter, " How often muft you depart in the morning, without knowing where you will arrive in the evening! How often lofing yourfelf in thefe deferts, muft you fearch out your way amidft thorny brakes, thick forefts, and fteep rocks; fometimes ftopped by a river which you muft wade through, by a lake which you muft walk round, or by a marfh which you cannot crofs without danger! fometimes fcorched by the fun, or drenched by the rain, and at others dying with thirft, without being able to find the fmalleft fpring to quench it! If you carry no provi-fions with you, it will be impoffible for you to take any refrefhment before night. This is the only time at which the Moors make a regular repaft, or can offer any food to a ftranger. But when night arrives, that period of repofe for the traveller in Europe, it is not fo for the African tra-veller. He muft then choofe out a dry fituation, and well fheltered, to erect his tent; he muft unfaddle his horfes,

unload

In confequence of the indolence of my attendants, my baggage was not completely packed up
on the 8th till between ten and eleven in the morning, when I left the hofpitable roof of Mr De
Rocher, and proceeded on my journey for Dar
Beyda, the next town which offered itfelf on my
way to Mogodore.

With all the inconveniences which I had hitherto experienced, I had reafon to think myfelf very
fortunate in having fuch fine weather; for this
was the feafon when the heavy rains ufually come
on, and when a fhower of half an hour's continuance would wet more than the rain of a whole day
in England. Dry weather had accompanied us
the whole of the road from Tangier to Rabat,
and the heat from the hours of eleven to three
was violent; but, as I have juft before obferved,
previous to, and after thofe hours, the air was uncommonly cool. As an alleviation to the great
heat, we found the water-melons and pomegranates between Rabat and Mogodore of a moft delicious flavour, and of particular ufe in allaying
the exceffive thirft, and removing the fatigue we
experienced from the journey. Thefe fruits grow
common in the open ground, and we only paid two
blanquils, or three-pence Englifh a-piece, for water-melons, which were fufficiently large to ferve

unload his mules, cut wood, light fires, and take every
precaution that prudence dictates, to defend himfelf againft
ferocious animals and robbers. It is fafeft to encamp not
far from the tents of the Arabs, when one can find them.
They furnifh many fuccours when they are tractable, and
they are always fo when they fee one with a fufficient
guard."—See a tranflation of the Abbe Poiret's travels
through Barbary, Letter viii.

4

half

half a dozen people. I could not help obferving how provident nature has been, in granting in fuch plenty, fruits fo well calculated for the natives of warm climates. Indeed, many of the poor in this country have fcarcely any other provifions than fruit and bread.

At the time of our departure the appearance in the atmofphere promifed us a continuance of the fame fine weather we had hitherto experienced; and it continued fo till we had paffed three fmall ftreams which the Moors name the Hitcumb, Sherrat, and Bornica. Thefe, after the heavy rains have fallen, fwell out into deep and rapid rivers, and are frequently rendered totally impaffable, except in boats or on rafts. About five in the evening, however, very heavy and black clouds began to affemble, and very fhortly after followed a moft fevere ftorm. It was a dreadful union of wind, hail, rain, thunder, and lightning. From darknefs approaching faft upon us, we became very anxious to find out a place of fafety where we might pitch our tent, and for that purpofe fpurred our beafts; but no excitement from the fpur or whip could induce them to face the ftorm, and we were obliged to wait a full hour in a ftate of inactivity, till its violence was over. We then pufhed on till we arrived at a couple of Arab tents, pitched in an open country: bad as this fituation was, we however rejoiced in being able to fix our tent for the night, even in this unfociable fpot.

On the 9th of October, it having rained the whole night, we were detained till between ten and eleven in the morning in drying the tent,

which

which from its being quite wet, was become too heavy for the mules to carry with the other baggage; we then purfued our journey, and at twelve, arrived at the ruins of Menfooria. There was formerly a caftle on this fpot, which from the extent of its walls, and a fquare tower which form the whole of the ruins, appears to have been a very large building. My foldiers informed me, that it had been the refidence of a prince who was in oppofition to his fovereign; and who was obliged to defert it. The building was deftroyed by the then reigning emperor, and the intermediate ground is now inhabited by a few Negroes, living in fmall huts, who were banifhed thither for having on fome occafion incurred the difpleafure of the emperor. In an arbitrary country, where the poffeffion of the throne depends more on the will of the foldiers than on the rights of fucceffion, the defpot confiders that caftles may prove rather places of fecurity for his opponents, than of any great utility to himfelf; he therefore either fuffers them to decay, or deftroys them entirely, according to the dictates of his caprice. Indeed every town through which I paffed in the empire affords ftriking marks of the truth of this affertion.

Soon after our leaving Menfooria we came up to Fadala, having forded in our way the river Infefic. Fadala whilft its ruins exift, will be a lafting monument of Sidi Mahomet's caprice. It confifts of the fhell of a town, began by him in the early part of his reign, but never finifhed. It is enclofed within a fquare wall, and is furnifhed with a mofque (the only building that was com-

D

pleted

pleated) for the ufe of the inhabitants, who, like thofe of Menfooria, live in huts in the intermediate ground. To the right of Fadala we obferved a fmall but apparently neat palace, which my attendants informed me was built by the late emperor for his occafional ufe, when bufinefs led him to travel that way.

The remainder of our journey to Dar Beyda, where we arrived about fix in the evening, afforded nothing remarkable, excepting that we paffed over a double bridge, which is the only piece of architecture of the kind that I faw in the country. It is the work of Sidi Mahomet, and is built of ftone. The country between Rabat and Dar Beyda, a diftance of about forty-four miles, is one continuation of barrennefs and rock.

Dar Beyda is a fmall fea-port of very little importance; it poffefles, however, a bay which admits veffels of pretty confiderable burthen to anchor in it with tolerable fafety, except when the wind blows hard at north-weft, and then they are liable to be driven on fhore. Upon my arrival, I was immediately introduced to the governor, who was then in the audience-chamber, attending to the complaints of the inhabitants. After offering me his fervices, and begging my acceptance of a few fowls, he foon left us in the poffeffion of the room where we flept that night.

On the 10th of October we departed for Azamore, about fifty-fix miles diftant, between feven and eight in the morning; and after a journey of two days came up to the Morbeya, at the mouth and fouthern fide of which is fituated Azamore.

The

The river is so wide and deep here, that it is necessary to be ferried over, and a large boat is continually employed for that purpose.

We had no sooner got all our baggage, our mules, and ourselves into the boat, and were ready to row off, than a most violent dispute arose between my Negro soldiers and the ferrymen. As it was no new circumstance to me to be a witness to these altercations, I remained very quietly in the boat till I observed that one of the ferry-men was putting every thing on shore again, whilst another was collaring one of the soldiers. In fact, matters were proceeding to such extremities, that I thought it was full time to interfere.

Upon inquiry, I was informed that the proprietor of the ferry farmed the river from the emperor, and that in consequence of it he was allowed all the perquisites of the ferry ; that my soldiers insisted that as I was in the emperor's service, it was the duty of the people to ferry me, my baggage, &c. without receiving any reward for their trouble. Which of the two were in the right I could not pretend to determine ; but I was very glad to end the dispute, by paying the usual demand. After a few curses on both sides, the baggage and mules were replaced in the boat, and we were ferried over to Azamore.

In a country where arts and sciences are totally neglected, and where the hand of despotism has destroyed public spirit, and depressed all private exertion, it is obvious, that considerable tracts must occur which are productive of nothing deserving of notice. This was precisely the case in my journey from Dar Beyda to Azamore, which

 presented

prefented to our view one continued chain of rocks and barrennefs, unpleafant and fatiguing roads, without any one object to vary the fcene, or to intereft curiofity.

Azamore is a fea-port town on the Atlantic ocean, fituated at the mouth of the Morbeya; and though a large place, is neither ornamented with public buildings, nor has any thing remarkable in its hiftory or fituation.

In compliance with the particular requeft of one of my foldiers whofe near relations refide at Azamore, I continued here the remainder of the day, and was lodged in a room of a Moorifh houfe, which was fecluded from the family. Soon after my arrival I was vifited by a Jew in an European drefs, who had formerly lived with one of the Englifh confuls, and who fpoke the Englifh language with tolerable fluency. He took me to his houfe, and there received me with great hofpitality, infifting on my dining with him, and making ufe of his houfe as my own. After dinner he fhewed me the different parts of the town; and in the courfe of our converfation requefted me to be particularly cautious how I conducted myfelf with the prince whom I was going to attend; obferving, that the Moors were extremely fickle, and their conduct governed merely by the caprice of the moment. To enforce this caution, he related to me a ftory, from which I learned that an European furgeon had at fome former period, attended a prince of Morocco, who, neglecting his advice when under his care, had increafed his malady; that this circumftance fo alarmed the prince that he fent for the furgeon, and upon his appearance

produced

produced a piftol. The unfortunate man, alarmed and diftreffed by fuch unworthy treatment, haftily withdrew, and in a fhort time put an end to his exiftence.

On the 13th of October, having taken leave of my Jewifh acquaintance, and my foldiers of their friends, we fet off at eight in the morning for the town of Saffi, where we arrived on the evening of the 15th, after a journey of about fifty-feven miles. The country we paffed through was rocky and barren, producing fcarcely a tree, or indeed any verdure whatever.

Soon after leaving Azamore, the town of Maza-gan prefented itfelf to our view to cur right. This place was taken a few years fince by Sidi Mahomet from the Portugueze; a conqueft of which his Moorifh majefty made a very pompous boaft, though it is well known that the Portu-gueze, from the great inconvenience and expence of keeping up the garrifon, without deriving any material advantage from it, had come to a refo-lution to evacuate it before the emperor's attack, and for that purpofe had actually begun to em-bark their goods and property. As, however, the emperor was determined to exhibit fome fpe-cimen of his military prowefs and addrefs, this circumftance did not deter him from commencing a regular fiege. A magazine for military ftores (which may be feen from the road) was raifed with the utmoft expedition, and the attack was carried on with all the vigour and ability which his Moorifh majefty was capable of exerting. The Portugueze defended the town no longer than was neceffary to allow time to carry away

D 3

their

their effects and valuables; it was then furrendered, or more properly, abandoned, to the
Moors.

On the day of our arrival at Saffi, we passed by
the ruins of a town, which was once large and
considerable. It was built by a former emperor,
named Muley Ocom Monsor, and is now called
by the name of Dyn Medina Rabæa. Its only
remains at present are remarkably thick and extensive walls, which inclose gardens and huts,
inhabited by disbanded Negro soldiers.

Saffi is a sea-port town, situated at the bottom
of a steep and high mountain. It is a small place,
and is only remarkable for a neat palace, which is
the occasional residence of the emperor's sons,
and a small fort at a little distance to the north
of the town. Its vicinity is a mixture of mountains and woods, which gives it a wild and truly
romantic appearance. Saffi carried on a considerable commerce with Europe, before Sidi Mahomet
obliged the European merchants to reside at
Mogodore. It affords a safe road for shipping,
except when the wind blows hard at West,
and then they are subject to be driven on shore.

During my residence in this town, I took up
my quarters at a Jewish house, and was visited
by two Moors who had been in London, and
could speak a little of the English language.
Among other marks of attention, they contrived
to procure, unknown to me, a chair and a small
table; articles which I had not seen since I left
Tangier, except at the French consul's house, as
the Moors never make use of either.

At

At eight in the morning of the fixteenth, we fet off for Mogodore, a journey of about fixty miles, which we performed in two days.

Soon after leaving Saffi we paffed over a very high and dangerous mountain. The rocky, fteep, and rugged path, which was only broad enough to allow one mule to pafs at a time, and the perpendicular precipice which hung over the fea, filled our minds with a fenfe of terror and awe, which no pen can defcribe. Our mules, however, accuftomed to this mode of travelling, carried us with the moft perfect fafety, over parts where, with European horfes, we fhould probably have been dafhed to pieces.

From this mountain we in a fhort time entered a foreft of dwarf oaks, which is about fix miles in length, and the fouthern extremity of which reaches to the river Tanfif. This is a very broad river, which after the heavy rains have fallen, or when fwelled by the tide, is always paffed upon rafts. Thofe difficulties not prefenting themfelves to us now, we forded the river with great eafe, and on approaching its fouthern fide, obferved in the midft of a thick foreft a large fquare caftle, which my foldies informed me was built by Muley Ifhmael, who is immortalized by the pen of Mr. Addifon, in one of the numbers of the Freeholder. Sidi Mahomet neglected it, and it is now falling to ruin. The breadth and windings of the Tanfif, its high and woody banks, and the caftle juft difcoverable through the trees, afforded altogether a fcene, which though fomewhat gloomy, yet was truly romantic and picturefque.

D 4

The

The directions which I had received from Mr. Matra were, to continue at Mogodore, till the return of a meſſenger, who was to be diſpatched thence to Tarudant, informing the prince of my arrival.

The very hoſpitable treatment I experienced from Mr. Hutchiſon, Britiſh vice-conſul at Mogodore, during my ſtay at his houſe, with the ſympathiſing letters and friendly advice with which he afterwards favoured me, whilſt under the many embarraſſments and inconveniencies which I underwent at Morocco, have made the moſt forcible impreſſion on my memory; and I ſhould feel utterly diſſatisfied with myſelf if I omitted thus publicly to acknowledge my gratitude to that gentleman.

Before I proceed to deſcribe Mogodore it may not be improper to take a ſhort review of the general appearance of the country through which I paſſed in my journey from Tangier.

The firſt part of the journey, as far as Larache, preſented to us, as I before obſerved, a rocky, mountainous, and barren country, and, if we except the foreſt of Rabe a Clow, but few trees or ſhrubs. From Larache to Sallee the eye was agreeably relieved by the variety of objects which offered themſelves to its view. The evenneſs of the ground, the numerous lakes, and the verdure which ſurrounded them, indicated fully the fertility of the ſoil; and theſe, joined to the interſected clumps of trees, would lead the contemplative mind to conceive that nature had intended this ſpot for the reſidence of a more civilized people than its preſent inhabitants. From Sallee to Mogodore, and thence to Santa Cruz, we again meet

with

with the fame barren, mountainous, and rocky country, which prefented itfelf at the firft part of the journey.

Though I occafionally met with forefts of fmall treeks, fuch as the arga, the dwarf oak, the palm-tree, &c. yet the country produces no ufeful timber whatever. The Moors are therefore obliged to import that article from Europe; and it may be on this account that the emperor poffeffes fo few veffels, and is obliged to fend thofe to be repaired in foreign ports. As vegetation does not take place in this climate till fome time after the heavy rains have fallen, I had not an oportunity of obferving in this journey what plants were peculiar to the climate. The variety which diftinguifhes the more improved countries of Europe, and particularlar England, probably arifes as much from the land being diftributed into inclofures, as from local fituation. This advantage the emperor of Morocco does not enjoy; fince, excepting in the immediate vicinity of towns, no divifions of land are to be obferved; the Arabs indifcriminately chufing pieces of ground, without fences, for the purpofes of agriculture, which, as I before noticed, they change as occafion requires. The famenefs of fcene which arifes from this circumftance, is in fome degree leffened by the numerous fanctuaries which are ditfufed over the whole country; but otherways thefe chapels prove troublefome to an European traveller, fince the Moors, upon paffing them, always ftop a confiderable time to pay their devotions to the remains of the faints who are buried there. There is likewife a cuftom in this country, which is alfo prevalent in Portugal, of confecrating the fpot on which any perfon has been murdered, by heaping a large proportion of ftones on the place, where it is ufual for thofe who pafs that way to add another ftone to the number, and to recite a fhort prayer, adapted to the occafion.

All the towns through which I paffed in my way hither, were furrounded with high walls of Tabby, flanked with fquare forts, generally without any artillery, and having caftles, which feemed to be in a very ruinous ftate, fituated upon the moft eminent fpot, for their defence or attack. The houfes, from having no windows and but very few doors, had more the appearance of dead walls than inhabited places; and their ftreets were univerfally narrow, filthy to a degree, irregular, and badly paved. With all thefe inconveniencies, the inhabitatants enjoy an advantage of which many of the more civilized capitals of Europe cannot boaft, I mean that of good police. The ftreets are fo well watched at night, that robberies or even houfebreaking are but feldom heard of; and the general quietnefs which reigns through their towns after the gates are fhut, is a convincing proof of the attention of their patroles to their duty. Their detection, and fpeedy bringing to juftice the criminals, likewife deferves our attention. From having no publick houfes or other places to harbour thieves, and from no perfon being permitted to quit the country without leave, it is utterly impoffible for a culprit to efcape the hand of juftice, except by taking refuge in a fanctuary, by which he banifhes himfelf for ever from fociety. On the other hand, the vigilance of the governors and other officers of juftice is fo great, and conducted

with

with fo much addrefs, that unlefs the means of fafety which his religion points out are quickly adopted, the criminal in a very fhort time is detected, and as quickly punifhed.

According to the opinion of fome travellers, much danger is to be apprehended in traverfing this country, from the attacks of wild beafts; but it is only juftice to obferve, that during the whole of my progrefs to Mogodore, and indeed I may add afterwards in paffing over the Atlas, I met with no obftruction or moleftation whatever from thefe animals; and I was alfo informed, that a circumftance of the kind was very rarely known to have happened. The fact is, the wild animals confine themfelves principally to the interior parts of the country, and to thofe retreats in the mountains which are beyond the track of men.

Mogodore, fo named by Europeans, and Suera by the Moors, is a large, uniform, and well-built town, fituated about three hundred and fifty miles from Tangier, on the Atlantic ocean, and furrounded on the land fide by deep and heavy fands. It was raifed under the aufpices of Sidi Mahomet, who upon his acceffion to the throne ordered all the European merchants who were fettled in his dominions to refide at Mogodore, where, by lowering the duties, he promifed to afford every encouragement to commerce. The Europeans, thus obliged to defert their former eftablifhments, confidering this firft ftep of the emperor to be a mark of his attachment to trade and commerce, and having refided long in the country without any better views at home, univerfally fettled at Mogodore, where they erected houfes, and other conveniencies

veniencies for the purposes of trade. The hopes,
however, with which they had changed their situation, were considerably frustrated by the perfidy
of the emperor, who indeed fulfilled his promise,
till he observed the merchants so fixed as not to
be likely to remove; but he then began to increase
the duties, and by that means to damp the spirit
of commerce which he had promised to promote.
His caprice, however, or, what had still more
influence, valuable presents, induced him at times
to relax these severities. In consequence of this
circumstance the duties have been so frequently
varied, that it is utterly impossible for me to state,
with any degree of certainty, the usual burthens
laid upon articles of commerce in this port.

The factory at Mogodore consists of about a
dozen mercantile houses of different nations, whose
owners, from the protection granted them by the
emperor, live in full security from the Moors,
whom indeed they keep at a rigid distance. They
export to America, mules. To Europe, Morocco
leather, hides, gum arabic, gum sandarac, ostrich
feathers, copper, wax, wool, elephants' teeth, fine
mats, beautiful carpeting, dates, figs, raisins, olives,
almonds, oil, &c. In return they import timber,
artillery of all kinds, gunpowder, woollen cloths,
linens, lead, iron in bars, all kinds of hardware
and trinkets, such as looking-glasses, snuff-boxes,
watches, small knives, &c. tea, sugar, spices, and
most of the useful articles which are not otherwise
to be procured in this empire.

Besides the commerce carried on between this
empire and Europe, the Moors have also a trade
with Guinea, Algiers, Tunis, Tripoli, Grand
Cairo,

Cairo, and Mecca, by means of their caravans, of which I foon fhall have occafion to fpeak more particularly.

Mogodore is regularly fortified on the fea fide; and on the land, batteries are fo placed as to prevent any incurfions from the Southern Arabs, who are of a turbulent difpofition, and who, from the great wealth which is known to be always in Mogodore, would gladly avail themfelves of any opportunity that offered to pillage the town. The entrance, both by fea and land, confifts of elegant ftone arch-ways, with double gates. The market-place is handfomely built, with piazzas of the fame materials, and at the water port there is a cuftom-houfe and powder magazine, both of which are neat ftone buildings. Befide thefe public edifices, the emperor has a fmall but handfome palace for his occafional refidence. The ftreets of the town, though very narrow, are all in ftrait lines, and the houfes, contrary to what we meet with in the other towns of the empire, are lofty and regular. The bay, which is little better than a road, and is very much expofed when the wind is at North-Weft, is formed by a curve in the land, and a fmall ifland about a quarter of a mile from the fhore. Its entrance is defended by a fort well mounted with guns.

C H A P. IV.

General View of the Empire of MOROCCO.—*Situation
and Climate.*—*Provinces.*—*Soil.*—*Wonderful Fertility.
*—*Sea Ports.*—*Natural Productions.*—*Mines.*—*Animals.*—*Occasional Famines.*—*Famine in* 1778.—*Manufactures.*—*Buildings.*—*Roads.*—*Population.*—*Introduction of Negroes.*—MULEY ISHMAEL—*his Policy.*
SIDI MAHOMET.—*General Oppression of the People.
*—*Merchants.*

AS I had a better opportunity of being informed of the state of the country, and its productions, from the European merchants at Mogodore, than occurred at any subsequent period
during my tour, I shall now avail myself of that
information; and to this I feel myself induced by
a further motive, namely, that it will enable the
reader to peruse with more satisfaction and advantage the succeeding pages of this Narrative.

The empire of Morocco is situated between the
29th and 36th degree of North latitude. It is
about five hundred and fifty miles in length from
North to South, and about two hundred in breadth:
It is bounded to the North by the Straits of Gibraltar and the Mediterranean sea; to the East, by the
kingdoms of Tremecen and Sugulmuffa; to the
South, by the river Suz, and the country to the
South of Tafilet; and to the West, by the Atlantic
ocean. The empire is formed of several provinces
and nominal kingdoms, which, as in most countries, before their union were distinct and petty
sovereignties.

The

The climate, though in the Southern provinces very hot in the months of June, July, and Auguſt, yet is in general friendly to the conſtitutions of its inhabitants, as well as to thoſe of Europeans. To the North the climate is nearly the ſame as that of Spain and Portugal, with the autumnal and vernal rains peculiar to to thoſe countries; but to the Southward, the rains are leſs general and certain, and of courſe the heat is more exceſſive.

Moſt of the towns which Europeans are allowed to enter, being ſea-ports, have the advantage of being frequently refreſhed with ſea breezes; and Mogodore, though ſo far to the Southward, from being ſubject in the ſummer ſeaſon to have the wind regularly at North Weſt, is quite as cool as the more temperate climates of Europe. Morocco and Tarudant are inland, and therefore, though nearly in the ſame degree of Latitude as Mogodore, are much hotter; their great heats, however, are conſiderably leſſened by their vicinity to the Atlas, the higher parts of which are the whole year covered with ſnow, and often favour them with cool and refreſhing breezes.

The ſoil of the empire of Morocco is naturally very fertile, and with proper cultivation and attention is capable of producing all the luxuries of the Eaſtern and Weſtern worlds. It muſt, however, be confeſſed, that on ſome parts of the ſea-coaſt, particularly where it is mountainous, like every other country under ſimilar circumſtances, the ſoil is ſandy and barren; but wherever there is the leaſt appearance of a plain, ſuch as that between Larache and Mamora, and in the neighbourhood

bourhood of Morocco and Tarudant, the soil is black and rich. Indeed I am informed from the best authority, that at Tafilet, and throughout most of the interior parts of the empire, its fertility is beyond imagination.

From the slight cultivation it at present receives, which is merely the burning of the stubble before the autumnal rains come on, and ploughing it about six inches deep, the earth produces, at a very early season, excellent wheat and barley (though no oats) Indian corn, alderoy, beans, pease, hemp, and flax; oranges, lemons, citrons, pomegranates, melons, water-melons, olives, figs, almonds, grapes, dates, apples, pears, cherries, plumbs, and in fact all the fruits to be found in the Southern provinces of Spain and Portugal. The people here preserve their grain in Matamores, holes made in the earth, lined and covered with straw, on which earth is placed in a pyramidal form, to prevent the rain from soaking in. In these stores corn has been kept five or six years, without undergoing any very material change.

As little encouragement, however, is extended to industry in this country, many of their fruits which require attention, particularly their grapes, apples, pears, plumbs, &c. do not arrive at that perfection to which they are brought in Europe. Could, indeed, a proper spirit for agriculture and foreign commerce be introduced in the country, or, in other words, could the sovereign be persuaded, that by suffering his subjects to be enriched he would improve his own treasury, this empire, from its convenient situation with respect to Europe, and from the natural luxuriance and fertility

of

of its foil, might become of the higheft political and commercial importance. The only material impediment to commerce is the inconvenience and infecurity of the ports. I am well informed, however, that at Valedia there is a bafon formed by nature, capable of containing with fafety any number of fhipping; and the other ports might moft probably be improved.

It is·melancholy, in traverfing the immenfe tract of fo fine a country, to obferve fo much land lying wafte and uncultivated, which by a very little attention would be capable of producing an inexhauftible treafure to its inhabitants. From this reprefentation it would fcarcely be fuppofed credible, that Spain, which is alfo a fine country, and a civilized nation fhould be obliged to remit to the emperor, very large prefents of money, to induce him to allow his fubjects to export corn, as well as moft other kinds of provifions and fruits, from Tangier and Tetuan. Indeed the Southern provinces of Spain can hardly exift without this fupply. To what are we to attribute this circumftance? Is it that Morocco is fo much more fertile than Spain, that it produces a redundance with fcarcely any cultivation; or is the indolence of the Spaniards fuperior to that of the Moors themfelves?

The Jews in moft of the towns of the empire make wine; but, either owing to the grapes not being in fuch perfection as thofe of Europe, or to an improper mode of preparing it, its flavour proves but very indifferent. They alfo diftil a fpecies of brandy from figs and raifins, well known in that country by the name of aquadent.

This

This liquor has a difagreeable tafte, but in point of ftrength is little inferior to fpirits of wine. It is drank without dilution very freely by the Jews on all their feafts or days of rejoicing, and there are very few of the Moors who are difpofed to forego any private opportunity of taking their fhare of it alfo.

The Moors cultivate tobacco; there is a fpecies of it near Mequinez, which affords fnuff, the flavour of which is very little inferior to Maccaba. In my progrefs through the country I have noticed forefts of oak trees of a dwarf kind, which bear acorns of a remarkable fize and fweet tafte. To the Southward we meet with the palm or date tree, the arga, bearing a nut of the almond fpecies, with the olive, from both of which the inhabitants extract great quantities of oil, which conftitutes a confiderable part of their exports to foreign countries. There is alfo an infinite variety of fhrubs and plants, fuch as the prickly pear, the aloe, &c. all in fhort that are to be found in Spain and Portugal. Cotton, wax, honey, falt, tranfparent gum, and gum fandarac, are all productions of this empire.

In the mountains of Atlas there are numerous iron mines; but as the Moors do not underftand the mode of working iron, thofe mines prove of no ufe to them, and they are therefore obliged to procure that article from Europe. The neighbourhood of Tarudant produces mines of copper; and the Moors affert, that in the Atlas there are alfo fome of gold and filver, which the emperor will not allow to be touched. But I am inclined to imagine that if the affertion had any foundation in

truth,

truth, the Brebes, who inhabit thefe mountains, and who are mere nominal fubjects, and pay but little refpect to the government of Morocco, would long before this time have difcovered them. It is, however, probable that this vaft chain of mountains may contain productions which might be converted to very valuable purpofes; but, owing to a want of emulation on the part of the inhabitants, and Europeans not being allowed to attempt any new difcoveries, a knowledge of them is not to be attained.

The domeftic animals of Morocco are much the fame as thofe of Europe, excepting the camel, which is the moft ufeful animal in this quarter of the globe, both on account of the great fatigue which it is capable of undergoing, and the little fubfiftance it requires. Camels are employed here for all the purpofes of agriculture and commerce, and are very numerous. It has been afferted that dromedaries are indigenous to this country; but in the courfe of my whole tour I could hear of none, except thofe which are in the poffeffion of the emperor; and he, as I difcovered, procures them from the coaft of Guinea. Thefe are the fleeteft animals for travelling that are known, and are only ufed by the emperor on urgent occafions. I was informed that their pace is fometimes fo exceedingly fwift, that their riders are obliged to tie a fafh round their waifts to preferve the power of refpiration, and cover the whole of the face except the eyes, to prevent their fuffering from the ftrong current of air occafioned by the rapid motion of the animal. It is computed that, in an

ordinary

ordinary way, a dromedary will perform a journey of five hundred miles in four days.

The oxen and sheep of this country are small; but their flesh is well flavoured. The hides of the former, and the wool of the latter, are both articles of exportation. The sheep with large tails, distinguished in England by the name of Barbary sheep, are here very scarce, and are more indigenous to the Eastern parts of Barbary. The horses, for want of attention in keeping up the breed, are much less valuable than they formerly were; there are still however some few that are good in the country, and those are generally strong, and have great spirit. The mules are numerous and useful, though I do not think them equal to those of Spain, either in size or beauty.

Fowls and pigeons are remarkably plentiful and good in the empire of Morocco; but ducks are scarce, and geese and turkies I never saw there. The country abounds with the red-legged partridge. In the proper season the frankolin, a bird of the partridge species, of a delicious flavour, and beautiful pumage, is found here; also a few woodcocks, snipes in great numbers, all kinds of water-fowl, and a variety of small singing-birds. Storks are are very plentiful, and as they are never molested by the Moors, who are taught to believe it sinful to destroy them, they become quite domestic and tame. They are generally to be seen feeding among ruinous walls and castles, where they pick up insects and snakes. Hares, rabbits, antelopes, porcupines, apes, foxes, wild cats, &c. are all natives of this empire.

Among

Among the ferocious animals may be enumerated wolves and wild boars, which are spread over the whole empire; and in the southern provinces, there are lions, tygers, and monstrous serpents.

During my residence in the country, I had frequent opportunities of examining that most singular of the animal productions, the cameleon. Though it is hardly necessary to adduce any proof to the philosophers of the present day against the vulgar error that it feeds only upon air, yet it may afford some satisfaction to my readers to be told that I had an opportunity of seeing a complete refutation of this opinion at Mogodore. A gentleman of my acquaintance there had in his possession, a cameleon, the dexterity of which in procuring its food I had ample means of observing. The fact is, its principal support is flies, which it catches by darting at them an exceedingly long tongue covered with a matter so very glutinous, that if it but touches an insect it is impossible for it to escape. The most singular part of its conformation however, (if, perhaps, we except the power of varying its colours) is the eye, the muscles of which are so constructed that it can move the ball quite round; and I believe it exists the only known instance in all animated nature of a creature which is able to direct its vision to two different objects at the same time, however those objects may be situated. Except in the act of darting out its tongue to procure subsistence, its motions are remarkably slow.

Although it must be allowed that the climate of Morocco is delightful to a degree, yet it is

occasion-

occafionally fubject to great droughts, which naturally produce immenfe fwarms of locufts, the moft deftructive enemy to vegetation that exifts. In the year 1778 thefe infects came in fuch numbers from the South, that they perfectly darkened the air, and, by deftroying all the corn, produced a general famine. This calamity was increafed to fuch a degree in the year 1780, that feveral unfortunate perfons actually died in the ftreets for want of food; many were driven to the neceffity of digging in the earth for roots to fupply the urgent calls of nature; while others were happy to find fome undigefted corn in the dung of animals, which they moft eagerly devoured. Upon this occafion of public diftrefs the emperor generoufly opened his ftore of corn, and diftributed it, as well as money, among his fubjects; and every perfon who was known to poffefs ftores was obliged to follow his example. Thefe melancholy facts are fo recent in the memory of the people, that they ftill repeat them to the Europeans who vifit the country.

The manufactures of the empire are the haick, which, as was before obferved, is a long garment compofed of white wool and cotton, or cotton and filk woven together, and is ufed by the Moors for the purpofe of covering their under drefs when they go abroad, which they do by totally wrapping themfelves in it in a carelefs but eafy manner; filk handkerchiefs of a particular kind, prepared only at Fez; filks checquered with cotton; carpeting little inferior to that of Turkey; beautiful matting, made of the palmetto or wild palm tree; paper of a coarfe kind; Cordovan,

commonly

commonly called Morocco leather; gun-powder of an inferior nature; and long barrelled musquets, made of Bifcay iron. The Moors are unacquainted with the mode of cafting cannon, and therefore thofe few which are now in the country are prefents from Europeans. The manufacture of glafs is likewife unknown to them; as indeed they make great ufe of earthen ware, and have few or no windows to their houfes, this commodity may be of lefs importance to them than many others. They make butter, by putting the milk into a goat-fkin with its outward coat turned inwards, and fhaking it till the butter collects on the fides, when it is taken out for ufe. From this operation it proves always full of hairs, and has an infipid flavour. Their cheefe confifts merely of curds hardened and dried, and has uniformly a difagreeable tafte. The bread in fome of the principal towns particularly at Tangier and Sallee, is remarkably good, but in many other places, it is coarfe, black, and heavy.

Their markets are under more ftrict regulations than might be expected from a people who are fo deficient in moft other inftances. A proper officer, entitled Almotafon, or Mayor, is appointed to infpect all kinds of provifions and corn, and, according to their plenty or fcarcity, to fix the price on each article: it is alfo the duty of this officer to attend conftantly the markets, and to fee that no perfon is guilty of overcharging what he fells, for which, upon detection, the offender is punifhed, by having his hands tied behind him, and being publicly flogged through all the ftreets, the executioner occafionally exclaiming, " Thus do we treat thofe who impofe upon the poor." Provifions both of the animal and vegetable kind are fold by the Rtab, or large pound, confifting of the weight of twenty hard dollars, or Spanifh ounces; corn, by the Almood, four of which are equal to a Faneg Spanifh, or fack; and articles of merchandize, by the fmall pound of fixteen Spanifh ounces, when fold by weight; and by the Code, which is about two thirds of an Englifh yard, when by meafurement.

The Moors, agreeably to the Jewifh cuftom, cut the throats of all the animals they eat, at the fame time turning their heads towards Mecca, in adoration of their prophet. After fuffering them to bleed freely, they carefully wafh all the remaining blood away, and divide the meat into fmall pieces of about one or two pounds in weight. As they are unacquainted with the invention of pumps, and have but few fprings, it affords employment to a number of indigent people, who would probably be idle otherwife, to carry water in fkins from the neareft river or refervoir, and fell it to the inhabitants. From their being obliged to tar the fkins to prevent them from leaking, the water is frequently rendered very unpleafant.

Their looms, forges, ploughs, carpenter's tools, &c. are much upon the fame conftruction with the unimproved inftruments of the fame kind which are ufed at this time in fome parts of Europe, only ftill more clumfily finifhed. In their work they attend more to ftrength than neatnefs or convenience, and, like all other ignorant people they have no idea that what they do is capable of improvement. It is probable, indeed,

that

that the Moors have undergone no very material change since the revolution in their arts and sciences which took place soon after their expulsion from Spain. Previous to that period it is well known they were an enlightened people, at a time when the greater part of Europe was involved in ignorance and barbarism; but owing to the weakness and tyranny of their princes, they gradually sunk into the very opposite extreme, and may now be considered as but a few degrees removed from a savage state.

They use no kind of wheel-carriage, and therefore all their articles of burden are transported from one place to another on camels, mules, or asses. Their buildings though by no means constructed on any fixed principle of architecture, have at least the merit of being very strong and durable. The manner of preparing tabby, of which all their best edifices are formed, is, I believe, the only remains of their ancient knowledge at present existing. It consists of a mixture of mortar and very small stones, beaten tight in a wooden case, and then suffered to dry, when it forms a cement equal to the solid rock. There are always unaccountable discrepancies and inconsistencies in the arts of uncivilized nations. The apartments are if possible even more inconvenient than those of their neighbours the Spaniards; but the carved wood-work with which many of them are ornamented is really equal to any I have ever seen in Europe.

The Moors have no idea of making high roads, or repairing those which have been formed by the ancient possessors of the country, or perhaps by

E   the

the mere refort of paffengers, but are content to leave them in the fame ftate in which they found them. Indeed, they are even incapable of comprehending the fimple fact—that by improving the roads travelling would become more expeditious, and lefs expenfive.

If we look for any of the elegant appendages of luxury and refinement in this country, we fhall be grievoufly difappointed. Their gardens are mere tracts of inclofed ground, over-run with weeds, interfperfed with vines, figs, oranges, and lemons, without tafte or difpofition,. and having perhaps one ftrait walk through the whole. They fometimes fow corn in the intermediate ground; but their gardens are rarely productive of efculent vegetables, and feldom or never ornamented with flowers.

As there are few or no bridges in the country, I am inclined to believe the Moors are not thoroughly acquainted with the mode of conftructing large arches; and it is only at their fea-ports where they even ufe boats. Thefe circumftances, united to the bad roads, render this part of Barbary very inconvenient and dangerous to be travelled through.

The country throughout is ill-watered. Moft of the rivers, which, however, are very few in proportion to the extent of ground, except juft at their fea-ports, deferve only the name of rivulets, and in the fummer feafon are many of them dried up. From all thefe circumftances it may be conjectured that the population is not extraordinary. When on my return, in my journey from Morocco to Sallee, which required feven days to

accom-

accomplish, I met with no habitations but a few Arab tents scattered in different parts; and I had reason to believe that a great part of the interior country is nearly in a similar situation. The towns are very few in proportion to the extent of country, and those are but thinly inhabited, Indeed Morocco, which is a metropolis, has many of its houses in ruins and uninhabited.

The want of population in the empire of Morocco, at this period may have been occasioned, in some degree by the enormous cruelties exercised by its former sovereigns, who have been known, not unfrequently, through a slight disgust to abandon a whole town or province to the sword. In the character of Muley Ishmael, grandfather to Sidi Mahomet, we find the most singular inconsistencies; for it is certain, that although a tyrant of the class which I have been describing, yet in other respects, as if to repair the mischief which he committed, he left nothing undone for the encouragement of population. He introduced large colonies of Negroes from Guinea, built towns for them, many of which are still remaining, assigned them portions of land, and encouraged their encrease by every possible means. He soon initiated them in the Mahometan faith, and, had his plan been followed, the country by this time would have been populous, and probably flourishing. As the Negroes are of a more lively, active, and enterprizing disposition than the Moors, they might soon have been taught the arts of agriculture, and their singular ingenuity might have been directed to other useful purposes.

It is true Muley Ifhmael, when he adopted this plan, had more objects in view than that of merely peopling his dominions: he faw plainly that his own fubjects were of too capricious a difpofition to form foldiers calculated for his tyrannical purpofes. They had uniformly manifefted an inclination to change their fovereigns, though more from the love of variety than to reform the government, or reftrain the abufes of tyranny. In fhort, whatever revolutions took place in the country confifted merely in a change of one tyrant for another. Muley Ifhmael had difcernment enough to fee, therefore, that by forming an army of flaves whofe fole dependence fhould reft upon their mafter, he could eafily train them in fuch a manner as to act in the ftricteft conformity to his wifhes. He foon learnt that the great object with the Negroes was plenty of money, and liberty of plunder; in thefe he liberally indulged them, and the plan fully anfwered his expectations.

Though, however, Muley Ifhmael had no great merit in introducing fubjects for the purpofes of tyranny, yet the good effects of this new colonization were very generally experienced. By intermarrying among themfelves, and intermixing among the Moors (for the Moors will keep Negro women as concubines, though they feldom marry them) a new race of people ftarted up, who became as ufeful fubjects as the native inhabitants, and brought the empire into a much more flourifhing ftate than it had ever been in fince their great revolution.

Sidi

Sidi Mahomet had different views, and was actuated by different motives. From his inordinate avarice, he ceased to act towards his black troops in the generous manner which had distinguished his predeceffor Muley Ifhmael; and they foon fhewed themfelves difcontented with his conduct. They frequently threatened to revolt, and fupport thofe of his fons who were in oppofition, and who promifed them the moft liberal rewards. They offered to place his eldeft fon Muley Ali, who is fince dead, on the throne; but this prince, not unmindful of the duty which he owed his father and fovereign, declined their offer. They next applied to Muley Yazid, the late emperor, who at firft accepted of the affiftance they tendered, but in a fhort time relinquifhed the plan.

Sidi Mahomet, difgufted with this conduct of the Negroes, determined to curb their growing power, by difbanding a confiderable part of thefe troops, and banifhing them to diftant parts of the empire. This important mode of population has therefore been of late years neglected, while no better fyftem has been fubftituted in its room; for though the late emperor indulged in cruelty much lefs frequently than his predeceffors, yet population has, perhaps, been more completely impeded by the general poverty which he has introduced into the country by his fevere exactions, than if he had made a liberal ufe of the fword or of the bow-ftring. To acquaint Sidi Mahomet that any of his fubjects were rich, was equivalent to telling him that he had fo many ambitious opponents, who by their wealth would fupport his fons in rebellion, which it was neceffary to prevent, by depriving them of thofe riches.

E 3

The

The only maxim of government therefore a-
dopted by this monarch was to keep his subjects
as nearly as possible upon a level; that is, in a state
of poverty. This he most effectually accomplish-
ed. No man who had property one day could
with certainty call it his own the next. The most
devoted misers, with their utmost ingenuity, were
unable to evade the discovery of their treasure. If
the victim of tyranny manifested any reluctance
to reveal to his inquisitors the sacred depository
of his hoarded wealth, the emperor seldom hesita-
ted about the means of compulsion. The fortitude of several enabled them to resist every tor-
ture short of death; but the love of life was always found to prevail over even avarice itself.

But this perhaps was not the worst; the heavy
taxes and duties imposed by this impolitic monarch
impeded commerce, and discouraged manufactures; and on the whole I am inclined to believe
that the country was never in a greater state of
poverty than during his reign.

Power and weakness, rank and meanness, opulence and indigence, are here equally dependent,
equally uncertain. There are instances of the sul-
tan elevating at once a common soldier to the rank
of a bashaw, or making him a confidential friend;
the following day he would perhaps imprison him,
or reduce him again to the station of a private
soldier. It is surprising that men under these circumstances should be ambitious of rank, or desi-
rous of riches and power. Yet such is the disposition of these people, that they have an unbounded thirst for rank and power with all their
uncertainties; and, what is more extraordinary,
when they have obtained a high station they seldom

dom fail to afford their fovereign a plea for ill-treating them, by abufing, in fome way or other, their truft.

The only independent people in the country, if it be at all lawful to make ufe of the expreffion when fpeaking of Morocco, are to be found among the merchants who refide in towns at fome diftance from the feat of government. The neatnefs of their houfes and gardens, the furniture of their apartments, their rich difplay of china and glafs, and their liberal treatment of ftrangers, their better education, and more enlightened ideas, all ferve to point them out as a clafs of beings different from the reft.

I wifh this defcription would apply generally to all the people in trade; but I am forry to add it does not: it is confined to a particular clafs of merchants, who tranfact bufinefs upon a very large fcale. Even thefe, however, though diftant from the feat of government, befides, rigoroufly paying their quota of every fevere tax which the emperor chufes to impofe upon them, are not always exempt from plunder. If the bafhaw or Alcaide of the town can difcover a plea for imprifoning them, which he fometimes does without much regard to juftice, he feldom fails to turn it to his own advantage; and not unfrequently difgraces his mafter's royal name, by ufing it as a pretext for feizing their property.—Thus the empire of Morocco, in all its parts, prefents a ftriking picture of the wretched policy and miferable confequences of defpotic government.

E 4   C H A P.

CHAP. V.

Journey from MOGODORE *to* SANTA CRUZ.—*Some Account of the Origin of that Place.*—*Arrival at* TARUDANT.—*Introduction to the Prince.*—*Description of his Palace.*—*Singular Reception.*—*Accommodations.*—*State of the Prince's Health.*—*Absurd Prejudices of the Moors.*—*Altercation with the Prince.*—*Application from other Patients.*—*The Cadi.*—*Introduction into the Prince's Harem.*—*Wives of the Prince.*—*State of the Female Sex in this Secluded Situation.*—*Visible amendment in the Prince's Complaint.*—*His Affability.*—*Character of the Prince* MULEY ABSULEM.

I Had not rested from the fatigues of my journey above six days at Mogodore, before a new scene was opened, by the return of the messenger from Tarudant, with orders for my immediate attendance on my royal patient. In addition to my former party, I was allowed by the governor three Negro foot-soldiers, armed with muskets and sabres, an elegant tent, and a Jewish interpreter, who was perfect master of both Arabic and English, and from whom in the end I derived the most useful services. The Jew who had been pressed in so singular a manner into my service at Tangier was immediately, and doubtless much to his own satisfaction, sent home.

We performed a journey of seventy-six miles, from Mogodore to Santa Cruz, in about three

days,

days, which from the former part of this Narrative the reader will perceive is not remarkably flow travelling, in Morocco, however fingular fuch a progrefs would appear on the level turnpikes of England. Our journey, which was on the fea-coaft, prefented to our view one continued expanfe of wild, mountainous, and rocky country, and we had confequently very bad roads. Our progrefs indeed could be compared to nothing but the continual afcending and defcending of a feries of rough and uneven ftone fteps. At one place in particular the defcent was fo fteep, and the road fo choaked up with large pieces of ftone, that we were all obliged to difmount, and walk a full mile and a half with the utmoft caution and difficulty, before we could mount again.

Santa Cruz is a fea-port, fituated on the declivity of a high and fteep mountain, forming the Weftern termination of that chain of mountains, which nearly divides the emperor's dominions into two parts, fo well known by the name of the Atlas. It formerly belonged to the Portugueze, and till the acceffion of Sidi Mahomet was the principal place whence Europeans were allowed to trade. It is at prefent a deferted town, with only a few houfes, wich are almoft hourly mouldering to decay. The port appears to be much more fecure than that of Mogodore; and from the vicinity of Santa Cruz to the Southern provinces, it appears to me to be the part of the empire which is beft adapted to all the purpofes of commerce*.

* As Santa Cruz, before the reign of Sidi Mahomet, was, and is ftill capable of being made of great commercial importance to Europe; and as its origin will afford fome idea.

how.

E. 5.

On the 26th of October we departed for Tarudant, which is diftant forty-four miles from Santa Cruz, where in two days we arrived. Our journey to this place was immediately inland, be-

how the Portugueze came to fettle upon this coaft; I muft trefpafs upon the reader's patience, while I relate, from an eminent Spanifh author, in what manner it was firft raifed; as well as its fubfequent ftate while poffeffed by the Moors, in the year 1737, from the manufcript of an Englifh gentleman who was refident in the country at that period.

" Agader Aguer, which the Europeans call Santa Cruz, is a town of modern fabric ; nor can I any where find that the fpot of ground on which it ftands was ever actually inhabited, till the beginning of the fixteenth century. Then, or very foon before, in the reign of Don Manuel, King of Portugal, a certain Portugueze adventurer undertook to fettle there, on account of the quantity of excellent fifh with which its bay abounded; and found means to build himfelf a timber fort or caftle, which he garrifoned with his fellowers, naming his fettlement Santa Cruz, or Holy Crofs; his African neighbours calling it Dar al Rumi, or the Chriftian Houfe.

" Don Manuel foon after forefeeing the great importance of this place to the navigation of thofe feas, and to his projected conqueft of the weftern parts of Barbary, took it into his own hands, reimburfing the adventurer who had founded it, all his expences, and making him other gratuities. Santa Cruz being thus annexed to the kingdom of Portugal, it was foon enlarged, fortified, and well inhabited ; and as this part of the world was at that time divided among feveral petty fovereigns, generally at variance with each other, it afforded the new colony, as well as many others upon the fame coaft, an opportunity of eftablifhing a firm footing in the country, inducing a number of difcontented Arabs and Moors, with a view of revenging themfelves on their various adverfaries, to fwear allegiance to his Portugueze Majefty.

" The affiftance which was afforded by thefe people to the Chriftian garrifons, enabled them to make frequent incurfions a confiderable way up the country, plundering and feizing upon a great number of the inhabitants, whom
they

ing in the direction, and within half a day's ride to the South of the Atlas. We enjoyed the whole way from Santa Cruz a fine level road, through a woody and uncultivated country.

they fent over to Europe as flaves. At this period, the Portugueze had eftablifhed themfelves fo firmly on the African coaft, that had not the family of Sharifs ftarted up, and the attention of thefe Chriftian adventurers been diverted to their new acquifitions in America, the greateft part of the country would in a fhort time have been completely depopulated, and the Portugueze would have eftablifhed in it a permanent fovereignty.

"Thefe Sharifs, from whom the prefent royal family of Morocco are immediately defcended, obferving the variance between the people and their different fovereigns, and taking advantage of their credulity, pretended that they were lineally defcended from Mahomet, and that they were fent by him to protect his followers from the oppreffions of their fovereigns. They foon made converts to their ftandard, and in a fhort time eftablifhed themfelves in the fovereignty of all the fouthern parts of Barbary. In order to add importance to their government, and knowing that it would flatter the prejudices of their fubjects, who had been fo continually haraffed by their Chriftian neighbours, they determined upon expelling the Portugueze from Santa Cruz, and if fuccefsful, to carry on their attacks againft the other Chriftian garrifons upon the Barbary coaft.

"For this purpofe, in the year 1536, an army of 50,000 men, horfe and foot, was raifed with all expedition, and put under the command of Muley Hamed al Haffan, who with this force completely invefted the garrifon. After many unfuccefsful attacks on the part of the Moors, Santa Cruz at laft owed its deftruction to the negligence of one of its own people; who carrying a lighted match into the powder-magazine, it unfortunately blew up, and by its concuffion made a large breach in the wall; of which the Moors availing themfelves, they immediately recovered their fpirits, and, headed by their commander, haftened in force up to the breach, before the aftonifhed Portugueze

had

Upon my arrival at Tarudant, without being allowed time to difmount, I was immediately carried to the refidence of the prince, which is fituated about half a mile to the South of the town.

had time to apply a proper remedy to this unforefeen accident. They now attacked their enemy with fo much energy, and with fuch fuperior numbers, that they foon reduced the garrifon, and put every perfon in it to the fword.

"Thus did Santa Cruz fall into the hands of the Moors, by whom it has ever fince been poffeffed. The lofs of this important place proved extremely injurious to the Portugueze navigation to Guinea and India, by affording a harbour to their European enemies, whofe fhips were accuftomed to flip out from this port, and to plunder and take the Portugueze as they paffed by; while they fupplied thofe barbarians with powder, cannon, and other warlike ftores, enabling the Moors by that means, in the courfe of time, to attack the other poffeffions of the Portugueze in Africa."

My Englifh author, who dates his manufcript in January 1737, gives the following account of Santa Cruz:—

"Santa Cruz is a city of Africa, in the kingdom of Suz, fubject to the Emperor of Fez and Morocco, fituated in a temperate air, on a mountain diftant about half a league from the fea, in the latitude 30 deg. 35 min. North, feven leagues from Cape de Guerra, fixty from Morocco, one hundred and forty from Fez, and one hundred and fifty from Mequinez. It is in circumference about three quarters of a mile, of a fquare form, the four fides fronting the four quarters of the world. On the eaft, it has a fpacious plain of fand; on the weft, the fea; to the north, about the diftance of a quarter of a mile, is a fmall village, containing about twenty inhabitants; and on the fouth is its entrance, oppofite to the mount of Tylde.

"The town is encompaffed with walls defended by feven baftions, having artillery mounted on them which carry between four and fix pound balls; there are alfo fome fixteen and twenty-four pounders, but, owing to their not having proper perfons to work them, thofe pieces of ordnance

At a fhort diftance, the houfe, which is fmall, and was built by the prince, has a great appearance of neatnefs; but that want of tafte and convenience, which is univerfally the characteriftic of the Moorifh buildings, is prefently difcernable when it is narrowly infpected.   It is compofed of tabby, and is furrounded with a high fquare wall, which allo enclofes two tolerably neat gardens, planned

nance are fuffered to lie on the ground half buried, rendering them by that means entirely ufclefs.   The walls indeed are only of fufficient ftrength to refift an attack from their neighbouring enemies, the Arabs, who have no ordnance to oppofe them with, but they could by no means withftand even a weak cannonade from a regular appointed artillery.

" Santa Cruz is a place of confiderable trade, owing to the great quantities of copper which they procure from mines in the neighbourhood of Tafilet.   It is alfo plentifully ftored with various other merchandizes, fuch as wax procured from Heja Saxit and Morocco, the beft in the country, Morocco leather, yellow leather of Tafilet, almonds, gum arabic, gum fandarac, oftrich feathers, elephants teeth, gold duft, and falt petre, wh ch is exported with fome difficulty owing to its being contraband.   There are alfo other merchandizes of European Manufacture, fuch as iron, leather from Buenos Ayres, mufquets, fwords, and all kinds of hard-ware, &c. as well as thofe of Afia and the eaftern parts of Africa, brought thither by caravans. The people are for the moft part of a tawny, fun-burnt complexion, fpare and lean in body, but active, ftrong, and capable of undergoing any labour or hardfhip, pretty good œcononiifts, not much addicted to prodigality or vanity, and are dexterous and active in their trade and bufinefs."

Such was the ftate of Santa Cruz before Sidi Mahomet ordered it to be evacuated by the European merchants: and it is impoffible to read this account without being convinced that what I have advanced, with refpect to its importance in a commercial view, is not beyond the truth.

by

by an European, and now under the care of a
Spanish renegado. The apartments, which are
all on the ground-floor, are square and lofty,
opening into a court, in the centre of which is a
fountain. The entrance is through a small arched
door-way, which leads into a court-yard, where
on one side are a few out-houses; on the other,
the space allotted for the horses of the prince.
As the climate is open and fine, there are few or
no stables in this country, but the horses are kept
out in an open yard, and held by pins fixed in the
ground.

There is not much of magnificence, it must be
confessed, in this introduction, nor did any thing
occur to counteract the unfavourable impression,
previous to our entering the apartment of the
prince. The chamber into which I was conducted,
I found a small room with seats in the walls; and
there it is customany for all persons to wait till
their names are announced. I observed a number
of singular looking persons attending here; and
as I was not much disposed to make one of their
company, instead of sitting, I amused myself, as
Europeans do, with walking about the room. In
this exercise, however, I was a solitary perfor-
mer; for the Moors, whatever be their object,
whether business, coverfation, or amusement, are
generally seated; and indeed so novel to them was
my deportment in this respect, that they concluded
I was either distracted in my intellect, or saying
my prayers.

After being detained in this disagreeable situation for about an hour, orders were brought from
the prince for my immediate introduction with my
                                      interpreter.

interpreter. From the chamber where we had been waiting, we paffed through a long and dark entry, which at its termination introduced us to a fquare court-yard, floored with checquered tiling, into which the prince's room opened, by means of large folding-doors. Thefe were curioufly painted with various colours, in the form of checquers. The immediate entrance to the room was neat; it was a very large arched door-way, curioufly ornamented with checquered tileing, and forming a fmall porch, or antichamber. The room was lofty, fquare, and floored with checquered tiling; the walls ftuccoed, and the cieling painted of various colours. Much of the beauty of the room was loft for want of windows, which is a defect obfervable in moft Moorifh houfes.

I found the prince fitting crofs-legged, on a matrafs covered with fine white linen, and placed on the floor; this, with a narrow and long piece of carpeting that fronted him on which were feated his Moorifh friends, was the only furniture in the room. Upon my firft entrance, and delivering the conful's letter of introduction, which acccording to the cuftom of the country, was prefented in a filk handkercief, I was addreffed by the prince with the falutation *Bono tibib, bono Anglaife*; which is a mixture of Arabic and Spanifh, meaning, " You are a good doctor, the Englifh are good ;" and was ordered with my interpreter to fit down on the floor, between the prince and his vifitors ; when I was immediately interrogated by every one prefent, each having a

queftion

queſtion to put to me, and that of the moſt inſignificant kind.

The prince expreſſed great pleaſure at my arrival, wiſhed to know whether I came voluntarily or not, and whether the Engliſh phyſicians were in high repute. To the firſt queſtion I replied, that I was ſent by order of the governor of Gibraltar : to the ſecond, I felt it a duty which I owed to truth and to my country, to anſwer in the affirmative. He then deſired me immediately to feel his pulſe and to examine his eyes, one of which was darkened by a cataract, and the other affected with a paralytic complaint ; and requeſted me to inform him, whether I would undertake to cure him, and how ſoon ? My anſwer was, that I wiſhed to conſider his caſe maturely before I gave my opinion ; and in a day or two I ſhould be a better judge.

One of his particular friends obſerved to him, from ſeeing me without a beard, for I had ſhaved in the morning, I was too young to be an able phyſician. Another remarked, that I had put powder in my hair on purpoſe to diſguiſe my age ; and a third inſiſted, that it was not my own hair. But what ſeemed to produce the greateſt aſtoniſhment among them, was my dreſs, which from its cloſeneſs, the Mooriſh dreſs being quite looſe, they were certain muſt occaſion pain, and be diſagreeably warm.

The reader may be aſſured, that a part of this converſation was not very entertaining to me ; and indeed after the great fatigue which I had undergone, I could well have diſpenſed with moſt

of

of their interrogatories; but inftead of the dif-
miffion and repofe which I wifhed and expected,
my patience was exhaufted by the abfurd curiofity of the whole court, who one after another
intreated me to favour them with my opinion,
and inform them of the ftate of their health,
merely by feeling the pulfe. Having acquitted
myfelf to the beft of my ability in this curious enquiry, the prince informed me, he had prepared for
my reception a good houfe, whither he defired me
to retire, and vifit him the following morning early,
when I was to examine his cafe more particularly.

The good houfe promifed me by the prince,
proved to be a miferable room in the Jewdry, that is, the part of the fuburb inhabited by
the Jews, fituated about a quarter of a mile
from the town. It was however, the habitation
of the prince's principal Jew, and the beft in the
place. This apartment which was on the ground
floor, was narrow and dirty, having no windows,
to it, but opening by means of large folding-
doors into a court, where three Jewifh families,
who lived all in the fame houfe, threw the whole
of their rubbifh and dirt. I fuppofe my feelings
might be rendered more acute by the difappointment, for on being introduced into this wretched
hovel, I was fo ftruck with horror and difguft, that
I was on the point of mounting my horfe, for the
purpofe of afking the prince for another apartment; but upon being told it was the beft in the
town, and reflecting that I had voluntarily entered
upon thefe difficulties, I determined to ftruggle
through them as well as I could, and confented
for the prefent to acquiefce in this indifferent fare.

I took

I took, however, the firſt opportunity of repreſenting my diſagreeable ſituation to the prince, who gave orders for apartments to be fitted up for me in his garden; but from the ſlowneſs of the maſons, they were not finiſhed in time for me to occupy them before I left Tarudant. The prince's Jew had directions to ſupply me with every thing that was neceſſary; and while at Tarudant I had no reaſon whatever to complain of any inattention on the part of the prince.

As ſoon as my baggage was unpacked, the firſt object that occurred to me was to endeavour, under theſe circumſtances, to make my ſituation as comfortable as the nature of it would admit. At one end of my room I placed my three folding ſtools, which I had uſed as a bed on the road, and ſcreened it off as well as I could with mats, which I fixed acroſs the apartment as a partition. One of my boxes were ſubſtituted for a table, and another for a chair, not being able to procure either of thoſe articles in Tarudant. At the other end of the room my interpreter placed his bedding on the floor, where he ſlept during the whole of our ſtay.

Having furniſhed our room, our next object was to conſider in what manner our cookery was to be performed. The whole of our kitchen furniture conſiſted of one ſmall iron ſauce-pan, one pewter diſh, two pewter plates, a horn to drink out of, and two knives and forks. As the Moors are many of them accuſtomed to the uſe of tea, breakfaſting articles we were not at a loſs for. On the road the iron ſauce-pan had ſerved very well to boil our eggs and fowls, which, as I be-

fore

fore obferved, were the only food we could procure. But at Tarudant we found ourfelves in a
a land of plenty, without having it in our power
to avail ourfelves of fuch an advantage. After a
few days inconvenience on this account, I found
out a Jew, who contrived to drefs me a few
hafhes and ftews fomething in the Spanifh ftile,
with which fare I was obliged to be fatisfied during my refidence at Tarudant.

Two hours before my arrival, the whole of the
Englifh people who had been fhipwrecked, except
the captain and a Negro, paffed through the town
in their way to the Metropolis. They had been redeemed from the wild Arabs, by Muley Abfulem,
with an intent, I prefume, of complying with his
promife, but by the emperor's orders were fent up
to Morocco.

Upon my vifiting the prince the following day,
and examining into the nature of his complaint,
I found it to be of the moft defperate kind; but
as I had travelled near five hundred miles to fee
him, I could not be fatisfied to return back without attempting fomething; I therefore gave a
formal opinion to the prince in writing, ftating,
that I could by no means abfolutely undertake to
cure him; that I could not even flatter him with
very great hopes of fuccefs; but that if he chofe
to give my plan of treatment a trial for a couple
of months, we could then judge whether the difeafe was likely to be removed. This plan was
approved of, and he immediately began his courfe
of medicines.

I have already intimated, that the prince had
totally loft the ufe of one eye by a cataract; and
I may

I may add, that he had nearly loft that of the other by a paralytic affection, which threatened to end in a gutta ferena*, and which had drawn the eye fo much towards the nofe, as fometimes entirely to exclude the appearance of the pupil. The only remains of fight left, were merely fufficient to enable him to fee large bodies without diftinguifhing any of them particularly. The fpafm was the difeafe which I was ordered to cure.

But thefe were by no means the limits of the prince's complaints. For in truth, his whole frame was fo enervated by a courfe of debauchery, that I found it neceffary to put him under a ftrict regimen; to enforce the obfervance of which, I committed from time to time my directions to writing. They were tranflated into Arabic, and one copy delivered to the prince, and the other to his confidential friend, who undertook, at my requeft, to fee them carried into execution.

As I adminiftered internal as well as topical remedies, I made a point of giving them to my patient with my own hand. The prince made no difficulty of fwallowing the medicine, however naufeous; but it was a long time before I could make him comprehend, how a medicine introduced into the ftomach could afford any relief to the eye. I muft, however, do him the juftice to fay, that I found him a more apt difciple than any of his attendants. Many of them could not be made at all to underftand the action of medicines,

---

* By this difeafe is to be underftood, fuch a ftate of the optic nerve as renders it infenfible to the rays of light.

and

and of confequence were full of prejudices againft my mode of treatment.

In a few days after my firft attendance on the prince, one of his prejudiced friends perfuaded his highnefs, that I had adminiftered medicines to him intended to produce a certain effect upon his conftitution, of which I had never entertained fo much as an idea before it was mentioned to me. What this effect was I cannot with decency explain. Suffice it to fay that thefe malignant infinuations had too powerful an effect on the mind of my patient, and he expreffed himfelf to me upon the fubject in terms which I could not hear without the moft poignant indignation and uneafinefs.

I vindicated my conduct as well as I was able, under the difadvantages of an interpretation by explaining to him how impoffible for the medicines to have the effect he fufpected; and how much more to my credit, as well as advantage, it would be to re-eftablifh his health than to do him a prejudice; that a profeffional man had a character; which when once loft was irrecoverable; and that therefore I trufted he would reflect on my fituation, and confider me in a more favourable light than his refentment at firft had led him to fuggeft. The prince began now to retract his calumny, by faying that he believed the medicines had produced an effect different from what I intended, but that it was the duty of the patient to inform his phyfician of every circumftance which related to his health. In fhort, after a variety of explanations, I at laft brought him to confent to give my plan a few days longer trial, and if then

there

there appeared any objections to the purfuing of it, I would willingly confent to give it up entirely. Thofe days being elapfed, and none of the fufpected effects appearing, the prince proceeded regularly in the courfe agreeably to my directions.

The intermediate time between my attendance on the prince whom I vifited twice a-day, was employed in reading a few books which I brought with me from Mogodore, making little excurfions into the country, and vifiting patients at Tarudant.

Among the latter was the Cadi, or judge of the town. This I found to be a venerable old man, of about feventy years of age, whofe beard was become perfectly white, and whofe countenance, though doubtlefs altered by time, yet ftill retained a great expreffion of vivacity and fenfe, mixed with more apparent goodnefs of heart than any I had feen in the country. He received me with the greateft refpect, and expreffed his gratitude for my vifit in a manner that appeared ftrongly marked with fincerity. He feemed fully aware tnat his complaint was merely a decay of nature, and only wifhed me to adminifter fomething to him which might palliate his moft urgent fymptoms. With a great fhare of feeling he expatiated on the inconveniences I muft undergo, from being at fo great a diftance from my friends, and in a part of the world where the manners of the people were fo different from what I had been accuftomed to, expreffing his wifh at the fame time to render me every fervice that a perfon in his fituation could offer. Such an uncommon fhare of fenfibility and reflection, from one whofe countrymen are in general in a very fmall degree removed from the favage ftate, excited in me a warm defire of rendering my patient a fervice; among the many queftions he put to me, he afked what was cuftomary for our judges in England to receive as a reward for their fervices. Upon my informing him, the Cadi was in perfect aftonifhment: " Good God!" he exclaimed, " the emperor allows me only fifty " ducats (about twelve pounds fterling) a year !"

I wifh I could have it in my power to give as favourable an account of my other patients at Tarudant, as of this refpectable old man. The generality of them proved infolent, ungrateful, and many, who vifited my habitation, notorious thieves. From my apartment being in the houfe of a Jew, none of whom dare venture to prevent a Moor from entering, I was from morning to night peftered with Arabs, mountaineers and the worft defcription of towns-people, who were feldom fatisfied with my advice, but infifted on my either giving them money, or fomething elfe equal in value. Many I turned out of my room by force, while with difficulty they reftrained their refentment at my conduct, and every moment threatened to draw their knives upon me; to others, who behaved a little better, I gave fomething to get rid of them; and to a third who, were real objects of diftrefs, I with pleafure extended my utmoft affiftance. On the whole, my fituation was fuch as to oblige me to complain of it to the prince, who afterwards allowed me a foldier to mount guard conftantly at my door, who
had

had directions to permit no person to enter my room without my particular permission.

It was with the greatest pleasure that in about a fortnight after my first attendance on the prince, I observed an amendment in his complaint. His eye now evinced a disposition to recover its former position; at first he was able only to discern light from darkness, but he could now distinguish an apple at about ten yards distance.

These flattering appearances entirely removed every prejudice which at first arose in the minds of the prince's attendants; and his highness himself acknowledged that he had been too hasty in forming his opinion of me. The confidence which this success occasioned, induced the prince to admit me into his Harem, where there were several ladies who had occasion for my services.

Though this afforded me an opportunity of seeing the Harem, I shall wave a particular description of it, as it only differed from that of the the emperor (which I shall hereafter very particularly describe) by being on a smaller scale.

Upon receiving the prince's orders to attend his ladies, one of his friends was immediately dispatched with me to the gate of the Harem; with directions to the Alcaide* of the eunuchs to admit myself and interpreter whenever I thought it necessary.

The eunuchs, who have the entire charge of the women, and who in fact live always among them, are the children of Negro slaves. They are generally either very short and fat; or else

---

* An officer in the general idea of the word.

tall,

tall, deformed, and lame. Their voices have that particular tone which is obfervable in youths who are juft arriving at manhood; and their perfons altogether afford a difgufting image of weaknefs and effeminacy. From the truft repofed in them by their mafters, and the confequence which it gives them, the eunuchs exceed in infolence and pride every other clafs of people in the country. They difplayed indeed fo much of it towards me, that I was obliged, in my own defence, to complain of them once or twice, and to have them punifhed.

Attended by one of thefe people, after paffing the gate of the Harem, which is always locked, and under the care of a guard of eunuchs, we entered a narrow and dark paffage, which foon brought us to the court, into which the women's chambers open. We here faw numbers of both black and white women and children; fome concubines, fome flaves, and others hired domeftics.

Upon their obferving the unufual figure of an European, the whole multitude in a body furrounded me, and expreffed the utmoft aftonifhment at my drefs and appearance. Some ftood motionlefs with their hands lifted up, their eyes fixed, and their mouths open, in the ufual attitude of wonder and furprize. Some burft into immoderate fits of laughter; while others again came up, and, with uncommon attention, eyed me from head to foot. The parts of my drefs which feemed moft to attract their notice were my buckles, buttons, and flockings; for neither men for women in this country wear any thing of the kind.

F

kind. With refpect to the club of my hair, they feemed utterly at a lofs in what view to confider it; but the powder which I wore they conceived to be employed for the purpofe of deftroying vermin. Moft of the children when they faw me, ran away in the moft perfect confternation; and on the whole I appeared as fingular an animal, and I dare fay had the honour of exciting as much curiofity and attention, as a lion, or a mantiger juft imported from abroad, and introduced into a country town in England on a market-day. Every time I vifited the Harem I was furrounded and laughed at by this curious mob, who, on my entering the gate, followed me clofe to the very chamber to which I was proceeding, and on my return univerfally efcorted me out.

The greateft part of the women were uncommonly fat and unwieldy; had black and full eyes, round faces, with fmall nofes. They were of different complexions; fome very fair, fome fallow, and others again perfect Negroes.

One of my new patients being ready to receive me, I was defired to walk into her room; where, to my great furprife, I faw nothing but a curtain drawn quite acrofs the apartment, fimilar to that of a theatre which feparates the ftage from the audience. A female domeftic brought a very low ftool, placed it near the curtain, and told me I was to fit down there, and feel her miftrefs's pulfe.

The lady, who had by this time fummoned up courage to fpeak, introduced her hand from the bottom of the curtain, and defired me to inform her of all her complaints, which fhe conceived I

might

might perfectly perceive by merely feeling the pulfe. It was in vain to afk her where her pain was feated, whether in her ftomach, head, or back; the only anfwer I could procure was a requeft to feel the pulfe of the other hand, and then point out the feat of the difeafe, and the nature of the pain.

Having neither fatisfied my curiofity by exhibiting her face, nor made me acquainted with the nature of her complaint, I was under the neceffity of informing her in pofitive terms, that to underftand the difeafe it was abfolutely neceffary to fee the tongue, as well as to feel the pulfe; and that without it I could do nothing for her. My eloquence, or rather that of my Jewifh interpreter, was, however, for a long time exerted in vain; and I am perfuaded fhe would have difmiffed me without any further enquiry, had not her invention fupplied her with a happy expedient to remove her embarraffment. She contrived at laft to cut a hole through the curtain, through which fhe extruded her tongue, and thus complied with my injunction as far as it was neceffary in a medical view, but moft effectually difappointed my curiofity.

I was afterwards ordered to look at another of the prince's wives, who was affected with a fcrophulus fwelling in her neck. This lady was, in the fame manner as the other, at firft excluded from my fight; but as fhe was obliged to fhew me her complaint, I had an opportunity of feeing her face, and obferved it to be very handfome. I was informed that fhe had been at one period the favourite of the prince, but owing to this defect

he

he had in a great meafure deferted her; and this circumftance accounts for the extreme anxiety which fhe feemed to exprefs to get rid of this dif-agreeable difeafe.

As foon as I had examined her neck, fhe took off from her drefs the whole of her gold trinkets, which were very numerous, and of confiderable value, put them into my hand, and defired me to cure her; promifing a ftill greater reward if I fucceeded. Confcious of the uncertainty of render-ing her any material fervice, I immediately re-turned the prefent, and affured her that fhe might depend on my giving all proper remedies a fair trial, but that I could not be anfwerable for their fuccefs. There is nothing more unpleafant than the inability of giving reafonable ground for hope, when it promifes to be productive of fo much hap-pinefs to a fellow-creature. It was with pain I obferved that this poor lady, though fomewhat cheered, was yet diffatisfied with my reply; fhe could not refrain from fhowing evident marks of difappointment, and even difpleafure, at my hefita-tion, by faying, fhe always underftood that a Chriftian phyfician could cure every difeafe.

During the courfe of my attendance in the Ha-rem, I had an opportunity of feeing moft of the prince's women, who, exclufive of the four wives allowed him by his religion, were about twenty in number, and who did not, like his wives, dif-cover that invincible reluctance to the difplay of their beauty. They at firft proved very trouble-fome patients; for upon my not telling them all their complaints immediately upon feeling the pulfe, they confidered me as an ignorant empiric,

who

who knew nothing of my profeffion.   Befides this,
I found that each of them flattered themfelves
with almoft an inftantaneous cure.   In fhort, after
many fruitlefs efforts to teach thofe to reafon who
had hitherto never made the fmalleft ufe of their
underftandings, I was at laft obliged to adapt my
deportment to the capacities of my patients, and
foon acquired among them as much undeferved
commendation as I had incurred unmerited re-
proach.

Moft of the women in the Harem were under
thirty years of age, of a corpulent habit, and of
a very aukward gait.   Their knowledge of courfe,
from having led a life of total feclufion from the
world, was entirely confined to the occurrences
in their Harem; where, as they were allowed a free
accefs to each other, they converfed upon fuch
fubjects as their uninformed underftandings
ferved to furnifh them with.   They are never
fuffered to go out, but by an exprefs order from
the prince; and then only when removing from
one place of refidence to another.   I in general
found them extremely ignorant, proud, and vain of
their perfons, even to a degree which bordered upon childifhnefs.   Among many ridiculous queftions, they afked my interpreter if I could read
and write; upon being anfwered in the affirmative,
they expreffed the utmoft furprife and admiration
at the abilities of the Chriftians.   There was not
one among them who could do either; thefe rudi-
ments of learning are indeed only the lot of a few
of their men, who on that account are named
Talbs, or explainers of the Mahometan law.

F 3

Among

Among the concubines of the prince there were six female flaves of the age of fifteen, who were prefented to him by a Moor of diftinction. One of thefe was defcended from an Englifh renegado, another from a Spanifh, and the other four were of Moorifh extraction.

Where the more folid and ufeful accomplifhments are leaft cultivated, a tafte is often found to prevail for thofe which are purely ornamental and frivolous. Thefe devoted victims of libidnous pleafure received a daily leffon of mufic, by order of the prince, from a Moor who had paffed fome little time in London and Italy, where he had acquired a flight knowledge of that fcience. I had an opportunity of being prefent at one of thefe performances, but cannot fay I received much amufement, in a mufical view, from my vifit. It was a concert vocal and inftrumental: the inftruments ufed upon this occafion were the mandoline, a kind of violin with only two ftrings, and the tabor. The principal object in their performance feemed to be noife; it was without the leaft attention to melody, variety, or tafte, and was merely drawing out a wild and melancholy ftrain.

Converfation, however, forms the principal entertainment in thefe gloomy retirements. When I vifited the Harem, I never found the women engaged in any other employment than that of converfing on the ground in circles. In fact, as all their needle-work is performed by Jeweffes, and their cookery, and the managemet of their chambers, by their flaves and domeftics, of which they have a proportionable number, according to the favour they are in with the prince, it is not eafy

for

for them to find means of occupying their time, and particularly fince none of them are able to read or write. It is impoffible, indeed, to reflect on the fituation of thefe unfortunate women without the moft lively fentiments of compaffion. Excluded from the enjoyment of frefh air and exercife, fo neceffary for the fupport of health and life; deprived of all fociety but that of their fellow-fufferers, a fociety to which moft of them would prefer folitude itfelf; they are only to be confidered as the moft abject of flaves—flaves to the vices and caprice of a licentious tyrant, who exacts even from his wives themfelves a degree of fubmiffion and refpect which borders upon idolatry, and which God and nature never meant fhould be paid to a mortal.

After the lapfe of a third week, there was a confiderable amendment in the prince's complaint. He began to diftinguifh very large writing; and he affured me that he had written with his own hand a letter to the emperor, wherein he informed him of the relief my attendance had afforded him; affuring me, that his father would reward me very handfomely if I effected a cure.

Our intercourfe was at this time improved into intimacy. He ufed to fee me without referve, and often at a time when he had his women with him, which, I was informed, was a mark of confidence with which no other man had ever before been honoured. He made me feel their pulfes, and obliged one of them, who was remarkably fat and unwieldy, to be held on the floor by two of the others, while I dropped into her eye fome of the fame medicine which I had occafion to ap-

F 4

ply

ply to his. The violent but temporary pain brought on by this application produced an immoderate fit of laughter in the prince, as well as in the other ladies; and the object of it, though in moſt violent pain, to evince her reſpect to his royal highneſs, declared it to be a very pleaſant ſenſation.

Upon other occaſions he would detain me for two, and ſometimes three hours, enquiring concerning European cuſtoms, and particularly thoſe of the Engliſh, their religion, laws, and government. He made ſome comments upon what I told him, manifeſted an earneſt deſire of information, and appeared greatly intereſted in the converſation. At other times, when he had been put out of humour, after I had felt his pulſe, and adminiſtered to him the medicines, he would diſmiſs me without aſking me to ſit down, or even allowing me to aſk any further queſtions.—But the curioſity of the reader is probably by this time excited reſpecting the perſon and character of this prince; and perhaps it cannot be gratified at a more convenient part of the Narrative.

Muley Abſulem is of the middle ſize, of rather a corpulent habit, and about thirty-five years of age. His features are very much disfigured by the great defect in his eyes; the cataract having entirely obſcured one of them, and the other being drawn quite on one ſide by the violence of the paralytic affection. Theſe circumſtances, joined to the great natural ſize and prominency of both eyes, a bad ſet of teeth, and a ſallow complexion, will not allow me to ſay that the prince has the ſmalleſt pretenſions to the character of handſome.

His

His drefs was the fame as that of other Moors, which I fhall hereafter defcribe, except a filk taffel to his turban, which is in this country a diftinctive mark of royalty. When I firft faw him, he was covered with a loofe furtout, made of red woollen cloth, and edged with fur-fkin, which the Moors term a Caftan. Indeed the only diftinction of drefs in this country is in the good or bad qualities of the materials. I have feen inftances of private Moors, whofe drefs was much richer than that of any of the princes, or even of the emperor him-felf. The attendants of the prince confifted prin-cipally of foldiers, of which he has an unlimited number, pages, who are generally about his per-fon, black eunuchs, and a few black flaves.

The character of Muley Abfulem is marked with lefs of feverity and cruelty than that of the greater part of the Moorifh princes; it poffeffes however, at the fame time, lefs of that fagacity, acutenefs, and activity, which is fo neceffary for the government of fo uncivilized a people as the Moors. To be explicit, this prince is naturally of a mild and indolent difpofition; immoderately indulgent to his paffions, when he can enjoy them without much trouble; and very little ambitious of fame.

Till very lately he had accuftomed himfelf to drink, to a very great excefs, ftrong brandy; that he has now entirely relinquifhed, and his principal paffion fince has been the love of women, which engroffes the whole of his attention and time. I obferved, however, that he allowed his ladies much more indulgence than is in general cuftomary among the Moors; and I found that even in his

F 5   prefence

prefence they converfed among each other with as much freedom as if they had been by themfelves.

From the fketch which I have given of the prince's character, it will be no difficult matter to difcover the reafons why his father's wifhes for appointing him his fucceffor were difappointed. He was rich, it is true, but a great part of his wealth was fquandered on fenfual gratifications; and the total want of energy in his character prevented his fecuring friends in a country, where cruelty and great activity are confidered as the only characteriftics of fovereignty.

The advantages of hereditary fucceffion can only be feen by contemplating the ftate of thofe monarchs where it does not exift. In Morocco, where there is no regular fixed order of fucceffion, though the emperor is indulged in the formality of nominating his fucceffor, yet the fword fupplies the place of right; and that prince who can acquire the greateft number of friends, and confequently the ftrongeft army, fucceeds to the throne. This circumftance is often attended with the moft fatal effects, and has given rife to thofe bloody revolutions which from one period to another have fhaken and depopulated the empire of Morocco. The emperor Sidi Mahomet, from having no competitors, enjoyed a much more peaceful reign than any of his predeceffors. How far his fucceffor, who has feveral brothers, each feeling an equal claim to the throne, will be equally fuccefsful, time only muft determine.

C II A P.

CHAP. VI.

Description of TARUDANT.—*Country of* VLED DE NON.
—*Markets for the Sale of Cattle.*—*Extraordinary
Amendment in the Prince's Complaint.*—*Great Civility
from two Moors.*—*Singular Adventure.*—*The Prince
ordered on a Pilgrimage to* MECCA.—*Intercession in
Favour of the English Captives.*—*Unexpected Order
to repair to* MOROCCO.

AS it is quite unfashionable in this country to
go even to the next ſtreet on foot, and as
my ſituation was at ſome diſtance from that of
the prince, his highneſs made me a preſent of an
horſe, which, however, I could not ſay was one
of the beſt in the country. But as I had once
engaged in his ſervice, I conceived it my intereſt
to make the beſt of every ſituation. In the hours,
therefore, when my perſonal attendance on my
patient was not demanded, I frequently made uſe
of my Roſinante, both for the purpoſe of exerciſe,
and for the gratification of my curioſity in viſiting
every thing which appeared worthy of inſpection.
The following are the principal obſervations which
I was able to collect in the courſe of my excur-
ſions; and I flatter myſelf they will ſerve at leaſt
to give a general idea of the city where I reſided,
and its environs.

Tarudant, now the capital of the province of
Suz, was formerly, while the empire was divided into petty ſtates, the metropolis of a kingdom.
It lies in a fine but uncultivated plain, about twenty
miles to the South of the Atlas, and may be conſidered.

fidered as the frontier town of that part of the emperor's dominions. The emperor, it is true, claims the fovereignty of the defert of Zahara, and the territory of Vled de Non. But his authority over that part of the country is almoft nominal; as it entirely depends on the caprice and inclination of the Arabs who inhabit it; and who, from their diftant fituation from the feat of government, are more properly under the dominion of their own chiefs. They acknowledge the emperor to be their fovereign, and the head of their church, and occafionally pay him tribute as fuch; but they pay no attention whatever to his particular orders, and over their interior government he has not the leaft controul.

Thefe people confift of different tribes of Arabs, who live in tents without any fixed places of refidence. They wander over the country in fearch of plunder, and are fuppofed, on fome occafions, to extend their depredations as far as Nigritia, whence they carry off Negroes. They profefs the Mahometan religion, though they intermix it with a great portion of idolatry; and in the deferts, where no water can be procured for the purpofe of ablution, they fubftitute fand. Their manner of treating thofe unfortunate mariners who have the misfortune to be fhipwrecked on their coaft, I fhall hereafter have occafion to reprefent.

The walls of Tarudant, now half in ruins, are very extenfive, and enclofe a much larger fpace of ground than is occupied by the buildings. The houfes, which are compofed of earth and mud, beaten very tight in a wooden cafe, and

left

left to be dried by the fun, have only appartments on the ground floor; and as each houfe is furrounded by a garden and wall, the place altogether bears a greater refemblance to a well-peopled fpot of country, or a collection of hamlets, than a town. This idea is much increafed by the number of lofty palm, or date trees, which are intermixed with, and overlook the houfes, affording altogether a very rural appearance. The apartments are in general mean and inconvenient, and principally inhabited by the lower clafs of mechanics, as there are very few Moors of diftinction refiding at Tarudant. It is true, when the prince is there, he brings with him all his attendants and friends, but they generally live in the caftle, and are by no means to be confidered as the inhabitants of the town.

From the irregular and ftraggling manner in which the town is built, it is impoffible to form a conjecture concerning the number of houfes and inhabitants it contains. As its extent, however, is confiderable, it may be accounted an important and populous city, when compared with moft of the others in the emperor's dominions.

The principal manufactures at Tarudant are making of fine Haicks, and the working of copper, which is procured in great plenty from a neighbouring mine. They have a regular market twice a week, where all kinds of cattle and provifions are brought to be difpofed of. For the fale of horfes and mules, the proprietor of the market employs men on purpofe to ride, and exhibit the beafts to the beft advantage, and afterwards to put them up to public auction. In thefe fales,

if

if the higheſt bidder does not offer a price agreeable to the owners, they are at liberty to refuſe
ſelling them.   This cuſtom prevents many of thoſe
impoſitions in the ſale of cattle, which too frequently prevail in European fairs and markets.
By thus putting the cattle up to public auction,
thoſe perſons who have really good ones will in
general get their full price for them; and thoſe
buyers, who from their ignorance might be liable
to be impoſed upon, can without much difficulty
form a tolerable idea of the real value of the animal
by the price which others bid.

The Jewdry is a miſerable place, ſituated about
a quarter of a mile from the town. The inhabitants
are in the moſt abject ſtate of poverty and ſub-
jection, and when they enter the Mooriſh town
are obliged to go barefooted.   The caſtle, which
is very extenſive, and ſituated halfway between
the town and Dar Beyda, the reſidence of the
prince, is incloſed in a tolerably neat garden,
which was planned by a Frenchman.   It is divided into three parts; one for the prince, which
he occaſionally uſes, the other for his women,
named the Harem*, and the third for all thoſe
who are in the ſervice of the prince.

As the prince's recovery became daily obſerv-
able, I thought I might venture to try him with
a large watch which I had with me, to ſee whether he could point out the time of the day.
In this he ſucceeded very well, and had diſcern-

* Europeans have in general an idea, that the place allotted for the women to live in is named the Seraglio,
This is quite erroneous. Seraglio means properly a palace,
and the women's place of reſidence is the Harem.

ment.

ment enough to obſerve, that it was an old watch, and in part broken. He therefore begged my acceptance of a very elegant gold one, requeſting of me to wear it inſtead of the other. The handſome manner in which his highneſs made this preſent gave me a much more flattering idea of his character than his conduct afterwards warranted. But we are to recollect, that he was then in the act of receiving a benefit from me; that the journey which he was afterwards obliged to undertake, put it out of my power to render him any further ſervice; and therefore, to an illiberal and uncultivated mind, the motive for continuing any acts of generoſity or kindneſs no longer exiſted.

In the courſe of my viſits to the prince, I occaſionally met with two Moors, one of whom had been in Italy for ſome time, and the other in England, who could ſpeak a little of the Engliſh language. I mention theſe men not only from motives of gratitude, but alſo to evince, that it is by improving the mind and converſing with refined and civilized people only, that we are able to conquer illiberal prejudices. From an impulſe of benevolence, for it could proceed from no other motive, ſince they had not received the ſmalleſt favour from me, they in a ſhort time contracted ſo warm a friendſhip for me, that had I been their neareſt relation, they could not have ſhewn it in a ſtronger manner than I experienced. They not only expreſſed their diſtreſs at ſeeing me in a country where I muſt be continually ſubject to inſult, and where the manner of living muſt be ſo very different from that to which they knew by their own experience I had been accuſtomed,

tomed, but they alfo took me to their houfes, introduced me to their wives, and defired them to
take the fame care of me as of their own family.

This was not all; they urged me to allow one
of them to go into fome other apartments, which
they could obtain from the prince, and almoft
infifted upon my accepting of theirs. To this
friendly propofal, however, I could not accede.
Indeed I was in daily expectation of taking poffeffion of the apartments promifed me by the
prince; and had it been otherwife I could never
have intruded fo much upon their friendfhip as to
have confented to this requeft. They continually,
however, obliged me to accept of tea and fugar,
and many other articles, which from their fcarcity at Tarudant were very valuable. Of money
they knew I was not in want, as I drew upon Mr.
Hutchifon's agent for that article; but of thofe
little rarities which they frequently fent to the
prince, I was always kindly compelled to take my
fhare. Had thefe two eftimable perfons received
all the advantages of a liberal education, what
an ornament would they have proved to fociety,
and of what extenfive utility to their nation!

On returning home from one of my vifits to
the prince, and having paffed the gate-way, which
is very lofty, and leads to the town, I was furprized at hearing a number of voices, from above
calling out very loudly, "Tibib, Tibib!" (Doctor,
doctor!)—On looking back I obferved Muley
Omar, one of Sidi Mahomet's fons, and half-
brother to Muley Abfulem, fitting in great ftate
on the centre of the wall over the gate-way,
with a number of his attendants on each fide of
him,

him. I immediately rode up to the prince, and found him a tolerably good looking young man, of about two-and-twenty. He was rather of a dark complexion, and his features were ſtrongly marked with good-nature. After the uſual ſalutation, and having anſwered his queſtion, whether I approved of the horſe his brother had given me, I took my leave; but could not poſſibly conceive the reaſon why a perſon of his conſequence ſhould be ſeated in ſo ſtrange a place. I had not ridden far before I obſerved about an hundred Moors on horſeback, who were upon the full gallop, and firing at each other in a ſtrange and irregular manner. I was now informed that this was a ſham fight, performed for the amuſement of the prince, who had choſen the top of the gate-way for his place of obſervation.

As I found it an eaſier matter to keep my mind employed in the day-time than in the evening, I accuſtomed myſelf to go to bed, as well as to riſe, very early. One evening I had not retired to reſt more than three hours, when I was alarmed by a noiſe which I at firſt imagined was occaſioned by thieves getting into the houſe. There had been lately a great number of robberies at Tarudant committed by the Arabs, who, as the houſes in general were conſtructed of nothing but mud, had a cuſtom of making a hole in the wall large enough to admit themſelves through, without occaſioning the leaſt alarm to any of the family. This I conceived to be the caſe, and ſuppoſed that the noiſe I heard aroſe from the accidental falling down of part of the wall.

I im-

I immediately got up and flew to the door, which was already opened by my interpreter, who had rifen before me, and there I obferved the whole of my neighbours with lights in their hands, and in their fhirts and fhifts, in a perfect ftate of confternation. They were ftanding as if totally unconfcious where they were, and without the power of fpeech. Indeed the alarm had occafioned the fame apprehenfions in them that it had in me, and they had juft advanced as far as the fpot where I firft faw them, without having the refolution to examine any further into the caufe of the noife.

My interpreter, though but little better than the others, had fummoned up courage enough to approach the fpot whence the noife arofe; he there found that one fourth of the houfe, which was built in a fquare, with a court in the centre, had entirely fallen down, and buried in its ruins two Jews, who were fleeping in the fallen apartment. I immediately affifted, and we foon brought the two men into my room, where I examined them very particularly, and found them fpeechlefs—but fpeechlefs only from fright. I muft confefs this accident, which had occafioned a crack in my apartment increafed my anxiety to change it, as it was impoffible to fay how foon I might be in the fame predicament with the two Jews whom I and my interpreter had extricated from the ruins; but notwithftanding all my importunities, I could not perfuade the prince's mafons to work faft enough to prove of any utility.

Among the many inconveniences which I experienced at Tarudant, were the frequent infults I

received

received in the ftreets, for which I could certainly have received redrefs, but the number of new faces which were daily appearing, made applications for it entirely ufelefs.   One day in my way to the prince, I was infulted by an ill-looking Moor, who, under the fanction of a Sharif*, thought himfelf juftified in fo doing; and therefore in a very rude manner, ran his mule directly upon me, with an intention of either giving me a fevere blow, or of frighting my horfe.   I immediately expoftulated with him upon the impropriety of fuch brutal behaviour; upon which he told me I might go to the devil, for he was a Sharif.   Upon this I found it neceffary to explain to him that I was furgeon to his prince, who from being governor of the province, and having me under his immediate protection, would pay very little attention to his being a Sharif, but would punifh him as his conduct merited; that I was then going to his highnefs, and as I was well acquainted with his name, fhould make my complaint of him.   With a meannefs proportioned to his pride, this haughty Sharif turned back his mule, and offered any atonement. I could point out, even that of going down upon his knees, if I would forgive this offence, for he dreaded the idea of his infolence being made known to the prince. I immediately confented to accept his fubmiffion, but admonifhed him, though a Sharif, to be cautious in future how he committed fuch a breach of hofpitality as to infult a ftranger.

* Sharifs are men who profefs themfelves to be the defcendants of Mahomet, and on that account are held in great efteem.

At

At the end of the fourth week, the prince informed me that he had received orders from the emperor to prepare himself to proceed on a pilgrimage to Mecca, but that it was his intention to take me up to Morocco, where he would introduce me to his father, whence I was to accompany him to Fez, and Mecquinez, where he would give me a detachment of soldiers which should conduct me to Tangier. "By these means," added his highness, " you will have an opportunity " of telling your brother Christians what a num- " ber of fine places you have seen in this coun- " try." His departure from Tarudant, however, was not to take place for some weeks, so that it would not interfere with the plan of cure which I was at present pursuing.

In the course of our conversation, during the different times I visited the prince, I repeatedly urged him to redeem out of his captivity Captain Irving, the master of the shipwrecked Guineaman, agreeably to his promise, and always received the strongest assurances that my requests would be complied with ; but hitherto nothing had been done. I therefore proceeded upon another plan, which as it operated to the interest of the prince, I flattered myself would be attended with more success. I told him that Captain Irving was a physician, whom I knew to be a man of great abilities (for he really was brought up to the profession) and that his advice was highly necessary in order to promote and facilitate my plan of cure, and therefore I wished him to be sent for immediately. The prince, though satisfied with my conduct, was highly pleased

with

with the idea of novelty, and foon obtained the emperor's permiffion to fend for him up to Tarudant.

Having no European with whom I could converfe, and refiding among the very worft part of the Moors, who harraffed me at one time with their folicitations for relief, and at another with their infolence, it will eafily be conceived that my time was not fpent in the moft agreeable manner poffible at Tarudant. My attendance however on on the prince, and the apparently great amendment in his health, ferved in fome meafure to keep up my fpirits, amufe me, and enable me to bear my fituation with patience.

At the expiration of five weeks, during which time the prince expreffed the moft perfect fatisfaction at the relief which I afforded him, an order came down from the emperor, commanding my immediate prefence at Morocco. It may well be conceived that I could not receive this order without ftrong emotions of chagrin and furprife. From the well-known difpofition of thefe people, I was aware that had any accident happened to the prince during my attendance on him, fuch an order would probably have been the confequence; but to remove me from my patient, at a time when his highnefs was continually informing his father of his amendment, was a myftery which I could not unfold. I repeatedly urged the prince to explain the reafon of this extraordinary conduct in the court; but he was either unable or unwilling to afford me any information.

Confcious how ufelefs and abfurd the attempt would be to withftand a pofitive order of the emperor

peror in a government fo uncommonly defpotic, and reflecting upon the favourable ftate of the prince's health, after revolving the queftion again and again within my own mind, I in the end (fo ready are our imaginations to flatter us on every occafion) brought myfelf to hope that the journey might prove rather to my advantage than otherwife. How egregioufly deceived I was in thofe hopes the fequel will fufficiently prove. A gold watch, an indifferent horfe, and a few hard dollars forced into my hand contrary to my inclination, were the princely and magnificent rewards which I received for taking a journey of five hundred miles, and an affiduous attendance on an ungrateful defpot!

C H A P.

CHAP. VII.

Journey over Mount Atlas *from* Tarudant *to* Morocco.—*Retinue.*—*Dangerous Paffage over Mount* Atlas.—*Defcription of Mount* Atlas.—*Natural Productions.*—*Animals.*—*Beautiful Vallies.*—*Manners and Cuftoms of the* Brebes.—*Picturefque Views in the Mountains.*

ON the 30th of November, between feven and eight in the morning, I took my leave of the prince, having previoufly intreated him to continue his courfe of medicines, and left Tarudant, under the charge of an Alcaide, and two foldiers of the Negro cavalry, who carried up the annual prefent from the prince to the emperor, of fix horfes and three boxes of money. Thefe, with my interpreter, a Jew, who ferved both as cook and groom, and a muleteer, who had the charge of my baggage, were my party for the journey.

Between twelve and one at noon we arrived at the foot of Mount Atlas, about twenty miles from Tarudant, where we pitched a very elegant tent, which the prince had procured for me, adjoining to fome Moorifh huts. We found the country in our way hither a woody and uncultivated plain.

On the following day at fix in the morning we ftruck the tent, and immediately began to afcend Mount Atlas. For near four hours we had one continued, difficult, and fatiguing afcent, owing to the road being narrow, rocky, and fteep. From its abrupt and angular turnings the Moors diftinguifh it by an Arabic name, which fignifies the camel's neck.

2

In

In many places and particularly on the higher parts of the mountain, befides the inconvenience of a rocky road which was only broad enough to allow one mule with difficulty to pafs, we had a tremendous perpendicular precipice on one fide, and even in fome places, where the mountain confifted only of a narrow ridge of rock, on both. It was aftonifhing to obferve with what eafe and fafety our mules afcended and defcended the rough and uneven paths over the mountains without putting us to the neceffity of difmounting. By two in the afternoon we began to defcend, and arrived at a fmall village, in the centre of which we pitched the tent.

On the following morning, at a little before fix, we proceeded on our journey, and at five in the evening arrived at the termination of the mountains, where we flept that night. The firft part of this day's journey was a defcent on a moft dreadfully fteep and rocky road, which at laft brought us into a beautiful vale, between two very high mountains, which immediately opens into the plains of Morocco, in a manner that is truly picturefque and fublime.

I confefs it would have gratified me to have prolonged my ftay for a little while in thefe mountains, fo fertile in objects interefting to curiofity. The few obfervations which I was able to collect in my paffage over them I fhall, however, prefent to my readers, without any further apology.

The Atlas are a chain of high mountains, interfected with deep vallies, which extend from the Eaftern to the Weftern parts of Barbary, dividing it into two parts or fections. Thofe to the

Weftward

Weftward, from their height, are named the Greater Atlas, and thofe to the Eaftward the Leffer. So immenfe is the height of thefe mountains, and particularly of thofe in the neighbourhood of Morcco, that though fo far to the Southward, their fummits are perpetually covered with fnow. When Muley Abfulem, the following January, paffed over the fame track which I had paffed in December, it fnowed the whole way; and from Morocco we at that time could not difcover any part of the mountains which was not completely white.

The atmofphere near their fummits is intenfely cold, to a degree indeed which is frequently found to be deftructive to animal life. I was well informed that fome Brebes, who had attempted to afcend the higheft part of the mountain, died immediately on the fpot, while others who were engaged in the fame attempt were obliged to return with the utmoft precipitancy.

As December was not the moft favourable feafon for botanical refearches, I faw little vegetation on the mountains, except the arga-tree, on which I have already made fome remarks when fpeaking of the natural productions of the country in general; but I am informed from the beft authority, that in the fpring thefe mountains abound with an innumerable variety of curious plants. Indeed I have great reafon to believe the natural philofopher would find a nobler fcope in this country for his enquiries than in almoft any part of the globe; and that the knowledge of medicine, as well as of botany, would be improved by a philofophical tour over the Atlas.

G   In

In the interior parts of the mountans there are, as I have before obferved, numerous iron-mines, and the Moors have an opinion that there are gold ones alfo; but the truth of this has not been af-certained.   I was informed of feveral volcanoes which exifled in different parts, but as I did not fee them, I only give this as a mere report; though from the nature of things I cannot help repeating, that I think it highly probable many curious and valuable articles are concealed in the bowels of thefe unknown mountains, which indolence and want of emulation, fo ftrongly interwoven in the difpofition and chara&ter of the Moors, will not fuffer them to explore.

With refpe&t to animal produ&tions, Mount Atlas abounds with lions, tigers, wolves, wild boars, and monftrous ferpents.   But except when the neceffity produced by an extremely fevere winter drives the animals into thefe vales or tracks of men, they generally confine themfelves to the moft inacceflible parts of the mountains.   This remark, however, is not to be underftood without exceptions; for when I was at Tarudant a tiger was killed quite clofe to the town; and there have been many inftances of their ranging far beyond limits of the Mountains.   The means made ufe of by the inhabitants to fecure themfelves from their attacks at night are, by making large and numerous wood-fires, which the wild beafts fel-dom venture to approach.   When I paffed over the mountains, I met with no animals of prey, except fome remarkably large eagles.

On the upper parts, in fome places, there was nothing to be feen but an huge mafs of barren

and

and rugged rocks, whofe perpendicular and immenfe heights formed precipices, which, upon
looking down, filled the mind with inexpreffible
horror; in others, we paffed through thick and
extenfive forefts of the arga-tree, which, though
it afforded an agreeable variety, being the only
vegetable on the mountains, very little leffened the
general appearance of barrennefs.

The vallies, however, prefented us with a very
different fcene. Here we obferved numerous villages, gardens, and inclofures, which, though in
December, were beautifully covered with verdure,
and filled with fruit-trees of every defcription.
Corn grew at this feafon in the greateft abundance,
intermixed with plantations of olives and oranges,
and ferved as the refort of a variety of finging
birds of every defcription. In fome places fmall
cafcades of water iffued from the rocks and mountains above, uniting and forming one continued
ftream, which plentifully watered the plain. In
fact, this fcene afforded the moft pleafing relief to
the mind, after the fatigues and dangers we had
experienced in the higher parts of the mountains.

The villages confifted of huts, rudely conftructed of earth and mud, and walled in. They
are very numerous, and are inhabited by a fet of
people who are named Brebes. Thefe people differ entirely from the Arabs and Moors. They
are the original inhabitants of the country, who
at the time of the conqueft by the Arabs fled into
thefe mountains, where they have ever fince continued, and in a great meafure maintained their
independence. Each village is under the direction
of a Shaik, who, contrary to to the practice in the

 encamp-

encampments of the Arabs, is an officer of their own choice.

The Brebes are a very athletic and ſtrong-featured people, patient, and accuſtomed to hardſhips and fatigue, and ſeldom remove far from the ſpot where they reſide. They ſhave the fore part of the head, but ſuffer their hair to grow from the crown as far behind as the neck. They wear no ſhirt or drawers; they are only covered by one woollen garment without ſleeves, and belted round the middle, though I have ſeen ſome few cover it with the haick. Their principal amuſement is in the uſe of their muſkets; they are indeed excellent markſmen, and are very dexterous in twirling their muſkets round, throwing them very high in the air, and afterwards catching them. So attached are they to theſe inſtruments, that they frequently go to the expence of ſixty or even eighty ducats, to ornament them with ſilver and ivory.

Their employment conſiſts principally in cultivating the vallies, looking after their cattle, and hunting wild beaſts, the ſkins of which become a very valuable article for ſale. Like the Arabs they have their regular markets for the diſpoſal of cattle, &c. where they either receive money or ſome other article in exchange. They have fallen, in a great meaſure, into the cuſtoms and religion of the Moors, but they ſtill retain their original language; and a Moor is frequently obliged to uſe an interpreter to enable him to converſe with them.

Beſides thoſe who reſide in huts in the vallies, which are numerous, there are alſo others who
live

live in caves in the upper parts of the mountains; so that the number of the whole must be very considerable.

From their secure situation, the Brebes, although inhabiting a considerable tract within the bounds of the empire, have frequently proved very troublesome to the Moorish monarchs, sometimes paying them tribute, and at others refusing it, according to the dictates of their inclination. It is not long since a general revolt took place among the Brebes, which obliged the emperor to send a large army to subdue them; but he succeeded no farther than to oblige them to disperse, without either conquering them, or gaining the point at which he aimed, which was to compel them to the payment of the tribute he demanded. The situation indeed of these mountains does not admit of the operations of a large army; for the mountaineers, accustomed to climb up into the almost inaccessible recesses, soon get beyond the reach of enemies who never before had made the attempt.

Beside the Brebes, many Jews reside in the vallies, and possess separate habitations or villages. These people are employed in the trifling mechanical occupations which the Brebes require. Indeed I believe, there is no part of the world where the Jews are so completely diffused over the face of the country, or where they are so severely oppressed, as in Barbary.

In one of the places where I slept in these vallies, soon after I got under my tent, I was amused with the sound of an instrument very much resembling the bagpipe, and producing a wild and

G 3

melancholy

melancholy ſtrain. Curious to know the nature
of the inſtrument, I ſent for the perſon who was
playing upon it, and immediately purchaſed it.
It proved to be made of a common cane, about
eight inches in length, perfectly hollow, without
any cork or ſtop to it, with ſix holes before, and
one behind for the thumb, between which was a
narrow braſs plate by way of ornament; it had
a common cord fixed to it, for the purpoſe of
hanging it round the neck. It in fact altogether
ſo well correſponded with the deſcription of the
pipe which was uſed by the antient ſhepherds,
that I have little doubt of this deſcription reviving
a few claſſical and romantic ideas in the minds of
ſome readers.

It is by no means a very eaſy matter to deſcribe
the different ſenſations which are experienced in
paſſing over theſe wonderful mountains. Their
immenſe height, the dangerous precipices, the
vales, which form their depth appeared like ſo
many abyſſes, inſpired altogether an emotion of
awe and terror, which may be better conceived
than expreſſed. On the other hand, the unlimited
and great variety of proſpects diſcoverable from
their ſummits, the numerous herd of goats and
ſheep which were ſcrambling over the almoſt perpendicular cliffs, and the univerſal barrenneſs of
the mountains, contraſted with the beautiful verdure of the vallies immediately below, formed on
the whole a ſcene ſufficiently beautiful and pic-
tureſque, to counterbalance the inconveniences we
otherwiſe ſuffered.

C H A P.

CHAP. VIII.

Arrival at Morocco.—*Difficulty of obtaining an Audience.—Description of the Metropolis.—Buildings.—House of the Prime Minister.—The Castle.—The Jewdry.—State of the Jews in Barbary.—Account of* Jacob Attal, *the Emperor's Jewish Secretary.—Manners of the Jews in Barbary.—Jewesses.—Dress.—Marriages.—Disposition for Intrigue in the Jewish Women.—The Emperor's Palace described.*

ON the 3d of December, betwen five and six in the morning, we proceeded on our journey, and foon reached a fine plain, on which we continued the whole way to Morocco, where we arrived on the following day about noon, having performed altogether a journey of about one hundred and twenty-five miles.

My firſt objeċt on my arrival was to fecure myfelf a convenient place of refidence in the Jewdry; and having accompliſhed that to my fatisfaċtion, I immediately took poffeffion of it, expeċting anxioufly every hour to be fummoned before the emperor. Though, however, his Mooriſh majeſty was repeatedly informed of my arrival, yet to my great aſtoniſhment I continued a whole month in a ſtate of uncertainty and expeċtation, without having it in my power to obtain an audience, or to be informed of the caufe which removed me from Tarudant.

The number of anecdotes in circulation through the town to my prejudice, excited in me continual uneafinefs, which even increaſed in proportion to

G 4   the

the length of time that had elapfed fince my arrival. By one of the emperors confidential friends
it was infinuated to me, that his imperial majefty
had heard I was young; that I was adminiftering
internal medicines for difeafes of the eye, which
was a practice totally new and unaccountable to
them; that European medicines were always pow-
ful and violent, and that if I had been fuffered to
attend the prince much longer, his conftitution
would have been ruined for ever. Another even
went fo far as to fay, that the emperor fufpected
me of having been employed by my countrymen
with a view to poifon his fon.

After much perplexing inveftigation into the
truth of thefe affertions, I now difcovered that my
journey to Tarudant was a private affair, fettled
between the conful and the prince; that the emperor, who at that time was not upon the beft
terms with the Englifh court, and who had already
ftopped all communication between his dominions
and the garrifon of Gibraltar, was highly difpleafed
that an Englifhman fhould be introduced, unknown
to him, for the purpofe of attending his fon in a
medical capacity; that his Moorifh phyfician, out
of pique, had perfuaded the emperor, that European medicines were too potent for the prince's
conftitution, and that in reality his fon was in extreme danger while under my care;—that in fine,
all thefe arguments weighed fo powerfully with
the emperor, that he not only determined on immediately removing me from the prince, but at
the fame time ordered fome of my medicines to
be privately fent up to Morocco, where they
were to undergo a ftrict examination by his phyfician.

fician. The caufe of my not being honoured with an audience, I found to arife from a defire in the emperor, to be thoroughly informed of the ftate of the prince's health before he faw me, that according to circumftances he might give me a favourable or a cool reception.

As fome alleviation to the uneafinefs occafioned by this ftate of fufpenfe, I was now much more comfortably fituated than I had been before at Tarudant. The apartment which I had procured was one ftory high, in the houfe of a very refpectable family, and was fpacious, clean, and retired. From a Genoefe gentleman in the fervice of the emperor, I was enabled to procure a table, two chairs, two difhes, a few plates, fome knives and forks, and a couple of tumblers. In addition to this, a Jew offered his fervices as cook, who had lived fome time with an European, and who proved an adroit and ufeful perfon. Provifions of every kind were remarkably plentiful, good, and cheap. For beef and mutton I paid only about two pence Englifh a pound, for fine fowls about fix pence each, and pigeons were frequently fold at the rate of three halfpence a pair. Had I, in addition to all thefe comforts, been able to have procured a little agreeable fociety, my fituation would have been very fupportable; but in that particular I fcarcely poffeffed more advantages than I had during my refidence at Tarudant.

The Genoefe gentleman, from whofe houfe I had borrowed a part of my furniture, was at Mogodore, and the only Europeans who were at that time at Morocco, if we except a few

Spanish artificers in the emperor's service, were part of the English seamen who had been shipwrecked, a French officer, with some French seamen, who were also captives from a similar accident, and three Spanish friars. Out of these I could only chuse for my society the French officer and the friars.

With the first, as I was acquainted with the French language, I could converse pretty fluently, and I really found him a most agreeable companion: he had taken his passage on board a vessel bound for the French settlements on the coast of Guinea, whither he was proceeding to join his regiment, and was shipwrecked on that part of the coast of Africa which lies in the direction of the Canary Islands. This misfortune, united to the hardships which followed it on his being carried into slavery by the wild Arabs, and the little prospect which then appeared of his redemption, had made a deep impression upon his spirits, and subjected him to occasional attacks of hypochondria. The emperor, it is true, could not be accused of ill treating any of the captives; on the contrary, he allowed them daily a small sum of money, and permitted them to walk about at liberty. His detention of them, however, in the country, without any immediate prospect of returning home, was a sufficient reason for them still to consider themselves in no other light than that of slaves.

The Spanish friars, who have a small convent in the Jewdry, and who were originally placed there for the purpose of redeeming captives, as they distributed medicines to the poor gratis, considered themselves as being engaged in the same profession

profeffion with myfelf, and received me very hof-
pitably; but as, from my not underftanding their
language, I was obliged to converfe with them
by means of my interpreter, who fpoke Spanifh,
the fociety enjoyed with them was very limited indeed. I cannot avoid expreffing my concern for
the fate of thefe worthy men, who are diftined
to fpend the whole of their lives on a fpot deftitute
of all civilized fociety, where they are continually
fubjected to the caprice and infolence of the emperor, as well as of the worft part of his fubjects.
They appeared to me to be men who had received
much information from reading, as well as from
obfervation, and they very properly employed
their times in the duties of their profeffion, in
the offices of devotion, and adminiftering medicines
to the poor, in ftudy, and in fuch innocent re-
creations as the limited fociety of Morocco affords.

'To divert my thoughts from the great uneafinefs
which my fituation naturally infpired, during fo
long a ftate of fufpence, I made daily excurfions
through different parts of Morocco; though, from
the continual infults which I experienced when
in the ftreets, even this amufement was attended
with confiderable inconvenience.

The city of Morocco, which lies about one
hundred and twenty miles to the North of Tarudant, ninety to the eaft of Mogodore, and three
hundred and fifty to the South of Tangier, is
fituated in a beautiful valley, formed by a chain
of mountains on the Northern fide, and thofe of
the Atlas, from which it is diftant about twenty
miles, on the South and Eaft. The country which
immediately

immediately furrounds it is a fertile plain, beautifully diverfified with clumps of palm trees and
fhrubs, and watered by fmall and numerous
ftreams, which defcend from Mount Atlas. The
emperor's out-gardens, which are fituated at the
diftance of about five miles to the South of the
city, and are large plantations of olives walled
in, add confiderably to the beauty of the fcene.

Morocco, though one of the capitals of the
empire—for there are three, Morocco, Mequinez,
and Fez—has nothing to recommend it but its
great extent, and the royal palace. It is inclofed
by remarkably ftrong walls, built of tabby, the
circumference of which is about eight miles.
On thefe walls there are no guns mounted, but
they are flanked with fquare towers, and furrounded by a wide and deep ditch. The city has
a number of entrances, confifting of large double
porches of tabby, in the Gothic ftyle, the gates
of which are regularly fhut every night at certain
hours. As polygamy is allowed by the Mahometan religion, and is fuppofed in fome degree to
affect population, it would be difficult to form
any computation near the truth with refpect to
the number of inhabitants which this city may
contain.

The mofques, which are the only public buildings except the palace, worth noticing at Morocco, are more numerous than magnificent; one of
them is ornamented with a very high and fquare
tower, built of cut ftone, which is vifible at a confiderable diftance from the city.

The ftreets are very narrow, dirty, and irregular, and many of the houfes are uninhabited, and

falling to ruin. Thofe which are decent and refpectable in their appearance are built of tabby, and enclofed in gardens. That of the Effendi, or prime minifter, was among the beft which I vifited in Morocco. This houfe, which confifted of two ftories, had elegant apartments both above and below, furnifhed in a ftile far fuperior to any thing I ever faw in that country. The court, into which the lower apartments opened, was very neatly paved with glazed blue and white tiling, and had in its centre a beautiful fountain. The upper apartments were connected together. by a broad gallery, the balluftres of which were painted of different colours. The hot and cold baths were very large, and had every convenience which art could afford. Into the garden, which was laid out in a tolerably neat ftile, opened a room adjoining to the houfe, which had a broad arched entrance, but no door, beautifully orna-mented with checquered tiling; and at both ends of the apartment the walls were entirely covered with looking-glafs. The flooring of all the rooms was covered with beautiful carpeting, the walls ornamented with large and valuable looking-glaffes, intermixed with watches and clocks in glafs cafes. The ceiling was carved wood-work, painted of different colours, and the whole was in a fuperior ftile of Moorifh grandeur. This and a few others are the only decent habitations in Morocco. The generality of them ferve only to imprefs the traveller with the idea of a mifer-able and deferted city.

The Elcaifferia is a particular part of the town where ftuffs and other valuable articles are expofed to fale. It confifts of a number of fmall fhops, formed in the walls of the houfes, about a yard from the ground, of fuch a height within as juft to admit a man to fit in one of them crofs-legged. The goods and drawers are fo arranged round him, that when he ferves his cuftomers, who are ftanding all the time out in the ftreet, he can reach down any article he wants, without being under the neceffity of moving. Thefe fhops, which are found in all the other towns of the empire, are fufficient to afford a ftriking example of the indolence of the Moors.

There are three daily markets in different parts of the town at Morocco, where provifions are fold, and two weekly fairs or markets for the dif-pofal of cattle, where the fame cuftom is obferved as at Tarudant.

The city is fupplied with water by means of wooden pipes connected with the neighbouring ftreams, which empty themfelves into refervoirs placed for the purpofe in the fuburbs, and fome few in the centre of the town.

The caftle is a large and ruinous building, the outer walls of which enclofe a fpace of ground about three miles in circumference. It has a mofque built by Muley Abdallah, father to Sidi Mahomet, on the top of which are three large balls; thefe, the Moors allege, are formed of folid gold, but as no perfon is permitted to afcend to them, we muft truft to their word for the truth of this affertion. The caftle is almoft a town of itfelf; it contains a number of inhabitants, who in fome department or other are in the fervice of the emperor, and all under the direction of a par-

ticular

ticular Alcaide, who is quite independent of the governor of the town.

On the outside of the castle, between the Moorish town and the Jewdry, are several small, distinct pavilions, enclosed in gardens of orange-trees, which are intended as occasional places of residence for such of the emperor's sons or brothers as happen to be at Morocco. As they are covered with coloured tiling, they have at a small distance rather a neat appearance, but upon approaching or entering them, that effect in a great measure ceases.

It is a singular circumstance, that in the immediate vicinity of Morocco, for some distance round the city, the ground is totally occupied by a great number of rats, of a larger species than any I had ever before seen, which burrow under ground, and like rabbits, allow strangers to approach very near before they retire to their holes. They indeed gave me every idea of a rabbit-warren in miniature.

The Jews, who are at this place pretty numerous, have a separate town to themselves, walled in, and under the charge of an Alcaide, appointed by the emperor. It has two large gates, which are regularly shut every evening about nine o'clock, after which time no person whatever is permitted to enter or go out of the Jewdry, till they are opened again the following morning. The Jews have a market of their own, and, as at Tarudant, when they enter the Moorish town, castle, or palace, they are always compelled to be barefooted.

The Jews in general are obliged to pay to the emperor a certain annual income, in proportion to their numbers, which is a confiderable income, independent of his arbitrary exactions. Thofe of Morocco were exempted by Sidi Mahomet from this tax, and in its room he compelled them to take goods of him, of which they were to difpofe in the beft manner they could, and pay him five times their value; by which means they were far greater fufferers than if they paid the annual tax.

Every part of the empire more or lefs abounds with Jews, who orignally were expelled from Spain and Portugal and who fled into Barbary as a place of refuge. Thefe people are not confined to towns but are fpread over the whole face of the country, Mount Atlas itfelf, as was before mentioned, not excepted.

In every country where they refide, thefe unfortunate people are treated as another clafs of beings; but in no part of the world are they fo feverely and undefervedly oppreffed as in Barbary, where the whole country depends upon their induftry and ingenuity, and could fcarcely fubfift as a nation without their affiftance. They are the only mechanics in this part of the world, and have the whole management of all pecuniary and commercial matters, except the collecting of the cuftoms. They are, however, intrufted in the coinage of money, as I myfelf have witneffed*.

* Doubloons and hard dollars are current in this country: but the coins peculiar to it are, gold *ducats*, of the value of ten hard dollars, fome of five, of one and a half, and others of only one; ounces, of the value of about five pence En-

The Moors difplay more humanity to their beafts than to the Jews. I have feen frequent inftances where individuals of this unhappy people were beaten fo feverely, as to be left almoft lifelefs on the ground, and that without being able to obtain the leaft redrefs whatever, as the magiftrates always act with the moft culpable partiality when a Moor and a Jew are the parties in a fuit. What they lofe by oppreffion, however, they in a great meafure make up by their fuperior addrefs and fagacity, which frequently enables them to over-reach the Moors—as I cannot compliment the Jews of Barbary in general upon their probity and principle.

Jacob Attal, the emperor's Jewifh and favourite fecretary, had more influence with his royal mafter, and did more mifchief by his intrigues and addrefs, than all the other minifters put together. This young man who was a native of Tunis, and who was tolerably well acquainted with the Englifh, Spanifh, Italian, French, and Arabic languages, was of an active and enteprizing mind, and had fo well informed himfelf of the natural difpofition of the Moors, and particularly of that of Sidi Mahomet, that he had gained an entire afcendency over the emperor. As he knew that an unbounded love of money was the ruling paffion of his royal mafter, he not only

glifh; and blanquils, of five farthings, both filver coins; fluces, which are of copper, twenty-four being equal to a blanquil; but ounces are the money in which bills are ufually drawn in the country. All the emperor's coins have his name in Arabic ftamped on one fide, and on the other the date, and place at which they were coined.

furren-

furrendered to him half of his own gains, but also furnifhed the emperor with the earlieft and beft information concerning thofe who were in poffeffion of wealth, as well as with a projeft for extracting it from them. By thus attacking the emperor on the weakeft fide, he fecured his friendfhip; but he fecured it by means which expofed him to the refentment and revenge of thoufands as foon as the emperor died, which has been fince too fatally proved. I muft, however, do this young man the juftice to add, that throughout the whole of his adminiftration, though in fome inftances, perhaps, contrary to his own intereft he fhewed an exclufive preference to the Englifh; and of this the Moors in general were fo fenfible, that they gave him the appellation of the Englifh ambaffador.

The Jews in moft parts of this empire live entirely feparate from the Moors; and though in other refpects oppreffed, are allowed the free exercife of their religion. Many of them, however, to avoid the arbitrary treatment which they conftantly experience, have become converts to the Mahometan faith; upon which they are admitted to all the privileges of Moors, though they lofe their real eftimation in the opinion of both fects.

In moft of the fea-port towns, and particularly at Tetuan and Tangier, the Jews have a tolerable fmattering of Spanifh; but at Morocco, Tarudant, and all the inland towns, they can only fpeak Arabic and a little Hebrew. . They nearly follow the cuftoms of the Moors, except in their religious ceremonies; and in that particular they

are

are by far more superstitious than the European Jews.

The Jews of Barbary shave their heads close, and wear their beards long; their dress indeed, altogether, differs very little from that of the Moors (which I shall hereafter describe) except in their being obliged to appear externally in black. For which purpose they wear a black cap, black slippers, and instead of the haick worn by the Moors, substitute the Alberoce, a cloak made of black wool, which covers the whole of the under dress. The Jews are not permitted to go out of the country, but by an express order from the emperor; nor are they allowed to wear a sword, or ride a horse, though they are indulged in the use of mules. This arises from an opinion prevalent among the Moors, that the horse is too noble an animal to be employed in the service of such infidels as Jews.

The dress of the Jewish women consists of a fine linen shirt with large and loose sleeves, which hang almost to the ground; over the shirt is worn a caftan, a loose dress made of woollen cloth, or velvet, of any colour reaching as low as the hips, and covering the whole of the body, except the neck and breast which are left open, and the edges of the Caftan as worn by the Jewesses of Morocco, are embroidered with gold. In addition to these is the Geraldito, or petticoats, made of fine green woollen cloth, the edges and corners of which are sometimes embroidered with gold. They are fastened by a broad sash of silk and gold, which surrounds the waist, and the ends of it are suffered to hang down behind, in an easy manner.

This

This is the drefs they wear in the houfe, but when they go abroad, they throw over it the haick. The unmarried women wear their hair plaited in different folds, and hanging down behind. They have a very graceful and becoming method of putting a wreath of wrought filk round the head, and tying it behind in a bow. This drefs fets off their features to great advantage, and diftinguifhes them from the married women, who cover their heads with a red filk handkerchief, which they tie behind, and over it put a filk fafh leaving the ends to hang loofe on their backs. None of the Jewifh women ufe ftockings, but wear red flippers, curioufly embroidered with gold. They wear very large gold ear-rings, at the lower part of their ears, and at the upper three fmall ones fet with pearls or precious ftones. Their necks are loaded with beads, and their fingers with fmall gold or filver rings. Round each wrift and ankle they wear large folid filver bracelets; and the rich have gold and filver chains fufpended from the fafh behind.

Their marriages are celebrated with much feftivity for fome time previous to the ceremony, and the intended bride with all her female relations, go through the form of having their faces painted red and white, and their hands and feet ftained yellow, with an herb named henna. A variety of figures are marked out on them with a needle, and then this herb, which is powdered and mixed with water into a pafte, is worked into the holes made by the needle, and thefe marks continue on the hands and feet for a long fpace of time. Upon the death of a Jew (before and after burial) all

the

the female relations, with other women hired for the purpose, affemble in the room of the deceafed, and for feveral days lament his lofs by moft dreadful fhrieks and howlings, and tearing their cheeks and hair.

The Jewelfes of this empire in general are very beautiful and remarkably fair.—They marry very young, and when married, though they are not obliged to hide their faces in the ftreet, yet at home they are frequently tre ted with the fame feverity as the Moorifh women. Like the Moors, the Jewifh men and women at Morocco eat feparate; and the unmarried women are not permitted to go out except on particular occafions, and then always with their faces covered.

A difpofition for intrigue in the female fex is always found to accompany tyrannical conduct and undue reftraint on the part of ours; and this difpofition is again made the excufe for the continuance of thefe reftraints. Thus the effect becomes a caufe, and when the women ceafe to be the guardians of their own honour, they derive no credit from the prefervation of it, and incur in their own eftimation but little difgrace by its lofs. The Jews allege, in extenuation of their feverity, the licentious inclinations and artful difpofitions of their women, and that a fingle act of criminality in a daughter would be an effectual bar to her ever forming a legal connection. The fame objection not being fo applicable to their married women, they are permitted to go out without reftraint. Indeed many of their hufbands, from interefted motives, are too apt to connive at a conduct, which, in other countries would infallibly

fallibly bring down upon them well-merited contempt.

The palace of Morocco is an ancient building,
surrounded by a square wall, the height of which
nearly excludes from the view of the spectator
the other buildings. Its principal gates are constructed with Gothic arches composed of cut
stone, which conduct to several open and spacious
courts ; through these it is necessary to pass before we reach any of the buildings. These open
courts were used by Sidi Mahomet for the purposes of transacting public business and exercising
his troops.

The habitable part of the palace consists of several irregular square pavilions, built of tabby,
and whitened over; some of which communicate
with each other, others are distinct and most of
them receive their names from the different towns
of the empire. The principal pavilion is named
by the Moors the Douhar, and is more properly
the palace or seraglio than any of the others. It
consists of the emperor's place of residence, and
the Harem, forming altogether a building of considerable extent. The other pavilions are merely
for the purposes of pleasure or business, and are
quite distinct from the Douhar.

The Mogodore pavilion, so named from the
emperor's partiality to that town, has by far the
fairest claim to grandeur and magnificence. This
apartment was the work of Sidi Mahomet, and is
lofty and square. It is built of cut stone, hand-
somely ornamented with windows, and covered
with varnished tiles of various colours; and its
elegance and neatness, contrasted altogether with
the

fimplicity and irregularity of the other buildings, produce a moft ftriking effect. In the infide, befides feveral other apartments, we find in the pavilion a fpacious room, floored with blue and white checquered tiling, its ceiling covered with curioufly carved and painted wood, and its ftuccoed walls varioufly ornamented with lookingglaffes and watches, regularly difpofed in glafs cafes. To this pavilion Sidi Mahomet manifefted an exclufive preference, frequently retiring to it both for the purpofes of bufinefs, and of recreation.

The apartments of the emperor have in general a much fmaller complement of furniture than thofe of the Moors in the inferior walks of life. Handfome carpetting, a matrafs on the ground, covered with fine linen, a couch, and a couple of European bedfteads, are the principal articles they contain. The gardens within the walls of the palace, of which he has feveral, are very neat; they contain orange and olive trees, varioufty difpofed and arranged, and interfected with ftreams of water, fountains and refervoirs. Thofe on the outfide are nothing more than large tracts of ground, irregularly planted with olives; having four fquare walks, and furrounded by walls.

In introducing the defcription of the palace in this place, I have rather deviated from the chronological feries of my narrative, as the events which brought me acquainted with this facred refidence of the Moorifh princes were pofterior to my vifiting all the other quarters of the metropolis.

C H A P.

CHAP. IX.

Introduction to the Emperor.—Conversation with his his Moorish Majesty.—Account of the Emperor SIDI MAHOMET—his Character—his extreme Avarice—. his miserable Situation.—Anecdotes relative to the late Emperor.—Anecdotes of SIDI MAHOMET—his Deceit and Hypocrisy—his Charity.—Pusillanimous Conduct of the European Powers.—Ceremonies of the Court of MOROCCO.—Exactions from Strangers.—Account of the principal Officers of State.—Character of the late Prime Minister.—Revenues of MOROCCO.—Wealth of the Emperor, less than generally imagined.—The Army of the Emperor—how commanded—his Navy. —Internal Government of the Empire.—Bashaws.— Alcaides.—Ell hackum.—Cadi.—Mode of administering Justice.—Criminal Punishments.

AFTER the lapse of a month without a prospect of obtaining an audience, my anxiety was increased to a degree which in the end proved extremely injurious to my health. From the attention which I had paid to most of the emperor's ministers, who all of them in their turn had occasion for my services, I thought I had a right to expect some little return. With all that deceit which has characterized the inhabitants of Barbary * from the earliest periods, they professed the warmest friendship for me, and assured me that they would exert their influence upon the emperor to persuade him to see me. Among the number was a Moor named Sidi Brahim, to whom

2

* Punica fides.

the

the prince had given me ftrong letters of recommendation, and who, during a tedious ficknefs which
had prevailed in his family, had received from
me the moft conftant attention. This Moor had
directions from the prince to introduce me immediately upon my arrival to the emperor, and
to fhew me every civility that was due to fuch
recommendation. All thefe circumftances I conceived gave me a fufficient right to expect that
Sidi Brahim, both from motives of duty to his
prince, and gratitude to me, would have exerted
himfelf in a manner correfpondent to fuch obliga-
tions. But that was far from being the cafe.
When his family was under my care, he certainly
did receive me with attention, and treated me
with kindnefs; but when my advice became no
longer neceffary, his friendfhip cooled in proportion; and latterly, when we happened to meet,
he fcarcely feemed to recollect me. Upon reflection, what was I to expect from a man, who for
his notorious crimes, though at that time in great
favour, had been punifhed by his fovereign,
having had the greateft part of his beard pulled
up by the roots?

Unfuccefsful nd difappointed through this channel, I had recourfe to fome others of the emperor's
attendants, on whom I had conferred favours,
and who had perhaps ftill greater influence with
the emperor than even Sidi Brahim. Among this
number were thr prime minifter, and one of the
emperor's principal talbs. From thefe officers
I experienced, however, much the fame treatment
as from Sidi Brahim; and had I not accidentally
been called in to attend the wife of one of the em-

H	peror's

peror's principal Jews, it is probable I might have continued in the fame fame ftate of anxious uncertainty for fome weeks longer. As a return for my attendance, the hufband of this patient, agreeably to my requeft, had addrefs and influence enough to perfuade the emperor to appoint an audience for me the very day after the application.

On the day appointed for my reception at court, about twelve at noon, three negro foldiers, with large clubs in their hands, came to my apartments to efcort me to the palace; telling me, that they had directions to return with me inftantaneoufly, and that they muft anfwer it with their heads, if they delayed a moment in the execution of their orders. Not fufpecting that my Jewifh friend, for fuch I muft certainly denominate him, could have effected my wifhes fo immediately, I was by no means prepared for the audience; and I requefted them to wait a few moments, till I could enable myfelf to appear in a decent drefs before the emperor. Far, however, from acceding to my requeft, the foldiers became impatient, and acquainted me, that I muft either proceed with them immediately, or they would return and inform the fultan, that I had refufed to comply with his orders. I now found myfelf under the neceffity of fetting off, and we all actually *ran* together to the palace with the utmoft expedition. When we arrived there, I was introduced to one of the mafters of the audience, who defired me to wait on the outfide of the palace till I was called for.

From

From the abrupt and sudden manner in which I was forced away by the soldiers, I expected to be ushered immediately into the imperial presence; but so far was I still from the consummation of this expectation, that I remained on the spot where they first placed me, from twelve o'clock at noon till five in the evening, revolving in my mind, what kind of a person I should find the emperor, what reception I should meet with, and the answers which I ought to make to any questions he might propose. Situated as I was with respect to the prince whom I had been attending, and considering the malicious reports respecting my conduct which had been circulated about Morocco, the reader may well suppose that I was led to form a variety of conjectures, concerning what was likely to be the result of the audience. I however placed my whole confidence in the prince's recovery, which was a circumstance, when clearly known to the emperor, that must undoubtedly operate in my favour. This idea at last entirely removed a number of uneasy and anxious reflections, which had occured to me when I first entered the palace; and by the time the messenger came to introduce me to the emperor I had brought myself to be as calm and recollected as if my mind had been perfectly at ease, and had no reason to be otherwise.

From the court-yard into which I was first introduced, I was hurried with the greatest precipitancy through two or three others, till I arrived at the gate which opened to the court where the emperor was waiting to receive me. I was there

detained

detained for some time by the master of the audience, owing to my refusal of the present which Europeans are accustomed to make to the emperor upon being honoured with an audience. I had been previously acquainted that no person was ever permitted to appear in his majesty's presence, unless accompanied by a handsome present; but I conceived my situation to be in every respect so totally different from that of other strangers who visited the court, that I told the master of the ceremonies, if he persisted in refusing me entrance, I would immediately return home again.

The Moor, finding that I was determined not comply with his request, and knowing that the emperor was purposely waiting to see me, was afraid to defer my introduction any longer; I was therefore ushered into his majesty's presence very expeditiously, and directed to place myself and my interpreter in such a situation as to be seen without approaching too near his person.

The Moor who introduced me, upon appearing in sight of the emperor, prostrated himself on the earth, kissed it, and in a very humble manner exclaimed in Arabic, " May God preserve the king!" The emperor then ordered him to approach, and deliver what he had to say. He informed his majesty, that in compliance with his order, he had brought before him the English doctor; after which, having made a very low bow, he retired, and the emperor immediately desired me and my interpreter to advance towards him; but as soon as we had got within ten yards of the emperor, two foldiers came up, pulled us by the coat, and acquainted us that we muft not prefume to approach any further.

I found the fovereign feated in an European poft-chaife, placed in one of his open courts, and drawn by one mule in fhafts, having a man on each fide to guide it. Behind the carriage were foot foldiers, fome Negroes and others Moors, in two divifions, forming together a half-moon. Some of thefe foldiers were only armed with large clubs, while others had mufkets which they held clofe to their bodies, and pointed perpendicularly.

"The emperor, after furveying me minutely and with the greateft attention, accompanied with no fmall fhare of *hauteur*, demanded from my interpreter, in a very ftern manner, if I was the Chriftian doctor who had been attending Muley Abfulem? I defired him to anfwer, that I was. —" How came you into the country; and were " you fent by order of your own king, or by " whom?" To render my vifit of more importance, I anfwered, " By order of government."—" Where " did you learn your profeffion, and what is the " name of the perfon who taught it you?" I informed his majefty.—" What is the reafon that " the French furgeons are better than the Englifh; " and which do you think are beft?" I anfwered, "The French furgeons are very good, but it " muft certainly be allowed that the Englifh are " in general fuperior, being more fcientifically " educated."—The emperor then obferved, that a French furgeon had come into the country, and in the courfe of his practice had killed feveral perfons.

H 3

His

His majesty next asked, in a very austere manner, " What was the reason I had forbidden Muley " Abfulem the use of tea?" My reply was, " Mu-" ley Abfulem has very weak nerves, and tea is " injurious to the nervous system."—" If tea is " fo unwholesome," replied his majesty, " why do " the English drink so much?" I answered, " It " is true, they drink it twice a day; but then " they do not make it so strong as the Moors, and " they generally use milk with it, which lessens " its pernicious effects. But the Moors, when " once they begin to use it, make it very strong, " drink a great deal, and very frequently with-" out milk."—" You are right," said the emperor; " and I know it sometimes makes their hands " shake." After this conversation, about a dozen distilled waters, prepared from different herbs, were frought for me to taste, and inform the emperor what they were; which were hot, and which were cold, &c.

His majesty now condefcended to become more familiar and eafy in his remarks, and defired me to obferve the fnow on Mount Atlas, which his carriage immediately fronted, wifhing to know if we had the fame in my country. I anfwered, that we frequently had a great deal in the winter feafon, and that England was a much colder climate than Morocco. The emperor obferved, that if any perfon attempted to go to the top of the mountain, he would die from excefs of cold. He then informed me, that on the other fide of the mountain was a very fine, plain, and fertile country, which was named Tafilet.

Obferving

Obferving that the emperor was now in a good humour, I embraced the oportunity of mentioning to him, how much my feelings had been hurt by the malicious reports which had been for fome time paft circulating to my prejudice; that they were of fuch a nature as to make me very defirous of having my character cleared up, by a proper examination into the prefent ftate of the prince's health, as well as into the nature of the medicines which I had been adminiftering to him. The emperor in reply faid, that he had already ordered his Moorifh phyfician to examine very particularly my medicines; who had declared that he could find nothing improper in them. It is very clear, however, that fome fufpicion muft have taken place in the breaft of the emperor, to have induced him to fend privately for thefe medicines, for the purpofe of having them fo nicely examined; from which circumftance I could not help feeling it as a very fortunate event for myfelf, that the prince's health was in fo favourable a ftate.

After a converfation of fome length, the heads of which I have endeavoured briefly to ftate, the evening being far advanced, the emperor commanded one of his attendants to conduct me home to his Jew, and defire him to take great care of me; adding, that I was a good man, I was Muley Abfulem's phyfician, and that he would fend me home to my entire fatisfaction. He then ordered his carriage to drive on.

Confidering myfelf as now acquitted of the charges which had been infinuated againft me, and elevated by the emperor's promifes at the audience, I muft confefs that I returned home with a much

                        lighter

lighter heart than I could boaft of when I went. I now only waited for the arrival of the prince at Morocco, which I conceived would confirm the emperor's good wifhes towards me, and make my fituation as agreeable as I could expect. Such are the fanguine hopes with which we are apt to flatter ourfelves, after having encountered difficulties, when the fmalleft profpect opens of relief.

In the evening my room was filled with a number of the attendants of the emperor, who came to congratulate me on the honour I had received by a fight of their royal mafter; at the fame time to demand prefents, which on fuch occafions, they alleged was a cuftom to which all Europeans fubmitted. As therefore I faw there were no other means of relieving myfelf from their impertinent importunities, I was obliged in fome degree to comply with their demands.

I found the emperor Sidi Mahomet to be a tall thin old man, of near eighty years of age, and of a fallow complexion. From a vifage naturally long, and a diftortion of one eye, united with an acquired habit of aufterity, his appearance at firft was rather difgufting to ftrangers; but that impreffion was foon worn off by the affability of his converfation, which he generally confined to thofe fubjects he thought moft adapted to the perfon with whom he converfed. At the fame time he difplayed a great defire to acquire information, as well as to difcover the abilities of others. Some years ago he fo far loft the ufe of his feet as to difable him from walking. This difagreeable effect was probably owing to want of ufe, and to his accuftom-

accuftoming himfelf conftantly to be either in his carriage or on horfeback.   When I faw him, his beard and eye-brows, though before, as I was informed, very dark, had acquired a perfect white-nefs, and his voice was much impaired.   His drefs was exactly fimilar to that of other Moors, differ-ing only in the finenefs of the materials, and he was only diftinguifhed from his fubjects by a lar-ger retinue, riding in a carriage, or when on horfeback having an umbrella carried before him.

From the general tenour of his conduct through-out his reign, and from his converfation, Sidi Mahomet appears to have poffeffed ftrong natural talents, to which had a good education been united, he might have proved a great monarch.   But the want of education, and the illiberality and fu-perftition of his religion, betrayed him frequently into cruelty; and the poffeffion of arbitrary power tinged his character with that intolerable caprice which has ever diftinguifhed and difgraced the Moorifh princes.

Avaricious from his youth, he gave his whole attention to the accumulation of wealth; and it was from that motive only that he appeared to give more encouragement to European merchants than any of his predeceffors.   It is at the fame time well known, that he occafionally oppreffed them with fuch heavy duties, that they have been obliged to fend home their veffels empty. In hopes of adding ftill more to his treafures, Sidi Mahomet became himfelf a merchant, took up goods from Europeans, and obliged the Jews to pay him five times their value for them; fo that there was not

H 5

a fingle

a single resource for becoming rich of which he did not avail himself. Avaricious to this excess, and naturally of a very timid disposition, his great object has been peace: well aware that war could neither enrich him, nor contribute to his enjoyments in any respect.

His reign, it is true, has been distinguished by fewer instances of cruelty than that of any of his predecessors, but he has certainly exceeded them all in the licentiousness of his attacks upon private property. He was always surrounded by people, who, for the sake of rising into favour, were at all times ready to give him information concerning any of his subjects who were rich. It was then his usual course of proceeding, to invent some plea for confining them in prison; and if that did not succeed, he put them in irons, chained them down, and proceeded in a course of severity and cruelty, till at last, wearied out with punishments and disgraces, the unfortunate victims surrendered the whole of their possessions; which alone procured them the enjoyment of liberty, an oportunity of again obtaining sufsistence, or perhaps of once more becoming the prey of the rapacious monarch. Such of his sons as were in friendship with him, were continually making him presents, as if apprehensive of the same fate; and since I left the country it has been strongly reported that my patient Muley Absulem, who was the only son for whom the emperor professed much affection, was plundered by his father of the greatest part of his riches; which indeed were reputed to be very considerable.

Vices

Vices are never solitary; and those which are most naturally connected with an avaricious and timid disposition, are jealousy and suspicion. Conscious how little he deserved the affection of his people, and latterly sensible of having totally lost it, Sidi Mahomet was in constant fear of assassination and poison. In this state he dragged on a miserable existence; an example to arbitrary kings, and a living proof that the picture exhibited of the Roman tyrant, by the sarcastic historian, was not overcharged. He seldom stirred out of his palace, unless accompanied by a numerous band of soldiers, and even of these he had always his suspicions. At night he had constantly six bloodhounds in his chamber, and relying more on the fidelity of the irrational creation than on man, he thought these a more certain guard than his soldiers. His victuals were dressed and tasted in his presence; and at dinner, though no person was permitted to eat immediately with him, yet he always had some of his sons and ministers in the same apartment, who were helped out of his dish. To complete the misery of this unfortunate old man, he lived under the continual apprehension of being conquered by his eldest son Muley Yazid, the late emperor, who, in consequence of some ill treatment received from his father, retired secretly from court, and took refuge in a sanctuary near Tetuan.

This prince, whose grandmother was an English woman, had acquired the universal esteem of the whole country by his generous conduct and his great abilities; and though at that time in a state of poverty, and with only four attendants about

him,

him, such was his influence that he had only to
step forward, and say he wanted money and
troops, and he would shortly have been at the
head of an army, that must at any time have
entirely overwhelmed the late government of
Morocco. From motives of duty, and perhaps
of policy, this however was a step he did not
wish to take, conscious that his father could not
long survive, and that upon his death he was
certain of the succession. The emperor, notwith-
standing, was still unable to subdue his appre-
hensions; and when I was at Morocco sent an
army of five thousand blacks, with an order to
violate the sanctuary, and carry off the prince.
This order was not obeyed, for the chief could
not place sufficient confidence in his troops; and
the prince continued quiet in the sactuary till his
father's decease.

To evince the policy, as well as the sagacity
of Muley Yazid, I must beg leave to relate an
anecdote, which occurred a short time previous
to that period. The people who have the care
of the sanctuary received positive orders from the
emperor to expel the prince by force; which, if
they failed in doing, he assured them he would
send and put every man, woman, and child in
the neighbourhood of the sanctuary to the sword.
The people, though well disposed to the prince,
intimidated by these orders, related faithfully to
him the emperor's intentions, and informed him
that, as their lives were at stake, they expected
him to remove, at the same time recommending
him to another sanctuary at no great distance,
where he could equally take refuge. The prince,
who

who is one of the beft horfemen in the country, and who had a horfe of which he had the entire command, immediately promifed them to depart, and mounted his horfe for the purpofe. But what was their furprife, when they found the horfe would not ftir from the fpot, notwithftanding the apparently free ufe of whip and fpur? Upon this the prince exclaimed, " You fee plain-" ly that it is God's will I fhould continue here, " and therefore no other power fhall ever drive " me out." This had fuch an effect upon the fuperftitious multitude, that they preferred rifking the refentment of the emperor, to the violation of what, in their eftimation, was fo apparently the will of God.

With refpect to the other features of the emperor's character, his principal vices appear to have refulted from that great corrupter of the human heart, arbitrary power: for he was the moft arbitrary of monarchs, having at his abfolute difpofal the lives and properties of all his fubjects. In fuch circumftances, what man can be trufted, nay, who would truft himfelf? In fuch circumftances, can we wonder, when we obferve the occafional indulgence of intemperate revenge? Among thefe we are to account his treatment of an unfortunate Jew who had imprudently written fomething to his prejudice, and for this flight offence was quartered alive, cut to pieces, and his flefh afterwards given to the dogs.

Upon another occafion, a fimilar difpofition was manifefted by Sidi Mahomet. A Moor of fome confequence, and very opulent, gave a grand entertainment on the marriage of one of his fons.
The

The emperor, who happened to be in the neighbourhood, and who well knew that magnificence
was a ftriking proof of wealth, was determined
to be prefent at the feftival, in order that he
might more fully inform himfelf of the circumftances of the Moor. For this purpofe he difguifed himfelf in a common drefs, and entered the
houfe in the midft of all the jollity, and perhaps
the licentioufnefs of the entertainment. The mafter
of the ceremonies obferving a perfon of mean appearance intrude himfelf into the room fo abrupt-
ly, ordered him out; and upon the refufal of the
ftranger, he gave him a kick, and pufhed him by
violence out of the houfe. For a fhort fpace of time
after this occurrence the whole affair paffed without notice, and probably had efcaped the memory
of moft; and it was a matter of the utmoft furprize
to the mafter of the houfe, to receive an order commanding him immediately to repair to Morocco.
Upon being introduced to the emperor, he was
afked if he recollected the circumftances which
have juft been related, to which he replied in the
affirmative. " Know then," fays the emperor,
" I was that Moor whom you treated thus con-
" tumelioufly; and to convince you that I have
" not forgot it, that foot and that hand which
" infulted me fhall perifh."—I have feen this unfortunate victim of tyranny walking about the
ftreets with one leg and an arm.

The emperor was as ready to revenge the imaginary or the real injuries of his fubjects. To
elucidate this affertion; an Englifh and French
gentleman were amufing themfelves by the diver-
fion of courfing, in the vicinity of Mogodore,
when

when one of their dogs unfortunately attacked the calf of a Moor. This accident foon brought out the villagers, who immediately fhot the dog, and entered into a very ferious quarrel with the Chriftians, which terminated in a general conteft. The women of the village now thought it a proper occafion for their interference; and among their number was one, who from old age had loft all her teeth except two, and thefe were fo loofe that they could be with difficulty retained; and another, who had upon a former occafion fractured her arm, the bone of which had never been reduced or united. In the courfe of the difpute, thefe two women were unintentionally thrown down, and by this accident the old lady loft both her teeth, while the other infifted that the Chriftians had been the occafion of fracturing her arm. To be brief, the Chriftians were overpowered by numbers, and were obliged to retire to Mogodore, where they immediately made a complaint to the governor of the infults they had received from the Moors, who in their turn alfo appeared before him with a complaint againft the Chriftians. The whole being referred to the emperor, both parties were ordered up to court, with the view of giving the matter an impartial hearing, and of adminiftering juftice accordingly. It is hardly neceffary to intimate, that in this uncivilized country, and with a man of Sidi Mahomet's prejudices, the Moorifh evidence would be certain of a favourable hearing. The circumftances indeed of one woman lofing her teeth, and another having her arm fractured, appeared in the eyes of the emperor fo plaufible, that upon their being made known

to

to him, without hesitation he ordered the Christians to be put in irons, and confined till he should determine upon the punishment which such apparent crimes merited. For this purpose, the Mufti, or high priest was desired to refer the matter to the Koran, with a view of punishing the delinquents according to its dictates. The priest soon found out a passage, where it species an eye for an eye and a tooth for a tooth. The English gentleman, whom the old lady fixed upon for the person who had been the occasion of her misfortune, was therefore directed to lose two of his teeth, which punishment was immediately put in execution in the presence of the emperor; while his French companion, as they could not find out a punishment in the Koran for breaking an arm, received the bastinado in a manner which disgraced humanity and the law of nations; the prisoners were then set at liberty.

This circumstance brings to my mind how narrowly I escaped falling into a similar predicament in the course of my detention at Morocco. One day, within the walls of the palace, I was grossly insulted by a Moor, at a time when, from the great anxiety I was under, my temper was much disturbed, and which so far had put me off my guard as to induce me to give the offender a blow on the face. Upon this a Moorish soldier, who, unobserved by myself, was sitting behind me in a corner of the wall, exclaimed in Arabic in a very austere tone, " Christian, how dare you strike that Moor ?" A full consciousness of having acted imprudently, and a recollection of the emperor's former treatment of Christians under similar circumstances,

cumftances, now preffed upon my mind with fuch force, that at firft I was at a lofs what part I fhould take to extricate myfelf from this difficulty. To walk away, would be an acknowledgment of guilt, and would afford the Moor a greater plea for making a complaint; I therefore determined upon returning back and expoftulating with the man, by telling him that I had been grofsly infulted, and muft therefore be under the neceffity of making immediate application to the governor of the town to have the offender feverely punifhed for attacking one, who, from the nature of his employment, was in the emperor's fervice, and confequently under his particular protection. In reply, the Moor faid, that had I kicked him, horfewhipped him, or punifhed him in any other way but that of flapping his face, he fhould have over-looked it; but a blow on the face was in their law a crime of fo ferious a nature, that he thought it his duty to acquaint the emperor of it, who had hitherto never pardoned any perfon convicted of fo heinous an offence, but had always cut off that hand of the Moor which had offered the infult; what then could a Chriftian expect from him? From the knowledge I had already learned of the Moorifh character, I ftill thought it neceffary to continue in the fame ftrain, by informing the Moor, that he might act as he thought proper, but that I fhould ftill fulfil my refolution, and had no doubt but it would have its proper effect. The man now began to foften, and faid, that as I was in the emperor's fervice, he would for this time look over the offence, but cautioned me to be careful how I acted in future.

Upon

Upon confidering every circumftance I thought it moft prudent to let the matter drop here; and I acknowledge that this affair proved a fufficient leffon to me to avoid in future entering into fimilar contefts with the Moors.

Sidi Mahomet was fufficiently confcious of his own power and dignity, and kept every perfon at the moft abject diftance; no perfon daring to approach or fpeak to him without his permiffion. Senfible alfo of the exceffes into which he might be betrayed by ungoverned paffion, if at any time he found his temper difcompofed, he indifcriminately ordered every perfon out of his fight. It may eafily be conceived that the monarch had no difficulty in fecuring obedience to this mandate, fince all were fenfible that to have continued in his prefence would have been highly dangerous, if not fatal.

The only perfons who poffeffed any confiderable influence over the emperor were his women; and it was through that channel that the moft fuccefsful bufinefs was tranfacted with him.

Thus far for the vices of arbitrary power. But deceit, hypocrify and falfehood were qualities which could not be immediately afcribed to that fource, unlefs we confider them as the neceffary effects of an education in a defpotic court. As a cloak to actions which he knew muft excite difapprobation and difguft, Sidi Mahomet attempted to perfuade his fubjects that they proceeded from motives of religion and juftice; and to give them a greater fanction he enrolled himfelf in the fraternity of faints, and paid a ftrict attention to all the fuperftitions and forms peculiar to his religion.

This

This conduct anfwered well with the ignorant part of the community, but the more enlightened could not but obferve that he attended more to the ceremonial of his religion than to its principles, which he made no fcruple of violating whenever it fuited his convenience. What he promifed one day he would refufe the next, fo that no dependance was ever placed upon his word. Added to thefe, he poffeffed a large portion of that low cunning which is common to perfons whofe minds and fentiments have not been elevated or refined by literature or fcience. He perhaps, indeed, found this quality not without its ufes in governing fuch a people as the Moors; and no man underftood their character and difpofition better than he did. He was aware that refpect is frequently deftroyed by unfeafonable familiarities, and therefore kept at a moft ftately diftance from his fubjects, and but feldom appeared among them. By thefe means his confequence was preferved, and his conduct, and his talents were involved in that impenetrable and awful mift that furrounds the feraglios of Eaftern monarchs.

The few rebellions which occurred during his long reign, proved decifively that he knew how to govern his fubjects. Whenever a difpofition for revolt prevailed in any of the provinces, a body of troops was immediately difpatched to plunder the whole of the difcontented province, and to feize the infurgents, who were immediately conducted to court, and punifhed according to the magnitude of their refpective offences. Some were put to death, others were deprived

of

of their hands and legs; and for leffer crimes the difcontented parties underwent the baftinado. This monarch employed perfons in different diftricts to watch the motions of his fubjects, and to inform him of every fymptom of revolt; and thus, by a well-timed interference, he was enabled to crufh rebellion in the bud.

In his conduct towards foreign powers, Sidi Mahomet difcovered the fame difregard to truth and juftice, the fame adroitnefs and cunning. He readily promifed to grant every demand, provided he was to be well paid for the conceffion. But it muft have been valuable prefents indeed which would induce him to perform his promife. He protracted negociations in order that he and his minifters might be enriched by them; but always as much as poffible avoided bringing them to a final determination, by either granting or refufing a favour.

If foreign powers omitted to pay him the tribute he demanded, he immediately threatened in the fevereft manner to commence hoftilities; yet in this he was never in earneft, for he was more afraid of his enemies than they had reafon to be of him. When he found they were not difpofed to contend the matter with him, he increafed his demands accordingly.

In order to enhance his confequence, he endeavoured to perfuade his fubjects that he was remarkably fkilled in matters of which they were entirely ignorant. To preferve an appearance of ability, when he was vifited by Europeans, if the ftranger was a merchant, the fubject of converfation was on manufactures, foreign commerce,
&c.

&c. If he was a military officer, fortifications, attacks, &c. were the topics; and if a seafaring person, he would then scratch on a piece of paper a plan of his coasts and harbours. Though he rarely advanced any thing to the purpose on these subjects; yet as foreigners who visited the court generally appeared there with a view of obtaining some favour, and as it was never customary for any person to contradict the emperor, they always coincided with his opinions, and pretended at least to admire his extensive abilities. This fully answered the intention of the emperor; it induced his subjects to form a good opinion of his understanding, and he often collected some real information from the answers which his visitors returned to his questions.

Sidi Mahomet paid more attention to military affairs than to his navy, though if any power refused to repair a frigate, it was a sufficient inducement for him to threaten a war. He thought himself perfectly acquainted with the art of fortification, but his knowledge of it extended no farther than a few loose hints which he had received upon the subject from those Europeans who had visited the court.

In his court and personal appearance, Sidi Mahomet affected great simplicity of manners, not allowing even his own sons to appear in his presence except in a plain Moorish dress. They then were obliged to uncover their cap or turban (for a Moor never pulls off either except when going to bed) and to wear instead of the Haick the Sulam, which is a cloak made of white or blue woollen cloth, the front parts of which they were obliged to throw over their shoulders, and as

obliged

foon as they faw the emperor, to proftrate their heads to the ground, and kifs it, exclaiming, " God " fave the king!" He then ordered them to approach, and fpeak to him.

Though in general of a ftately demeanour, he was fometimes known to unbend, and occafionally took pleafure in converfing with his courtiers on various fubjects; but they were permitted to advance no opinion of their own, but merely to approve of what he faid. He frequently talked upon the fubject of religion, and confidered himfelf as well informed in that particular. He fometimes endeavoured to explain to them different parts of the Koran, pointing out its beauties, and impreffing on the minds of his auditors the moft intolerant prejudices againft Chriftians.

The mixture of good and evil fo incident to all human characters, was alfo to be found in Sidi Mahomet. Notwithftanding what has been remarked of his avarice, his duplicity, and abfurd pretenfions to religion, there are fome circumftances which ferve to leffen our indignation, and thefe it is only confiftent with juftice and candour to ftate. It is generally allowed, that though he muft neceffarily fuffer in a comparifon with the princes of free and civilized nations, yet when compared with his defpotic predeceffors, his character greatly rifes in the fcale of humanity. He was feldom or never wontonly cruel. He was certainly fometimes too hafty in pronouncing fentence on criminals, for which he has been often known to exprefs the ftrongeft fentiments of remorfe; and his defire to prevent any ill effects from his paffions has been already remarked.

In

In his adminiftration of juftice he generally
acted very impartially, except indeed when his
own intereft was immediately concerned, and
then every other feeling gave way. It muft,
however, be acknowledged, that though himfelf a moft notorious violator of the laws, he fo
far refpected them that he never would permit
others to follow his example. Though fo extremely avaricious, it has been already ftated that
in fome fevere inftances of public diftrefs, he generoufly difpenfed his treafures to adminifter relief
to the fufferers; and the number of poor people who were daily fed at his palace, of which I
was an eye-witnefs, plainly evinced that he was
not deftitute of charity. Europeans met with
greater encouragement, and the wheels of commerce were lefs clogged, during the reign of Sidi
Mahomet than at any preceding period.

Thus was this monarch a fingular compound of
liberality and intolerance, of avarice and benevolence, of cruelty and compaffion. It is perhaps
only a ftate of defpotifm that we behold this confufion of character. The legal reftraints of civilized life, form themfelves into habits; and the
eccentricities and caprices to which circumftances,
fituation, the ftate of the health, or perhaps the
variations of the climate, difpofe the human
mind, are no longer found to exift in European
countries, or to exift in an inferior degree. Happy
it is, when any reftraints are impofed upon us,
to prevent us from doing evil. Man is a creature
not formed for arbitrary power. So limited are
his views, fo variable his difpofition, fo violent
and

and tyrannical his paffions, that the wifeft of men would certainly not wifh for abfolute authority, and the beft, if entrufted with it, would probably abufe it.

The conduct of the emperor towards foreign courts has already been noticed. His means of extracting money from them by threatining a war, which perhaps in reality he dreaded, has been likewife ftated. It will probably not be unfeafonable in this place to introduce a few remarks on their conduct towards him.

The obfervation that firft and moft naturally prefents itfelf upon this occafion is—that nothing but grofs neglect or inexcufable ignorance could induce the European princes in general to remain in a kind of tributary ftate to a prince, who had neither an army nor a fleet which deferved the name, and a a people whofe difpofition is lefs fuited to enterprize than perhaps any other.

What had they to fear from him? His whole fleet confifted only of a few fmall frigates and row-boats, ill managed and worfe manned, the whole of which might have been deftroyed in one day by two or three well-appointed European frigates. The entrances of thofe ports where he laid up his fhipping, if we except Tangier and Larache, are, as I before obferved, fo continually choaking up with fand, that in a fhort time they will only admit fifhing-boats, or the very fmalleft craft. The towns are none of them regularly fortified, except Mogodore, and that hardly produces half a dozen men who underftand the leaft of working the guns. And yet this contemptible power gives

laws

laws to all the coasts of Portugal and Spain, and may be said in some measure to command the entrance of the Mediterranean!

It may be said, he was too trifling a power to notice; if so, why lavish immense presents for the purpose of keeping him in temper? Those who imagined they secured his friendship by these means were much mistaken; on the contrary, they only added fuel to that flame of avarice which was not to be extinguished, if he was one day presented with a frigate, he asked for two the next; and the more his requests were indulged, the more his inordinate desires were increased.

It is well known to those who have been conversant with the Moors, that to secure their friendship you must first assert your own superiority, and then if you make them a trifling present, its value is trebled in their estimation. The same disposition would have been found in Sidi Mahomet, as in the common Moor. So far from courting an alliance, it would rather have been good policy at once to quarrel with him; the loss of a few towns and particularly Mogodore, to which he was much attached, from its being raised under his own auspices, would soon have reduced him to good humour and submission.

The emperor's title is, " Emperor of Africa; " Emperor of Morocco; king of Fez, Suz, and " Gago; lord of Dara and Guinea; and great " Sharif of Mahomet."

The principal amusement of the emperor was latterly observing his soldiers fire with musquets at targets, and rewarding those who were successful with small pieces of money. He also occa-

I   sionally

fionally entertained himfelf with falcons; but in general he fpent the greater part of his time with his women.

The emperor received foreigners, and tranfacted all public bufinefs, either in his carriage or on horfeback, in fome of the open fpaces within the palace. Formerly, indeed, on fuch occafions, it was fometimes cuftomary to admit ftrangers into one of the rooms; and then he obliged them to conform to the cuftom of the country, by pulling off their fhoes when in his prefence: but fome fpirited Europeans a few years ago having refufed to pay that homage, he ever afterwards gave them audience in one of his court-yards. The Spanifh friars at Morocco only were an exception to this rule, for upon their informing him that they never pulled off their fhoes to any power under God, he always permitted them to enter his room with them on.

Previous to a ftranger, whether an European or Moor, obtaining an audience of his Moorifh Majefty, a prefent was always made to one of his minifters, as an inducement to him to acquaint his fovereign that a ftranger folicited that honour. The firft prefent, unlefs it was fomething very handfome, did not always fucceed; and it was frequently neceffary to apply to two or three minifters to procure a fpeedy audience, or even to fend in a prefent to one of the Sultanas, none of whom entertained any very uneafy fenfations about accepting the compliment. The latter was indeed the moft certain mode of fucceeding.

After having fo far accomplifhed his wifhes, the ftranger was next liable to be detained a longer or a fhorter time before the capricious monarch would

would fix on a day for receiving him.   Even after.
this he would frequently fend for him in a violent
hurry to the palace, and when there keep him ftanding in one of the open courts feveral hours; he
would then fend an excufe for not admitting him
on that day; and this agreeable procefs was in many
inftances repeated three or four times.   The tar-
dinefs, infolence, and irregularity, of the court
of Morocco, is indeed beyond conception; and
thofe who have bufinefs there, ought to be poffeffed of all the philofophy and patience of a Stoic,
if they would avoid the deprivation of their fenfes.

No perfon whatever, whether Moor or Chriftian, was admitted into the prefence of the fovereign, but when accompanied with a handfome
prefent, more or lefs valuable, in proportion to
the favour to be requefted.   Even the emperor's
own fons were not exempted from this cuftom,
upon paying their firft vifit after a previous abfence.   The generofity of the fuitor muft not even
ftop here; for when the audience is over, the
mafter of the ceremonies with his fervants, and
the porters of all the gates of the palace, which
are rather numerous, have a claim for their perquifites, and are not to be got rid of till they obtain fomething.   Indeed, as they receive no pay
from their royal mafter, thefe perquifites were
the only means they had of obtaining a fubfiftence*.

* For the fatisfaction of thofe who may have occafion
to vifit the court of Morocco upon bufinefs, I have with
difficulty obtained an account of the fees which are ufually paid by European merchants to the emperor's attendants. Confuls and ambaffadors of courfe pay more in
proportion.

                    Expen-

After having completed the bufinefs at court, the obtaining of the final difpatches was commonly attended with the fame difficulties as the obtaining of an audience. The emperor was not

Expences at Court.

To the emperor— { A more or lefs valuable prefent, according to the favour which is expected.

To the mafter of the ceremonies for public audience, who introduces ftrangers to the emperor — } The fame in proportion.

	Ounces.
To the man who attends the emperor at the Machoire	20
To — who cleans his mufkets	20
To — who has the care of his horfes	20
To — who makes tea for the emperor	10
To — who has the care of his lance	10
To — who has the care of his umbrella	5
To — who has the care of the emperor's faddles	10
To the emperor's coachman	5
To the man who has the care of the emperor's fpurs	5
To — who has the care of the emperor's tents	10
To — who has the care of the emperor's flippers	5
To — who gives the emperor water to drink	5
To — who takes care of the emperor's chair	5
To — who takes the flies off the emperor's face	5
To — who takes care of the emperor's fword	5
To — who takes care of the emperor's watch	5
To the porters of the Machoire, for ten gates	40
To the emperor's gardners	10
To calling for each audience	10
	——
Total	205

An ounce, as I have before obferved, is a filver coin of nearly the fame value as five pence Englifh.

only

only naturally very forgetful, but sometimes, from political motives, intentionally so. He was very well aware that the longer strangers were detained at Morocco, the more his ministers would be enriched by them; and as the money came at last, though by a circuitous course, into his own pocket, he used frequently to forget that strangers were waiting for their dispatches. The ministers, on the other hand, unless stimulated by substantial presents, were generally extremely dilatory in reminding him of them; and there have been many instances of foreigners being detained at Morocco five or six weeks, entirely owing to this circumstance.

With respect to the court of Morocco, it latterly hardly deserved that appellation. When the emperor was young, his faculties clear, and his abilities in their prime, he entrusted to his ministers a considerable share of the public business; but within the few last years of his life, when his strength of body as well as of mind were worn out by hard services and old age, either from suspicion or dotage, he took the reins of government entirely into his own hands. The ministers and secretaries not daring to notice the mistakes of the sovereign, were obliged to write out letters and send orders, which were contradicted almost every hour, and which occasioned the utmost confusion. The court of Morocco, indeed, under the most advantageous circumstances, was always notorious for its irregularity and contradiction; but a short time previous to the emperor's death, the government could scarcely be said to exist at all.

As an account of the officers employed about the court of the emperor has never been particularly detailed to the public, a fhort ftatement of them will probably not be uninterefting: I fhall therefore, in as few words as poffible, point out their refpective employments.

The emperor's court confifted of,

1. A prime minifter, named the Effendi, or friend; who was the refponfible man, and during that period when the government was carried on in a more regular manner, all letters and orders were figned by him before they were difpatched.

2. A principal fecretary to the treafury, united with the office of Effendi; who had the difburfement at large of the emperor's payments, with fix Moorifh and feven Jewifh under-fecretaries.

3. A mafter of the horfe, with one hundred and twenty affiftants.

4. A grand chamberlain, a place commonly united with that of prime minifter, with feventeen affiftants; nine of whom were fons of Spanifh renegadoes, three fons of negroes, and the others Moors.

5. A grand falconer, which is an hereditary place, and perhaps the only one in the country, with twenty affiftants.

6. A keeper of the great feal.

7. Two grand ftewards, with eight affiftants.

8. Five infpectors general of all the emperor's affairs, the principal of whom was the Effendi.

9. Three mafters of ceremonies for public audiences, with forty affiftants.

10. An

10. An interpreter general for the German, Dutch, English, French, Spanish, and Latin languages; this man was a German renegado.

11. A secretary for the Spanish and Italian languages, who was a Genoese.

12. Two grand keepers of the jewels and plate.

13. A grand master of the baths.

14. Two grand keepers of the arsenal.

15. Two keepers of the emperor's goods and warehouses.

16. Three inspectors of mosques, &c.

17. Five keepers of the provisions.

18. Two keepers of the library.

19. Two astrologers.

20. Four masters of the carriages with two assistants.

21. Twelve sons of renegadoes, who have never had beards, employed in drawing the small carriages.

22. Three principal assistants for prayers, with seventeen deputies, sons of the great people of the empire.

23. Three bearers of the umbrella, with nine assistants.

24. One bearer of the sabre.

25. Two bearers of the bason.

26. Two bearers of the lance.

27. One bearer of the watch.

28. Five bearers of the emperor's own firelocks, who are all Alcaides, with fifteen inferior assistants.

29. A bearer of the colours and standard.

30. A physician and a surgeon, with several tradesmen, too numerous to mention.

I 4

Upon

Upon taking a retrospective view of the employments under the emperor of Morocco, we shall find that they differ so much from those of other states, as might have been imagined, from the ignorance of the European customs observable in this people in other respects. The places of Effendi and principal secretary to the treasury being united in one person, bears considerable analogy to the union of the office of prime minister with those of chancellor of the exchequer and first lord of the treasury. The appointments of secretary of state, master of the horse, grand chamberlain, keeper of the great seal, and grand falconer, are all places which are well known in European courts; and many others have nearly the same correspondence.

The principal difference between the court of Morocco and those of Europe is, that the possessors of these appointments in European courts enjoy very lucrative incomes from their respective states, while those of Morocco receive none at all from the court. They depend solely on the perquisites which are paid them by those who have business to transact with the court. Even this, however, sometimes forms a very inconsiderable income, though always subject to defalcation from the rapacious hand of their sovereign, who seizes upon every thing with which he comes in contact.

The Effendi to the emperor had a degree of address, and an elegance of manners which would have done honour to an European courtier. He received a stranger with a pleasing smile and a respectful bow; shook him warmly by the hand,

enquired

enquired after his health, invited him to his houfe, and off red him his fervices. As he was rich, he w xtremely timid in the prefence of the er , notwithftanding he annually made him e prefent to keep him in temper. Some of e princes, and many others, followed his example in this refpect, judicioufly preferring the enjoyment of a little with a certainty, to the running a rifk of the whole.

The emperor of late had no regular court days, but fixed upon them as inclination or convenience dictated. On thofe days all the princes who were at Morocco, and every perfon in the immediate fervice of the emperor, were obliged to attend at the Machoire, an open part of the palace fo named, where they, with the foldiers, were arranged in the form of a crefcent; the minifters and ftrangers in front, and the fovereign, either on horfeback or in his carriage, in the centre. Upon thefe occafions the public bufinefs in general was tranfacted, foreigners were received, grievances were ftated, complaints heard (every perfon being at liberty to apply to the emperor for redrefs) and malefactors were punifhed in the prefence of the fovereign, and the whole court.

The revenues of the emperor of Morocco confift of a tenth on every article of confumption, being the natural production of the country, as allowed him by the Koran; an annual tax upon the Jews; his cuftom-houfe and excife duties; and the tributes which he exacts from his fubjects, foreign ftates, and European merchants, in the form of prefents. From the laft articles he derives the moft confiderable part of his income.

The

The want of fyftem, and the caprice of Sidi Mahomet, was fuch that it was utterly impoffible to fay what was the annual amount of all thefe branches of revenue. The duties were frequently changed three or four times in the courfe of a year, and the tributes were fubject to an equal degree of uncertainty. After all it has been a matter of great doubt and fpeculation whether Sidi Mahomet was wealthy. From the greater encouragement to commerce during his reign, the trifling expence of his court, every perfon engaged about it, receiving little or no pay from the emperor, the uncommonly fevere exactions he enforced, and the numerous voluntary prefents he received, the natural conclufion was, that he muft have been very rich.   On the other hand, however, his expences at the fieges of Melilla and Mazagan are known to have been very confiderable; and thefe, united to the valuable prefents he annually tranfmitted to the grand Seignior, and to the Sharifs* of Mecca, are to be placed in the oppofite fcale; and when this is done, it will perhaps appear that his wealth was far from confiderable.

The land forces of the emperor of Morocco, confift principally of black troops, the defcendants of thofe Negroes which Muley Ifhmael imported from Guinea, and fome few white, amounting altogether to an army of about thirty-fix thoufand men upon the eftablifhment, two thirds of which are cavalry. This eftablifhment, however, upon occafion admits of a confiderable increafe, as every man is fuppofed to be a foldier,

* See page 115.

and

and when called upon, is obliged to act in that capacity. About six thousand of the standing forces form the emperor's body guard, and are always kept near his person; the remainder are quartered in the different towns of the empire, and are under the charge of the bashaws of the provinces. They are all clothed by the emperor, and receive a trifling pay; but their chief dependance is on plunder, which they have frequent opportunities of acquiring.

The soldiers have no distinction in dress from the other Moors, and are only marked by their accoutrements, which consist of a sabre, a very long musquet, a small red leather box to hold their balls, which is fixed in front by means of a belt, and a powder-horn flung over their shoulders.

The army is under the direction of a commander in chief, four principal Bashaws, and Alcaides who command distinct divisions. With respect to the Alcaides it is proper to remark, that there are three descriptions of persons who bear this appellation: but those to whom I at present allude are military officers, who command soldiers from a thousand to five hundred, twenty-five, or even four men in a division.

The black troops which I have been describing are naturally of a very fiery disposition, capable of enduring great fatigue, hunger, thirst, and every difficulty to which a military life is exposed. They appear well calculated for skirmishing parties, or for the purpose of harrassing an enemy; but were they obliged to undergo a regular attack, from their total want of discipline, they would soon be routed. In all their man-

œuvres,

œuvres, they have no notion whatever of order and regularity, but have altogether more the appearance of a rabble than of an army.

Though thefe troops are fuppofed to be the ftrongeft fupport of defpotifm, yet from their avarice and love of variety, they frequently prove the moft dangerous enemies to their monarchs; they are often known to excite fedition and rebellion; and their infolence has fometimes proceeded to fuch exceffes, as nearly to overturn the government. Their conduct is governed only by their paffions. Thofe who pay them beft, and treat them with the greateft attention, they will always be the moft ready to fupport. This circumftance, independent of every other, makes it the intereft of the monarch to keep his fubjects in as complete a ftate of poverty as poffible. The Moors are, indeed, remarkable for infincerity in their attachments, and for their love of variety; a military force, in this kingdom efpecially, is therefore the only means which a defpotic monarch can employ for fecuring himfelf in the poffeffion of the throne. Ignorant of every principle of rational liberty, whatever contefts this devoted people may engage in with their tyrants, are merely contefts for the fucceffion; and the fole object for which they fpend their lives and their property, is to exchange one mercilefs defpot for another.

The emperor's navy confifts of about fifteen fmall frigates, a few xebecks, and between twenty and thirty row-gallies. The whole is commanded by one admiral; but as thefe veffels are principally ufed for the purpofes of piracy, they feldom
unite

uinite in a fleet. The number of feaman in the fervice, are computed at fix thoufand.

I have already noted the bad ftate of the ports of Morocco, and the probability of their becoming ftill worfe; it is therefore evident, that very little is to be apprehended from the emperor as a naval power; and indeed I am apt to believe, that though a confiderable part of his dominions is apparently maritime, he will in the courfe of fome years be deftitute both of fleets and harbours.

When defcribing the emperor's character, I obferved, that there cannot exift a more abfolute government than that of Morocco; the lives and properties of the fubjects depending entirely on the will or caprice of the monarch. The forms of order and juftice are, however, ftill preferved, though but very little of the fubftance remains.

An officer is appointed by the emperor for the government of every province, who, as I have already ftated, is named a Bafhaw; he is generally a Moor of fome diftinction, and frequently one of the emperor's fons. This officer, who is appointed or removed at the will of the fovereign, has almoft an unlimited power throughout the province which he commands; he can inflict every punifhment but death; can levy taxes, impofe fines, and in fhort can plunder any individual he pleafes; and indeed, if the reader will not fmile at the abufe of words, the plundering of the public and of individuals may be confidered as a part of his office. When by every fpecies of rapacity he has amaffed a large property, then it becomes the bufinefs of the emperor to divert this treafure into his own coffers. Some frivolous

plea

plea is therefore invented for the imprifoning of the bafhaw, which is immediately put into execution. The emperor then feizes upon all his property, and afterwards reinftates him in his government, in order that the fame game may be played over again. So perfectly acquainted with mankind in every ftate and fituation, was our inimitable Shakefpeare:

" *Rofencrantz.* Take you me for a fpunge, my " lord?

" *Hamlet.* Aye, Sir; that foaks up the king's " countenance, his rewards, his authorities. But " fuch officers do the king beft fervice in the end; " he keeps them, like an ape, in the corner of his " jaw; firft mouthed, to be at laft fwallowed. " When he needs what you have gleaned, it is but " fqueezing you, and fpunge, you fhall be dry " again."

Subordinate to the bafhaw, the emperor appoints governors to each town, named Alcaides, and officers with a fimilar authority in every Douhar or encampment, who are called Shaiks; thefe officers have the fame power invefted in them over their feveral diftricts as the bafhaws have in their provinces. But in other refpects their fituation is worfe, as they are not only fubject to the tyranny of the emperor, but alfo of the bafhaw.

The Alcaide, or governor, is invefted with both the military and civil authority in the town where he refides. As a military officer, he commands a number of foldiers, whom he employs for the public defence and tranquility, and alfo for enforcing the payment of taxes, for the punifhing of delinquents, and to convey his orders and mef-

fages

fages to court, or into the country. As a civil officer, he has the entire cognizance of all criminal matters, for which he di cretionally inflicts any punifhment fhort of death.

If we only reflect on the dangerous extent of this almoft unlimited power, it is eafy to anticipate the abufes of it in a country where fo little attention is paid to juftice or honour. For the moft trifling offences the Alcaide condemns the delinquent not only to be baftinadoed very feverely, and imprifoned, but alfo to pay him a fum of money, or prefent him with fome other article equal in value, which probably the prifoner has been half his life in acquiring. It frequently happens, indeed, that falfe accufations are invented purpofely againft individuals to plunder them of their property. This is not the only inconvenience arifing from an abufe of power ;—for let a perfon commit the moft notorious crime, if he can carry up a prefent to the governor of greater value than what was prefented by his accufer, he is not only forgiven, but if he has the leaft ingenuity, he will find very little difficulty in throwing the whole of the crime upon his antagonift. Indeed, in this country, juftice, or rather judgment, is moft eafily procured by purchafing it.

Under the Alcaide is an officer named Ell-hackum, or deputy governor, whofe office bears fome analogy to our principal bailiff or conftable.

Befides thefe officers, there is in every town a Cadi, who is both a civil judge and the chief prieft; for it is well known that the civil and religious inftitutions are united in the Koran. When any difpute happens between individuals, refpect-

ing

ing matters of right or property, debts, infults, &c. the perfon who fuppofes himfelf injured may apply for redrefs to the Cadi, who is to determine the matter agreeably to the principles of the Koran. In the abfence of the Cadi, any of the Talbs, who are common priefts, are equally authorifed to act for him. If the parties chufe to employ lawyers, the pleadings muft be carried on in writing, otherwife they plead orally their own caufes. Upon thefe occafions the Cadi or Talbs cannot openly receive any payment, but it is well known that they are too frequently influenced by private prefents.

The chief of the Cadis is the Mufti, who is alfo the fupreme head of the church.

When any party in a fuit conceives that he has reafon to complain of the jurifdiction of thefe officers, he has a right to appeal to the emperor, who gives public audiences for the purpofe of adminiftering juftice. This cuftom would be a great alleviation to the evils of defpotifm, were the emperor always to adminifter juftice impartially; but valuable prefents have fometimes too powerful an influence even over the fovereign himfelf. On this account, as well as on that of the great diftance of many of the provinces from the feat of government, the people feldom embrace this laft refource in applying for juftice.

The mode of punifhing criminals in this country depends entirely upon the will of the fovereign. Trifling offences are ufually punifhed by imprifonment and the baftinado, which is inflicting a certain number of ftripes on the back and legs by leather ftraps, and which is fometimes executed with

great

great feverity.   For crimes of a more ferious nature, in fome cafes the hands are cut off, particularly for ftealing, in others a leg and a hand.
When I was at Morocco four men who had committed murder had both their hands and legs cut
off, and were afterwards fhot.   Other criminals
are run through with fwords, knocked down
with clubs, or are beheaded.   Another mode of
punifhment is toffing, which is fo contrived that
the victim falls immediately upon his head.—
There were feveral perfons about Sidi Mahomet,
who from practice had acquired an habit of
throwing perfons up, fo as at pleafure either to
break the head, diflocate the neck, fracture an
arm, leg, or both, or to let them fall without receiving any material injury.   When I was at Morocco a man received the latter punifhment in the
morning, and in the afternoon the emperor made
him a handfome prefent as a recompence for what
he had fuffered.

To fum up all in a few words, there is no mode
of cruelty known which has not been practifed at
Morocco.   I am well aware that in the prefent
uncivilized ftate of the people, fevere and exemplary punifhments may be neceffary to keep them
in any degree of fubjection; but it muft be at leaft
allowed that fuch feverities fhould never be inflicted but when there is a full proof of guilt.   The
contrary of this I am afraid is too often the cafe
at Morocco.   The accufed is feldom permitted to
make his defence, but is fent out of the world
very frequently without knowing for what he
fuffers.

Thefe

Thefe punifhments were always inflicted in the prefence of the emperor. The former monarchs of this country were their own executioners, and Sidi Mahomet acted in the fame capacity when prince; but upon his acceffion to the throne he refigned this refpectable office to his Negro foldiers. I never was prefent at any of thefe executions, but was informed that legs and arms are taken off by a common knife and faw, and that the ftump is afterwards dipped in boiling pitch, which is the only mode of ftopping the hæmorrhage with which they are acquinted.

To evince in what a cool light all thefe things are confidered by the Moors, one of the emperor's fons had undertaken to put a memorial from me into his father's hands, praying to be fent home. Upon my calling upon him to afk if he had complied with my requeft, he informed me that when he laft faw his father an opportunity had not offered, as he was then very *bufy in putting fome perfons to death.*

C H A P.

CHAP. X.

Arrival of MULEY ABSULEM *at* MOROCCO—*his pompous Entry.*—*Adventures of some English Captives.*—*Account of wild Arabs.*—*Interview with the Prince.*—*Flattering Expectations—disappointed.*—*Unworthy conduct of the Prince—his departure for* MECCA.—*Disagreeable Embarrassments.*—*Efforts of the Author to procure Leave to return.*

ABOUT ten days after my interview with the emperor, Muley Abfulem arrived from Tarudant, in his way to Mecca. As this prince was fo diftinguifhed a favourite with the emperor, his public entrance into Morocco was conducted in a much more magnificent ftile than any other part of the royal family would perhaps have ventured upon. As foon as intelligence arrived that the prince was approaching the city, two of his brothers, Muley Slemma and Muley Ouffine, who happened to be at Morocco at the time, the Bafhaw, and all the principal perfons in the city, received orders to proceed on horfeback to meet him, which they did in great form, and found him encamped at the diftance of about four miles. As foon as he had dined, the cavalcade commenced, confifting firft, of all the prince's Alcaides, about twelve in number, in front, flanked on each fide by one ftandard-bearer, who carried each a red flag, and one lance-bearer, carrying a lance of an uncommon length. Behind them was Muley Abfulem in the centre; on the right of him Muley Slemma, and on the left Muley Ouffine. The next in order

was

was the Bashaw, with the principal persons of the city; and the rear was brought up by a troop of one hundred cavalry, all abreast, partly Negroes and partly Moors, who had the butt end of their muskets resting on their saddles, with the muzzles pointed perpendicularly. In this manner the prince advanced till he approached the walls of the town, where he received orders to halt till the emperor came to him; an honour which had never been paid by Sidi Mahomet to any person before. The emperor shortly after advanced on horseback, with his suite, consisting of about fifty soldiers. Upon his approach Muley Absulem dismounted and kissed the earth; upon which the emperor commanded him to rise, and approach close to his person. He then blessed him, laying his hand on the prince's head, and afterwards embraced him with all the affection of a fond father. Having made many enquiries concerning his son's health, the emperor took his leave, and each retired to their respective places of residence. As soon as the prince had got within the walls of his garden, his troops fired three vollies of musquetry in an irregular manner, as is customary on these occasions, and there the ceremony concluded.

It may easily be imagined, that I lost no time in waiting on his highness, and I received from him as flattering a reception as I could possibly wish. The prince informed me that he had continued recovering his sight gradually, and that he found himself in every other respect in good health. I took this opportunity of representing to him how disagreeably I was situated with respect to the emperor

emperor, and trusted that he would now clear up every doubt that might have arisen on my account; and with this request he promised to comply. On paying my second visit, the prince informed me that he had obtained the emperor's permission to have again recourse to his medicines, and that he was certain he should have influence sufficient with his father to persuade him to give me up the English captives, as a compliment for my services.

The prince had brought along with him to Morocco the English captain, the only Englishman that had been left in slavery, the black having died some time before. My reader will easily conceive the pleasure I felt at seeing my unfortunate countryman, who had been left alone in the hands of savages, now out of immediate slavery, and with the chearful prospect, according to the promises of the prince, of being immediately sent home to his friends and country. My sensations indeed on the occasion may be much more easily felt than described. But if this circumstance had such an effect upon me, what must it have had upon this unfortunate officer, who for some months past had been separated from his people, one of whom was a near relation, and without knowing whether they were dead or alive; who with the evils of slavery had experienced that of a severe fever, without having any person to console him, or afford him that assistance which is so necessary upon such occasions? To be redeemed under such circumstances from his inhospitable situation, to recover from his illness, and to meet with all his companions at Morocco, well taken

care

care of by the emperor, was a change which he had given up all expectation of ever beholding.

The captain was a well-informed young man, and an agreeable companion. He had been brought up, as I before intimated, to the profeffion of medicine and furgery, in both of which he had received a good education. His firft effay in the world was as furgeon to a Guinea-man; after having made feveral voyages in this capacity, however, finding it a difadvantageous employment, he obtained the command of a fmall veffel in the fame trade, and this was his firft voyage as commander.

Contrary to his inclination he was ordered by his owners to fail between the canaries and the coaft of Africa, which is at all times confidered as a dangerous navigation. As he approached towards the fpot where his misfortune happened, which is inhabited by wild Arabs, he got into a ftrong current, which drives directly towards the fhore, and a perfect calm fucceeding, the veffel unavoidably ran aground. The crew immediately took to their boat, carried off all the money on board, which was about five hundred dollars, with a good fhare of provifions and water, and got fafe to fhore.

The part of the country were they were wrecked confifted of deep and heavy fands. As upon their firft landing they faw nothing to moleft them, it was their intention to proceed on foot, along the coaft to the northward, till they could reach Santa Cruz or Mogodore, where they could make their fituation known. For this purpofe
they

they fet off with their money, provifions and water, and met with no difturbance till the end of two days. They then obferved a party of wild Arabs, armed with large clubs and knives, and rapidly advancing towards them: their firft object was to bury their money in the fands. Over-powered by numbers, they faw no chance of making a fuccefsful defence, and therefore every moment expected inftantaneous death. The favages, however, had a different object in view. They knew very well that what property the unfortunate people had about them was fufficiently fecure, without being under the neceffity of deftroying their lives in order to obtain it, and they were not ignorant of the value of their perfons when offered for fale; their ultimate object therefore was, to bring them to market as flaves.

As each of their conquerors conceived himfelf equally interefted in the capture, they were fome time before they could agree among themfelves how they fhould difpofe of their prifoners; in the mean time fome of the people were knocked down, others had their pockets cut out, and the buttons torn from off their coats. They were at laft feized on by different perfons, and carried away to different places of refidence.

As I had an oportunity of feeing fome of thefe favages at Morocco, and as they appeared to be in fome refpects different from thofe Arabs whom I had met with in my travels, I fhall beg leave to defcribe them. Contrary to the cuftom of the Moors, they wear the hair long, which is a dark black, and ftarting from their heads like porcupine's quills. Their complexions are off a very

dark

dark brown, their nofes very pointed, their eyes dark and ftaring, their beards long, and their features altogether fuggeft the idea of lunacy or raving madnefs. In their perfons they are very ftrong and mufcular; and many of them go quite naked; others wear only a fmall garment round t heir waifts.—But to return to my narrative.

The Englifh failors were put into miferable huts or tents, where for feveral days they could procure no fuftenance, but juniper-berries, brakifh water, and now and then a fmall quantity of milk.

From thefe people they were foon difpofed of to others, who put them into the immediate employments of flavery; thefe employments were the carrying of water in fkins, and performing various other kinds of drudgery, which was at all times accompanied with ftripes.

After continuing in this ftate between two and three months, they contrived to get a letter conveyed to the Englifh vice conful at Mogodore, expreffive of their fituation, who forwarded it to the conful general at Tangier, and at the fame time wrote to Muley Abfulem upon the fubject. This prince, who commanded the province adjoining to that where Captain Irving and his people were detained, at the expiration of eight months from the time this accident happened, obtained the emperor's permiffion to redeem them out of flavery, with orders to fend them up to Morocco, where his Moorifh majefty thought proper to keep them, till they were exprefsly fent for by our fovereign; or, in other words, till he received an handfome prefent.

About

4

About four days after the prince's arrival, the flattering affurances which he had at firft given me refpecting thefe unfortunate perfons were apparently confirmed, by his informing me, that he had fucceeded to his wifhes with the emperor, in what he had promifed relative to the Englifh captives; that in two or three days he was to fet off for Fez, in his way to Mecca, and that he was to take us all with him as far as Sallee, whence a party was to be difpatched to conduct us to Tangier.

Such agreeable intelligence, and from fuch authority, afforded me the moft pleafing hopes that my journey would yet end to my fatisfaction. I eagerly flew to the captain to acquaint him with it; but he feemed too much accuftomed to difappointments, to entertain any very fanguine expectations from my information. I think, however, his fpirits appeared fomewhat revived upon the occafion.

The day before the prince's departure I was defired to ftate the number of mules which would be neceffary to convey my baggage; at the fame time I was told, that in two days we were all to fet off. To my very great furprize, however, on the fame evening, I was for the firft time refufed permiffion to fee the prince; an excufe being made that he was then bufy, and therefore wifhed me to call in the morning. At the fame time I faw every preparation making for the journey, and was pofitively told that the prince was to depart from Morocco the very next day.

As I could not help feeling uneafy and alarmed at this circumftance, I repaired early in the morn-

ing

K

ing to the prince's habitation, to know the truth of what I had heard the day before; little enquiry, however, was neceffary, fince the firft object that prefented itfelf was the baggage mules ready loaded; and, in addition to this circumftance, I was informed, that the prince was to fet off in an hour's time.

It was in vain that I fent in repeated meffages to the prince, requefting that he would permit me to fee him. The only anfwer I could obtain was, that he was then engaged, and that I muft wait a little. Wearied out at length by the urgency of my folicitations, a particular friend of his highnefs came out and told me, that the prince had fent me ten hard dollars, with order to leave the garden immediately, as no perfon but the emperor could fend me home.

Enraged at this unworthy treatment, I defired the Moor to acquaint the prince, that it was not money I wanted; I wifhed him only to fulfil his engagement, and that till I had fome profpect of that being accomplifhed, I would not ftir from the garden, unlefs compelled by force. The refult of this meffage was, that the fame man returned with two dollars more, and faid that the prince had done all he could for me. If I chofe to go to one of the emperors fecretaries, whofe name he mentioned, he would give me the emperor's letter of difpatch, and then I might proceed home in what manner I pleafed, but that the prince had no further bufinefs with me. Finding that meffages were fruitlefs, I determined to watch the oportunity of the prince's coming out of his houfe, and as foon as he had mounted his

horfe

horfe, I placed myfelf directly before him.   In this laft refource, however, I found myfelf equally unfuccefsful as before, and experienced the laft extreme of rudenefs and ingratitude; for before my interpreter could pronounce a fingle fentence, the prince pufhed on, and rode haftily by me, leaving me in as difagreeable a fituation as can well be conceived.

To whatever point I directed my view, there appeared nothing comfortable in the profpect.   I had come purpofely into the country to attend the prince, with his moft pofitive affurances that I fhould be fent back again, when he had no further occafion for my fervices.   How great then muft be my mortification to find myfelt in a worfe fituation than the crane in the fable? fince inftead of obtaining from him this negative favour, in return for all the fatigues and inconveniences which I had experienced on his account, I found myfelf deferted entirely, and left in the charge of a haughty and perfidious emperor!   Doubt after doubt took poffeffion of my mind; and this, joined with the reflection of having fo completely difappointed the hopes of the unfortunate feamen, as well as the favourable accounts I had written to the conful on the prince's recovery, preffed fo forcibly on my feelings, that for the fpace of two or three hours I was in a ftate little better than that of infanity.

As foon as I found myfelf in fome degree recovered, I went to the perfon to whom I was directed for my letter of difpatch, and was informed that he had fet off early that morning for Fez; and had the further fatisfaction of difcovering that the prince had availed himfelf of this excufe,

in

in order to avoid my importunity. As no ſtranger who is ſent for by the emperor can ſtir from the court till he gets his diſpatches, I now conſidered myſelf in every reſpect a priſoner. Diſappointed in every hope of emancipation, I returned home, and immediately diſpatched expreſſes to the conſuls at Tangier and Mogodore, informing them of my ſituation, and earneſtly requeſting their immediate interference. In the mean time I omitted no other means which occurred to procure my diſpatches, but all without ſucceſs. The moſt probable ſtep which I could deviſe, or at leaſt which I could carry into effect, was to convey to the emperor's hands the following memorial, by means of one of his ſons.

To his Imperial Majeſty of Morocco.

Moſt auguſt ſovereign,

With all the reſpect and ſubmiſſion due to your majeſty's exalted ſtation, I take the liberty of informing your majeſty, that I had particular orders from the governor of Gibraltar, under whoſe command I have the honour to ſerve, to return immediately to my duty, upon my ſervices being no longer neceſſary to your majeſty's ſon, the prince Muley Abſulem. That now being the caſe, I only wait to know whether I am to have the honour, of conveying your majeſty's commands to Tangier, either for your majeſty's ſon Muley Ilaſem, or for the Britiſh conſul-general.

I have the honour to be, moſt reſpectfully,
Your majeſty's moſt humble
and devoted ſervant,

W. Lempriere.

I got

I got the above letter tranſlated into Arabic, worded in the uſual compliments of the country, and having incloſed it in a ſilk handkerchief, the mode in which all letters are preſented to royal perſonages in Barbary, and carried to Muley Omar, whom I had ſeen at Tarudant, with a preſent of Iriſh linen, in value about ſix dollars, wrapped up alſo in a ſilk handkerchief; and requeſted him to deliver it into his father's hands the firſt opportunity. The prince firſt received the preſent, and then told me, that as we were old friends, I needed not have troubled myſelf with bringing one; but that I might be aſſured he would ſettle the buſineſs to my entire ſatisfaction in a very ſhort time. The reſult of this application was, a promiſe from the emperor of being ſent home immediately; but this was attended with the ſame inſincerity which I had uſually experienced.

My next effort was, by making preſents to the principal miniſters to bribe them over to my intereſt, as my delay might probably ariſe as much from the emperors want of memory as from any other cauſe; for his faculties were then ſo much impaired, that he was not able to recollect circumſtances from one hour to another. I was in hopes that by means of his miniſters he would be continually reminded of me; but, either becauſe my preſents were not ſufficiently large, or becauſe theſe rapacious miniſters were in hopes I would repeat them, I effected nothing by this plan.

K 3   C H A P.

CHAP. XI.

Departure of Captain IRVING.*—Infolence of the Populace to Chriftians.—Manners and Character of the Moors. —Education of the Princes.—Perfons and Drefs of the Moors.—Houfes and Furniture.—Ceremonies.—Couriers.—Anecdotes illuftrative of Moorifh Cuftoms.— Topics of Converfation at* MOROCCO.*—Horfemanfhip. —Mufic and Poetry.—Religion.—Mofques.—Slaves. —Marriages.—Funerals.—Renegadoes.—Caravans to* MECCA *and* GUINEA.

IN a fortnight after the prince's departure all the Englifh captives were ordered to Mogodore, to remain under the care of a gentleman of that place, till our court fhould think proper to fend for them. Deprived by this circumftance of the fociety of the captain, whofe good fenfe and agreeable converfation leffened in a great degree the uneafinefs I experienced from the irkfomenefs of my fituation, I muft confefs my fpirits did not receive much benefit from the change. My only refource at prefent for fociety was the French officer whom I formerly mentioned.

Limited as our fociety was to that of each other, there exifted a further impediment to amufement; for we could not leave the jewdry without being faluted with repeated fhowers of ftones, opprobrious names, and every infult that bigotry and brutality could devife. The ignorant of every nation are intolerant; and there can fcarcely exift a more defperate or favage defcription of people than the Lazzaroni of Morocco: they are a mixed

race,

race, confifting of the bafeft of the citizens, with a number of ferocious mountaineers and wild Arabs, who have wandered thither in hopes of acquiring a fubfiftence either by labour or by theft.

The defcription indeed of a mingled race will ftill more extenfively apply even to the more civilized inhabitants of this country. In the towns particularly, the defcendants of the different tribes from which they are fprung may ftill be traced, viz. thofe of the native Moors, of their Turkifh conquerors, and of the negroes who have been introduced in the manner already related.

The complexion of the two firft is a fallow white, and from this circumftance, and from their intermarrying with each other, it is not poffible always to determine the origin of each individual; I fhall therefore clafs them both under the general appellation of Moors. But the negroes, though they form a large proportion of the emperor's fubjects, are now by no means fo numerous as in the reign of Muley Ifhmael, who firft introduced them into the country. They are better formed than the Moors, and as they are more lively, daring, and active, they are intrufted with an important fhare in the executive part of government. They conftitute in fact the moft confiderable part of the emperor's army, and are generally appointed to the command of provinces and towns. This circumftance naturally creates a jealoufy between them and the Moors, the latter confidering the negroes as ufurpers of a power which they have no right to affume.

K 4   The

The negroes are blood-thirfty, capricious, and revengeful. As foldiers they manifeft fuff.cient ardour when commanded by popular officers; but their attachment depends on the generofity of their chief, and the energy, feverity, and cruelty of his difpofition: if he flackens in any of thefe particulars, they either defert him, or deliver him up to his enemy.

Befides the negroes which form the emperor's army, there are a great many others in the country, who either are or have been flaves to private Moors: every Moor of confequence, indeed, has his proportion of them in his fervice. To the difgrace of Europe, the Moors treat their flaves with humanity, employing them in looking after their gardens, and in the domeftic duties of their houfes. They allow them to marry among themfelves, and after a certain number of years fpontaneoufly prefent them with the invaluable boon of liberty. They foon are initiated in the Mahometan perfuafion, though they fometimes intermix with it a few of their original fuperftitious cuftoms. In every other refpect they copy the drefs and manners of the Moors; of which I fhall endeavour to give the reader fome general idea.

To think juftly and with candour of the Moorifh character we muft take into our confideration the natural effects of a total want of education, a moft rigidly arbitrary government, and a climate calculated, as far as climate has influence, to ftimulate and excite the vicious paffions, as well as by its debilitating and relaxing influence to weaken and deprefs the nobler energies of the mind.

To

To thefe we may add the difadvantages arifing from the want of a free intercourfe with other nations, and the influence of an abfurd and uncharitable religion.

In fuch a ftate of things the traveller is not to be furprifed if he finds moft of the vices of favage nations grafted upon thofe of luxury and indolence; if he obferves fuperftition, avarice, and luft the leading features of character, with their natural concomitants, deceit and jealoufy; he is not to be furprized if he finds but little of the amiable attachments and propenfities, little of friendfhip or focial union with each other, fince the nature of the government, and the habits of his private life, are calculated to infpire each man with a diftruft and fufpicion of his neighbour.

I will not affert, however, that this character will univerfally apply.—However the cuftoms and government of a nation may militate againft virtue and excellence, there are always fplendid exceptions to the prevalent vices of every fociety. There are certainly among the Moors many whofe private virtues would do honour to any civilized nation; but I am forry to add, that thofe characters are not numerous. Groaning under the fevereft oppreffions of defpotifm, they lofe all fpirit for induftry and improvements, and fuffer indolence and ignorance to reign without controul. Senfible of the uncertainty of enjoying the fruits of labour and ingenuity, the great majority of the people remain content with the bare neceffaries of life, or when in power endeavour to enrich themfelves by the fame means which had before kept them in a ftate of poverty.

Arts

Arts and sciences seem to be almost unknown here, or, if at all cultivated it is only by the Jews, who indeed are the only industrious and ingenious people in the country. The Moors in general may be considered as existing in the pastoral state, following only a few mechanical trades and leaving every thing that requires invention to the Jews, who have likewise the principal management of their commercial and pecuniary matters; and even those few of the Moors who are merchants are obliged to have Jew agents for the purpose of transacting their business.

Fearful of having it discovered that they are rich, sooner than part with money, which, under such circumstances, is of little or no use to them, they deprive themselves of the luxuries and even comforts of life; they hoard up and conceal their treasures, though seldom so artfully but they are at length detected, and consequently plundered by the bashaw, the prince, or the emperor. To conceal more effectually their riches, they are obliged to have recourse to every form of dissimulation and deceit; and being exercised in these qualities during the early part of life, at a more advanced period they become an established part of their character.

The Moors are naturally of a grave and pensive disposition, fervid in professions of friendship, but very insincere in their attachments. They have no curiosity, no ambition of knowledge; an indolent habit, united to the want of mental cultivation, renders them perhaps even more callous than other unenlightened people to every delicate sensation, and they require more than ordinary

excite-

excitement to render them fenfible of pleafure or
of pain.   It is to this circumftance, and to their
religion, which teaches them to impute every
thing to a blind predeftination, that we may attribute that paffive obedience which the Moors difcover under all their misfortunes and oppreffions.
This langour of fentiment is, however, unaccom-
panied with the fmalleft fpark of courage or fortitude.   When in adverfity they manifeft the moft
abject fubmiffion to their fuperiors, and in profperity their tyranny and pride is infupportable.
They frequently fmile, but are feldom heard to laugh
loud.   The moft infallible mark of internal tranquillity and enjoyment is when they amufe themfelves with ftroking or playing with their beard.
When roufed by refentment, their difputes rarely
proceed farther than violently to abufe each other
in the moft opprobrious language.   They never
fight or box with their fifts, like our peafantry,
but when a quarrel procceds to great extremities,
they collar each other, and fometimes terminate a
difpute by affaffination.

It has been fomewhere remarked, that whatever
debafes the human fpirit, corrupts and at the
fame time depraves the heart.   That abjectnefs
of difpofition, which a ftate of flavery induces,
eradicates every noble, every generous fentiment.
The Moors are difhonourable and unfair in all
their dealings; nor are the greateft among them
exempt from propenfities which would difgrace
the meaneft of the civilized inhabitants of Europe.
When the emperor's army was at Tangier, one
of the confuls invited the Moorifh general and his
particular friend to tea.   Soon after their departure

ture the conful miffed one of his tea-fpoons, and knowing the difpofitions of the Moors, fent to the general for it; who immediately returned it, and fimply apologized, by faying he had put it into his pocket by miftake.

When we treat of national genius and character, it were to be wifhed that language fupplied us with fome term which might ferve to indicate that habit and cuftom is the great framer of the characters of nations. Of this truth there can be no ftronger evidence than Morocco affords. Torpid and infenfible as I have reprefented the Moors in general to be, this character is by no means applicable to them in early life. In the ftate of childhood they poffefs an uncommon fhare of vivacity and acutenefs, but they fink gradually into indolence and ftupidity as they advance in life. It is evident, therefore, that to the want of education only this circumftance is to be attributed. While at fchool they are fcarcely lefs remarkable for attention than ability; and as they commit their leffons to memory, no fmall fhare of application is required. This courfe is, however, extremely limited, and continues for a very fhort period; it confifts at moft of being inftructed in certain parts of the Koran, and perhaps learning to write. After this all attention to learning ceafes; and though their parents never indulge them, yet they are rarely chaftifed, and are left to themfelves in general almoft in a ftate of nature.

A late eloquent writer has remarked, that " the " antients did not like Archimedes, want a fpot " on which to fix their engines, but they wanted " an engine to move the moral world. The prefs
" is

" is that engine."—and to the want of it may
fairly be attributed the ignorance, the ſtupidity,
the ſlavery of the African nations. The art of
printing is entirely prohibited and unknown in
Barbary; and, from ſome inexplicable cauſe, moſt
of the manuſcripts which were poſſeſſed by their
Saracen anceſtors are loſt to the preſent generation of Moors. A few indeed are ſtill in being,
which treat of aſtronomy, aſtrology, and phyſic;
but thoſe on aſtrology only are are at preſent
ſtudied.

If any thing could effect an important and be-
neficial change in theſe people, it would be the
example of ſome great and magnanimous monarch, who by ſome ſingular revolution might be
raiſed to the throne of Morocco. In ſo deſpotic
a government, where religion conſpires with habit in teaching the ſubject to conſider his prince
as ſomething more than man, much more might
be effected by example, than in a free country;
where the ſovereign is merely conſidered as an individual placed on the throne for the public good,
ſubject to all the imperfections and frailties incident to human nature, and where the mind, by
being allowed a free ſcope for reflection, diſdains
all authority but that of reaſon and truth.

The plan adopted, however, for the education
of the princes of Morocco, ſo far from tending
to the improvement of their minds, or the en-
largement of their ideas, ſerves on the contrary,
too frequently to render them ſtill more remarkable for vice and brutality than even the worſt of
their ſubjects. As ſoon as they become of an age
that renders it imprudent to truſt them any longer

within

within the walls of the harem, they are taken out, and put under the care of one of their father's confidential Negroes, with whom they foon form a clofe intimacy, from whom they imbibe all the bad qualities which are infeparable from a ftate of flavery, and by whom they are alfo initiated in vices of every kind, in debauchery, cruelty, and oppreffion.   Their education extends no further than to read and write; and their knowledge of the world is confined to what they can obferve and learn in the courfe of a pilgrimage to Mecca.   They are totally unacquainted with the political hiftory of every foreign power; and their knowledge of their own government is confined principally to its worft parts.   To acquaint themfelves with the refources of the country, and the improvements which from its fituation it would admit of, or to direct any part of their attention to thofe regulations in their government which might tend to the advantage and eafe of their fubjects, or to their own real aggrandizement, is as much out of the line of their education, as the Principia of Newton.   Thus they afcend the throne with all the prejudices of ignorance, with all the vices of barbarifm, with a pride that teaches them to look upon their fellow creatures as inferior beings, and without any fentiments of tendernefs, compaffion, or true policy, to reftrain the arm of defpotifm from its moft cruel and fatal exceffes. Thus ill-qualified in general are the fovereigns of Morocco for effecting a reformation in the manners and character of their people.

The ignorance of the Moors is, however, no bar to their loquacity.   They fpeak very loud,

and

and generally two or three at a time, as they are
not very exact in waiting for a reply.   Ufelefs as
the forms of politenefs may appear in the eye of
the philofopher, there are fome of them which
probably conduce in no trifling degree to even
our intellectual excellence and improvement.

Perfonal cleanlinefs has been pointed out by
modern philofophers as one of thofe circumftances which ferve to mark and determine the
civilization of a people.   It was in vain that Mahomet enjoined the frequency of ablution as a religious duty to the Moors.   Their drefs, which
fhould be white, is but feldom wafhed, and their
whole appearance evinces that they perform this
branch of their religious ceremonies in but a
flovenly manner.   With this degree of negligence
as to their perfons, we may be juftly furprifed to
find united a moft fcrupulous nicety in their habitations and apartments.   They enter their chambers barefooted, and cannot bear the flighteft degree of contamination near the place where they
are feated.   This delicacy again is much confined
to the infides of their houfes.   The ftreets receive
the whole of their rubbifh and filth, and by thefe
means the ground is fo raifed in moft parts of the
city of Morocco, that the new buildings always
ftand confiderably higher than the old.

The perfons of the Moorifh men are fo difguifed by their drefs, that it is impoffible to acquire any good idea of their form or proportion.
In height they are commonly above the middle
fize, and they are rather meagre than fat.   Their
complexions in general are fallow in the Northern
parts of the empire, but are darker in proportion

to

to their fituation towards the South. Their features have univerfally a great famenefs. Their
eyes are black and full, they have an aquiline
nofe, and in general a good fet of teeth.

The drefs of the men * confifts of a fhort linen
fhirt, with large and loofe fleeves hanging halfway down to the ground. A pair of loofe linen
drawers, reaching almoft to the ankle; over
which they wear another loofe pair, made of
woollen cloth. Over the fhirt they wear two or
three woollen cloth waiftcoats of different colours, and of European manufacture; thefe gar-
ments are made full as loofe as our great coats;
they are connected before by very fmall buttons,
and are faftened tight round the waift by a filk
belt. Over thefe waiftcoats they throw a velvet
cord, which croffes the right fhoulder, and fufpends on the left fide a curved dagger or knife,
fheathed in a brafs cafe. This is the drefs the
Moors wear when in their houfes; but when they
go abroad they cover it with the haick, a part of
drefs which has been already noticed. It is thrown
over the whole of their other clothing in a carelefs but eafy manner, fomething fimilar to the
Scotch plaid. When the weather is wet or cold,
inftead of the haick, the Moors fubftitute the
fulam; which is a large hooded cloak, reaching
to the heels, all of one piece, and made of blue
or white woollen cloth of European manufacture,
without feams, clofe before, and ornamented with

* The drefs, and general remarks on the Moorifh women will be introduced hereafter, when we fpeak of the
emperor's harem.

filk fringes at the extremities, on the breaft, and
the ends of the hood, terminating with a filk taffel. The latter part of the drefs is fixed on the
head by means of a ftrong cord of camel's hair;
and among the common people it often fupplies
the place of a cap or turban.

Thofe Moors who have performed a pilgrimage
to Mecca are entitled to wear a turban, and are
named El-hatch. They are always treated with
peculiar refpect. Even thofe beafts of burden
indeed which have performed this journey are
held in great veneration, and upon their return are
exempted from labour. The other clafs of Moors
wear only plain red caps. The Moors in general
fhave their heads clofe, leaving on the upper part
a fingle lock, and wear their beards long. They
ufe no ftockings or fhoes, but fubftitute in the
place of the latter, yellow flippers. They are very
fond of beads, of which the better order always
carry a rofary in their hands; but they ufe them
more as a matter of amufement than for any religious purpofe. Many alfo wear plain gold rings on
their fingers and thofe whofe circumftances will
allow them to go to that expence, poffefs likewife
watches, which, like the rofary they confider
rather as an ornament than an article from which
any great utility can be derived. Very few, in
fact, are properly acquainted with their ufe.

This may ferve to give fome idea of the drefs
of the rich; but among the poorer clafs of people fome wear the linen drawers, fhirt, and one
woollen waiftcoat, and over it the haick; and
others have merely a coarfe woollen frock, belted
round the waift, and covered with the haick.

The

The houfes in moft of the towns in this empire appear at a little diftance like vaulted tombs in a church-yard; and the entrance into the beft of them has but a mean appearance. They are of a fquare form, their apartments are feldom built higher than the ground floor, and their outer walls are univerfally white-wafhed, which, in the ftreets and particularly when the fun is out, produce a very unpleafant fenfation to the eyes. All thefe circumftances, united to the want of windows, the filthinefs and irregularity of the ftreets, the dirty appearance and rude behaviour of the inhabitants, and their total ignorance of every art and fcience, leaves at firft fight an unfavourable impreffion on the mind of the traveller, which perhaps while he continues in the country he can never do away. As the roofs of the houfes are all terraces, they ferve as *verandos*, where the Moorifh woman commonly fit for the benefit of the air, and in fome places it is poffible to pafs nearly over the whole town, without having occafion to defcend into the ftreet.

As the beft apartments are all backwards, a ftable, or perhaps fomething worfe, is the place to which vifitors are firft introduced. Upon entering the houfe the ftranger is either detained in this place, or in the ftreet, till all the women are difpatched out of the way; he is then allowed to enter a fquare court, into which four narrow and long rooms open by means of large folding doors, which, as they have no windows, ferve likewife to introduce light into the apartments. The court has generally in its cente a fountain, and if it is the houfe of a Moor of property, it is floored

with

with blue and white checquered tiling. The doors are usually painted of various colours in a checquered form, and the upper parts of them are frequently ornamented with very curious carved work.——None of the chambers have fire-places, and their victuals are always dressed in the court-yard, in an earthen stove, heated with charcoal.

When the visitor enters the room where he is received by the master of the house, he finds him sitting crofs-legged and barefooted on a mattrefs, covered with fine white linen, and placed on the floor, or else on a common mat. This, with a narrow piece of carpetting, is in general the only furniture he will meet with in Moorish houses; though they are not destitute of other ornaments. In some, for instance, he will find the walls decorated with looking-glasses of different fizes. In others, watches and clocks in glafs cafes; and in some the apartments are hung with the skins of lions or tigers, or adorned with a difplay of mufkets and fabres. In the houses of those who live in the very firft ftyle, an European mahogany bedftead, with one or two mattrrffes, covered with fine white linen, is sometimes placed at each end of the room. Thefe, however, are only confidered as ornaments, as the Moors always fleep on a matrefs, or a mat placed upon the floor and covered only with their haick, or perhaps a quilt.

As the law of Mahomet ftrictly profcribes the ufe of pictures of every defcription, this delightful fpecies of ornament finds no place in the houfes of the Moors. I was however, acquainted with

a Moor

a Moor at Morocco, who uſed to exhibit a raree-
ſhow to his friends and acquaintance, all of whom
appeared to exprefs infinite ſurprize and admiration
at his exhibition. This, indeed, was not the only
inſtance in which he was guilty of violating the
Mahometan law. He ſcrupled not to drink very
freely his bottle of port or claret, which, as it
was manufactured by Chriſtians, was from that
circumſtance an aggravated offence. He employed
me to procure for him from Mogodore three
dozen of claret, which appeared to adminiſter
to him infinite comfort and ſatisfaction. This affection indeed for the productions of Europe made
him perhaps more than uſually favourable to its
natives. However this may be, he was the only
man who ſhewed me much attention during my
reſidence at Morocco. He repeatedly took me
to his houſe, and made me little preſents of various
kinds, which at that place proved very accept-
able.

When a Moor receives his gueſts he never
rifes from his ſeat, but ſhakes hands, enquires
after their health, and defires them to ſit down,
either on a carpet or a cuſhion placed on the floor
for that purpoſe. Whatever be the time of day,
tea is then brought in on a tea-board with ſhort
feet. This is the higheſt compliment that can be
offered by a Moor; for tea is a very expenſive and
ſcarce article in Barbary, and is only drank by
the rich and luxurious. Their manner of preparing it is by putting ſome green tea, a ſmall
quantity of tanfey, the ſame portion of mint, and
a large portion of ſugar (for the Moors drink
their tea very ſweet) into the tea-pot at the ſame
time,

time, and filling it up with boiling water. When these articles are infused a proper time, the fluid is then poured into remarkably small cups of the best India china, the smaller the more genteel, without any milk, and, accompanied with some cakes or sweatmeats, it is handed round to the company. From the great esteem in which this beverage is held by the Moors, it is generally drank by very small and slow sips, that is flavour may be the longer enjoyed; and as they usually drink a considerable quantity whenever it is introduced, this entertainment is seldom finished in less time than two hours.

The other luxuries of the Moors are snuff, of which they are uncommonly fond, and smoaking tobacco, for which the greater part use wooden pipes about four feet in length, with an earthen bowl; but the princes or emperor generally have the bowls made of solid gold. Instead of the indulgence of opium, which, from the heavy duty imposed upon that article by the emperor, is too expensive to be used by the Moors, they substitute the Achicha, a species of flax. This they powder and infuse in water in small quantities. The Moors assert, that it produces agreeable ideas, but own that when it is taken to excefs it most powerfully intoxicates. In order to produce this effect, they likewise mix with their tobacco an herb, named in this country Khaf, which by smoaking, occasions all the inebriating effects of the Achicha. The use of spirits as well as wine is strictly forbidden by the Koran; there are, however, very few among the Moors who do not
joyfully

joyfully embrace every private opportunity of drinking both to excefs.

With refpect to the hours for eating, the people of this country are remarkably regular. Very foon after day-break they take their breakfaft, which is generally a compofition of flour and water boiled thin, together with an herb which gives it a yellow tinge. The male part of the family eat in one apartment and the female in another. The children are not permitted to eat with their parents, but take their meals afterwards with the fervants; indeed in moft other refpects they are treated exactly as fervants or flaves by their parents. The mefs is put into an earthen bowl, and brought in upon a round wooden tray. It is placed in the centre of the guefts, who fit crofs-legged either on a mat or on the floor, and who form a circle for the purpofe. Having previoufly wafhed themfelves, a ceremony always performed before and after meals, each perfon with his fpoon attacks vigoroufly the bowl, while they diverfify the entertainment by eating with it fruit or bread. At twelve o'clock they dine, performing the fame ceremonies as at breakfaft. For dinner, from the emperor down to the peafant, their difh is univerfally Cufcofoo, the mode of preparing which has been already defcribed. I believe I have intimated more than once that neither chairs, tables, knives or forks, are made ufe of in this country. The difh is therefore brought in upon a round tray and placed on the floor, round which the family fit as at breakfaft, and with their fingers commit a violent affault on its contents; they are at the

fame

fame time, however, attended by a flave or domeftic, who prefents them with water and a towel occafionally to wafh their hands. From the want of the fimple and convenient invention of knives and forks, it is not uncommon in this country to three or four people pulling to pieces the fame piece of meat, and afterwards with their fingers ftirring up the pafte or Cufcofoo, of which the often take a whole handful at once into their mouth. Their manner of eating indeed was to me fo difgufting, that though Cufcofoo is in reality a very good difh, yet it required fome time to get rid of my prejudice fo far as to be induced to relifh it. At fun-fet they fup upon the fame difh, and indeed fupper is their principal meal.

Such is the general mode of living among the principal people in towns. There are confiderable multitudes, however, who do not fare fo well, but are obliged to content themfelves with a little bread and fruit inftead of animal food, and to fleep in the open ftreets. This kind of exiftence feems ill calculated to endure even in an inactive ftate; far more fevere muft it therefore be to thofe who exercife the laborious employment of couriers in this country, who travel on foot a journey of three or four hundred miles, at the rate of between thirty and forty miles a day, without taking any other nourifhment than a little bread, a few figs, and fome water, and who have no better fhelter at night than a tree. It is wonderful with what alacrity and perfeverance thefe people perform the moft fatiguing journies at all feafons of the year. There is a regular company of them in every town, who are ready to be difpatched at a mo-

ment's

ment's warning to any part of the country their employers may have occasion to send them. They constitute in this empire the only mode of conveyance for all public and private difpatches; and as they are well known in the place to which they belong, they are very punctual in delivering every thing that is put into their hands. From their fteady pace in travelling, at the rate of about four miles an hour, and from their being able to pafs over parts which from the mountainous ftate of the country, and from the want of good reads, perfons on horfeback would find inacceffible, they are indeed by far the moft expeditious meffengers that could be employed. As a proof of the amazing exertions of which they are capable, I need only mention, that there have been repeated inftances of a courier proceeding from Morocco to Tangier, which is a journey of about three hundred and thirty miles, in fix days.

As none but the very vulgar go on foot in this country; for the purpofe of vifiting, mules are confidered as more genteel than horfes; and the greateft pride of a Moor is to have fuch as walk remarkably faft, and keep his footmen, of which the number is proportionable to the rank and confequence of the mafter, on a continued run.

As the Moors are not fond of admitting men into their houfes, except upon particular occafions, if the weather is fine they place a mat, and fometimes a carpet, on the ground before their door, feat themfelves upon it crofs-legged, and receive their friends, who form a circle, fitting in the fame manner, with their attendants on the outfide of the groupe. Upon thefe occafions they

either

I

either drink tea, or smoke and converse. The streets are sometimes crowded with parties of this kind; some engaged at playing at an inferior kind of chess or drafts, at which they are very expert; but the majority in conversation. The people of this country, indeed, are so decidedly averse to standing up, or walking about, that if only two or three people meet, they squat themselves down in the first clean place they can find, if the conversation is to hold but for a few minutes.

At Morocco, when I visited Muley Ouffine, one of Sidi Mahomet's sons, I was always received in the manner which I have now described. I found him sitting crofs-legged on a common mat, in the same open place where his horses were kept, and his friends forming a semicircle round him. I was immediately desired to form one of the groupe, and was helped to tea upon the occasion. In the course of our conversation, the prince told me, that the Christians and Moors were brothers; that the English were very good men; but that he had a particular aversion to the friars, for they were a determined set of knaves, and were neither friends to Christians or Moors.

I found this prince a handsome young man, of about the age of six-and-twenty, of rather a dark complexion, but accompanied with an open and generous countenance. He had been a few years ago appointed to the government of Tafilet, where he so far gained the affections of the people under his government, that they proclaimed him king; and he for some time governed with all the independent authority of a sovereign. This circumstance obliged the emperor to dispatch an army

against

againſt him, upon the arrival of which he immediately ſurrendered, and was brought to Morocco, where he was deprived of all his property, as well as his power; and when I was in the country, he lived in a very retired manner indeed. When at Tafilet, he had the character of acting very liberally towards every perſon with whom he was connected; at Morocco he manifeſted ſome proofs of the ſame diſpoſition towards me: merely for a trifling attention which I ſhewed to his favourite black, he preſented me with a horſe, that proved as good as any of which I had poſſeſ-ſion while in the country.

The only vice to which this young man was addicted was that of drinking to a very great exceſs. In this reſpect, however, he was not more culpable than all the reſt of his royal brothers. He told me, that if he did not daily take before dinner ſix tumblers of aquadent, a ſpecies of brandy ſomething weaker than ſpirits of wine, he would not be able to hold up his head the remainder of the day. He wiſhed to know if this cuſtom was bad for his health; and if ſo, what I would adviſe him to do. I recommended to him the diſ-uſe of ſpirits, and to ſupply their place with wine; which he might either procure from the European merchants at Mogodore, or he might uſe the wine which was made by the Jews. This advice, however, the prince obſerved he could not follow, ſince the Mahometan law more particularly forbade the uſe of wine, than that of ſpirits. This, I replied, might be true, in the ſtrict letter of the law; but when wine was uſed as a medicine, it became no longer wine. This

idea

iden I found satisfied the scruples of the prince, and he promised to follow my advice.

I was afterwards sent for to Muley Slemma, another of the emperor's sons, who with the late emperor Muley Yazid, were the offspring of a woman whose parents were English. This prince, who is about thirty-eight years of age, and of a tall and majestic appearance, with a very expressive and lively countenance, shewed me uncommon attention the whole time I was at Morocco. His pavillion, where he received strangers, and transacted business, was situated at the extremity of a long walk, in a garden of orange-trees. It consisted of one large room on the ground floor, fitted up in the same stile as that of Muley Absulem at Tarudant. The prince was sitting cross-legged on a large mattress, covered with fine white linen, and placed on the floor fronting the door-way, with his Moorish visitors on each side of him, forming a semicircle. Upon my first introduction he expressed uncommon pleasure at seeing me, exclaiming, *Bono, Bono, Anglais!* and added, that the English were his brothers and best friends. I was then directed to feel his pulse, and to inform him whether or not he was in health; as soon as I assured him he was perfectly well, he desired me to be seated on a narrow carpet, which was placed on the floor for the purpose, and he then ordered one of his pages to bring in tea, though so late as twelve o'clock at noon. Out of compliment to me, for the Moors seldom use it, the prince sent for milk, and said, as he knew the English always drank it with their tea, he would present me with a milch cow, that I might enjoy the custom of

my

my own country. This promise, however, entirely escaped his royal highness's memory, and the cow never made her appearance.

In the course of our conversation, the prince manifested many indications of good-nature and address; told me, that whilst he was on his travels in Turkey, he had been conducted from one port to another in the Mediterranean by an English frigate, the captain of which shewed him so much attention, that he should always bear it in remembrance. As soon as the ceremony of tea was concluded, the prince ordered out his horse, which was a very beautiful young animal, with a saddle ornamented with a rich velvet cover, and gold stirrups. He then mounted him, and went through all the manœuvers of managing a horse with which the moors are acquainted, such as putting him upon the full speed, and stopping him instantaneously, rising up on the saddle and firing a musket when the horse is on the full gallop, &c. in the performance of all which exercises he seemed very dexterous. The prince then asked me if we could do such things in England; and without waiting for a reply, ordered one of his attendants to catch a sheep out of his grounds, and take it home to my lodgings. He said, that as he always was fond of seeing his brothers the English, he wished I would visit him twice a day during my continuance at Morocco, and then gallopped off.——But to return to my observations.

The manner of salutation among the Moors is, when two equals meet, by a quick motion they shake hands, and afterwards kiss each each other's other's hand.   When an inferior meets a superior, such as an officer of rank, a judge, or a governor, he kisses that part of his Haick which covers the arm, and sometimes, as a higher mark of respect, he will kiss his feet.   But the compliment due to the emperor, or any of the princes of the blood, is to take off the cap or turban, and to prostrate the head to the ground.   When two particular friends or relations meet, they anxiously embrace and kiss each other's faces and beards for a few minutes, make a number of enquiries about the health of each party, as well as that of their families, but seldom allow time for a reply.

The common topics for conversation among these people, are the occurrences of the place, religion, their women, and their horses.   As curiosity is a quality which naturally attaches to all indolent people, it may easily be conjectured that the Moors are not deficient in this respect. It is incredible with what avidity they lay hold of any trifling circumstance which may occur in the neighbourhood; what pleasure and what pride they seem to take in communicating it; nor are they deficient in the arts of magnifying or adorning the tale with every addition which may serve to render it more palatable, or give it a greater appearance of plausibility.

Religion is also a favourite topic; but this subject is confined principally to those societies which are frequented by their Talbs, or men of letters.   As these gentlemen, however, are not a little proud of their acquirements in reading and writing, they do not fail to embrace every opportunity of manifesting their superiority over

L 3

those

thofe who are not fo happy as to be diftinguifhed by thofe accomplifhments.

Decency of manners and delicacy in converfa- tion are among the moft certain marks of refine- ment and civilization, and the contrary vices are equally univerfal charaCteriftics of ignorance and barbarifm. The converfation of the Moors con- cerning their women is of the moft trifling and difgufting defcription, and confifts of abfurd and vulgar obfervations, equally repugnant to decency and common fenfe.

The fubjeCt, however, on which, like our young men of fafhion in England, they appear moft calculated to fhine, is their horfes. It would indeed be truly difgraceful not to be accomplifhed upon this topic, fince it appears to occupy, both day and night, by far the greateft portion of their attention. I have formerly intimated that thefe animals are feldom kept in ftables in Morocco. They are watered and fed only once a day, the former at one o'clock at noon, and the latter at fun-fet; and the only mode which they ufe to clean them, is by wafhing them all over in a river two or three times a week, and fuffering them to dry themfelves.

Notwithftanding the attachment which the Moors manifeft to their horfes, they moft certain- ly ufe them with great cruelty. Their higheft pleafure, and one of their firft accomplifhments, is, by means of long and fharp fpurs to make the horfe go full fpeed, and then to ftop him inftan- taneoufly; and in this they certainly manifeft uncommon dexterity. The iron-work of their bridles is fo conftruCted that by its preffure on the

horfe's

horfe's tongue and lower jaw, with the leaft exertion of the rider it fills his mouth full of blood,
and if not ufed with the utmoft caution throws
him inevitably on his back. The bridle has only
a fingle rein, which is fo very long that it ferves
the purpofe of both whip and bridle. The
Moorifh faddle is in fome degree fimilar to the
Spanifh, but the pummel is ftill higher and more
peaked. Their ftirrups, in which they ride very
fhort, are fo formed as to cover the whole of the
foot. They either plate or gild them, according
to the dignity, opulence, or fancy of the pof-
feffor. Their faddles, which are covered with
red woollen cloth, or, if belonging to a perfon
of confequence, with red fatin or damafk, are
faftened with one ftrong girth round the body,
in the European ftyle, and another round the
fhoulders.

The Moors frequently amufe themfelves by
riding with the utmoft apparent violence againft a
wall; and a ftranger would conceive it impoffible
for them to avoid being dafhed to pieces, when
juft as the horfe's head touches the wall, they
ftop him with the utmoft accuracy. To ftrangers
on horfeback or on foot it is alfo a common fpecies
of compliment to ride violently up to them, as if
intending to trample them to pieces, and then to
ftop their horfes fhort and fire a mufquet in their
faces. This compliment I have experienced, and
could very well have difpenfed with their politenefs. Upon thefe occafions, they are very proud
in difcovering their dexterity in horfemanfhip,
by making the animal rear up, fo as almoft to
throw him on his back, putting him immediately

L 4

after

after on the full fpeed for a few yards, then ftopping him inftantaneoufly, and all this is accompanied by loud and hollow cries.

There is another favourite amufement, which
difplays perhaps fuperior agility :—A number of
perfons on horfeback ftart at the fame moment,
and accompanied with loud fhouts, gallop at full
fpeed to an appointed fpot, when they ftand up
ftraight in the ftirrups, put the rein, which I have
juft obferved is very long, in their mouths, level
their pieces and fire them off; throw their firelocks immediately over their right fhoulders, and
ftop their horfes nearly at the fame inftant. This
I am told, is their manner of engaging in an
action.

Though I am willing to allow the Moors the
merit of fitting a horfe well, and, as far as is neceffary for the above-mentioned exercife, of having
a great command over him, yet their horfes are
ill-bred, and they entirely neglect to teach them
thofe paces which in Europe are confidered as
the moft agreeable for the common purpofes of
riding. As none of thefe animals in Morocco are
geldings, and as the Moors are unacquainted with
the ufe of the ring, they are obliged to break them
in when very young, by taking them long and
fatiguing journies, particularly over the mountainous and rocky part of the country, where
they foon reduce their fpirit; they then take the
opportunity of teaching them to rear up, ftand
fire, gallop, and ftop fhort in the manner already
related; and having accomplifhed this they are
fatisfied without any farther qualification. For
this reafon a Barbary horfe feldom can perform
                                        any

any other pace than a full gallop or a walk; and from being broken in and worked hard before they have acquired their full ftrength, thefe horfes · in a very few years become unfit for fervice. 'The Moors feldom ride the mares, but keep them in the country for breeding; and, contrary to the general opinion in Europe, they confider them fo much more valuable than horfes, that they are never permitted to be exported.

Like all barbarous nations, the Moors are paf-fi⋅nately fond of mufic, and fome few have a tafte for poetry. Their flow airs, for want of that variety which is introduced when the fcience has attained a degree of perfection, have a very melan--choly famenefs; but fome of their quick tunes are beautiful and fimple, and partake in fome degree of the characteriftic melody of the Scotch airs. The poetry of their fongs, the conftant fubject of which is love, though there are few nations perhaps who are lefs fenfible of that paffion, has certainly lefs merit than the mufic.

Their inftruments are a kind of hautboy which differs from ours only in having no keys; the mandoline, which they have learnt to play upon from their neighbours the Spaniards; another inftrument bearing fome refemblance to a violin, and played upon in a fimilar manner, but with only two ftrings; the large drum, the common pipe, and the tabor. Thefe united and accompanied with a ce tain number of voices, upon many occafions form a band, though folo mufic is more common in this unfocial country.

Upon all days of rejoicing, this kind of mufic, repeated vollies of mufquetry, either by men on horfeback or on foot, and in the evening a grand

L 5

attack

attack upon the Cufcofoo, conftitute the principal part of the public entertainments. Mountebanks and jugglers alfo of every defcription meet with great encouragement from the Moors.

There are no other places of reception for the accommodation of travellers in this country except in their Fondaks, which are only to be met with in large towns. Thefe confift of a certain number of dirty apartments, with no other accommodation whatever, but the walls and roof, to protect the ftranger from the inclemency of the weath.r; and he muft furnifh himfelf with every article of which he may be in want, both in refpect to provifions and bedding. There is at the fame time, an open court, where the horfes of all travellers are intermixed.

In moft of the towns there are regular fchools, where thofe children whofe parents have the means of doing it, and have fenfe enough to fend them (which indeed are but few in proportion to the whole) are inftructed by the Talbs in reading and writing, and fometimes in the firft rules of arithmetic. The greater part of the people, however, learn very little more than to read a few prayers felected from the Koran, which are in common ufe, and are written in Arabic characters. on paper which is pafted on a board.

To fpeak particularly on the religion of the Moors would require a volume, and fuch a volume as would certainly be more extenfive than entertaining. It is well known they profefs the Mahometan faith, and I may add, that they attend very rigidly to all the bigotry and fuperftion which is peculiar to that religion.

Since every ftranger who enters a mofque is either put to death, or is obliged to conform to their religion, a very exact account of their places of worfhip is not to be expected from an European. The obfervations I made *en paffant*, the doors which are very large, being in the day-time always open, I fhall endeavour to relate.

The mofque is ufually a large fquare building, compofed of the fame materials as the houfes, confifting of broad and lofty piazzas, opening into a fquare court, in a manner in fome degree fimilar to the Royal Exchange of London. In the centre of the court is a large fountain, and a fmall ftream furrounds the piazzas, where the Moors perform the ceremony of ablution. The court and piazzas are floored with blue and white chec-quered tiling, and the latter are covered with matting, upon which the Moors kneel while re-peating their prayers. In the moft confpicuous part of the mofque, fronting the Eaft, ftands a kind of pulpit, where the Talb or prieft occa-fionally preaches. The Moors alway enter this place of worfhip barefooted, leaving their flippers at the door. On the top of the mofque is a fquare fteeple with a flag-ftaff, whither at ftated hours the Talb afcends, hoifts a white flag (for they have no bells,) and calls the people to prayers, repeating in Arabic three times, and addreffing him-felf each time to a different part of the town, *How great is God! Mahomet is his prophet! Come all ye faithful; Come to prayer.* From this high fituation the voice is heard at a confiderable diftance, and the Talbs have a monotonous mode of enuncia-tion, the voice finking at the end of every fhort

fentence,

fentence, which in fome meafure refembles the found of a bell.

The moment the flag is difplayed every perfon forfakes his employment and goes to prayers. If they are near a mofque they perform their devotions within it, otherwife immediately on the fpot where they happen to be, and always with their faces towards the Eaft, in honour of the prophet Mahomet, who, it is well known was buried at Medina. The prayer which is generally repeated on thefe occafions is a chapter from the Koran, acknowledging the goodnefs of God and Mahomet, and it is accompanied with various geftures, fuch as lifting the hands above the head, bowing twice, performing two genuflexions, bowing again twice, and kiffing the ground. The whole of this ceremony they repeat three times.

Their fabbath is on our Friday, and commences from fix o'clock the preceding evening. On this day they ufe a blue flag inftead of the white one. As it has been prophefied that they are to be conquered by the Chriftians on the fabbath day, the gates of all the towns and of the emperor's palaces are fhut when at divine fervice on that day, in order to avoid being furprifed during that period. Their Talbs are not diftinguifhed by any particular drefs.

The Moors have three folemn devotional periods in the courfe of the year. The firft, which is named Aid de Cabier, is held in commemoration of the birth of Mahomet. It continues feven days, during which period every perfon who can afford the expence, kills a fheep as a facrifice, and divides it among his friends. The fecond is the

Ramadam,

Ramadam.   This is a rigorous fast or lent, held
at the season when Mahomet disappeared in his
flight from Mecca to Medina; and is conducted
by the Moors with so much superstition, that for
thirty days, from sun-rise to sun-set, they lay aside
all worldly acts, and devote their whole attention
to exercises of piety; carefully abstaining from
eating, drinking, smoaking, washing their mouths,
or even swallowing their saliva; and they are indulged with their usual custom of bathing only,
upon condition, that they avoid suffering the water to approach their heads, lest any of it should
enter the mouth or ears.   To make amends for
this strict observance of their lent during the day,
they appropriate the whole night to the indulgence of every gratification, and at the expiration
of the fast, a general festival takes place, named
the Beyran which continues seven days.   The third
is named Llashore, and is a day set apart by Mahomet for every person to compute the value of his
property, in order for the payment of Zakat, that
is, one tenth of their income to the poor, and other
pious uses.   Although this feast only lasts a single
day, yet it is celebrated with far greater magnificence than either of the others.

'There is also a superstitious custom among the
Moors, when any thing of moment is to be
undertaken, such as going on a dangerous journey
or voyage, the disposal of their children in marriage, &c. for some grave person to make an har-
rangue to the multitude, upon which his auditors
call for the key of direction.   By this is meant
the performance of joining the hands, looking
steadfastly on the palms during the admonition,

then

then by a joint concurrence calling upon God and
and the prophet, and concluding the ceremony by
ftroaking their faces with both hands, and joining
in chorus, faying *Salem, Salem,* (peace be' with
you) with much devotion. The due perfoimance
of this ceremony, they conceive will enfure them
certain fuccefs in all their undertakings.

The Moors compute time by lunar months, and
count the days of the week by the firft, fecond,
third, &c. beginning from our Sunday. They
ufe a common reed for writing, and begin their
manufcripts from right to left.

The Moors marry very young, many of their
females not being more than twelve years of age
at their nuptials. As Mahometans, it is well known
that their religion admits of polygamy to the
extent of four wives, and as many concubines as
they pleafe; but if we except the very opulent,
the people feldom avail themfelves of this indulgence, fince it entails on them a vaft additional
expence in houfe-keeping and in providing for a
large family. Whatever infti ution is contrary to
truth and found morality will in practice refute
itfelf; nor is any further argument than this fingle
obfervation wanting to anfwer all the abfurdities
which have been advanced in favour of a plurality
of wives. In contracting marriage the parents of
both parties are the only agents, and the intended
bride and bridegroom never fee each other till the
ceremony is performed. The marriage fettlements
are made before the Cadi, and then the friends of
the bride produce her portion, or if not, the hufband agrees to fettle a certain fum upon her, in
in cafe he fhould die, or divorce her on account of

barren-.

barrennefs, or any other caufe.   The children of the wives have all an equal claim to the effects of the father and mother, but thofe of the concubines can each only claim half a fhare.

When the marriage is finally agreed upon, the bride is kept at home eight days, to receive her female friends, who pay congratulatory vifits every day.   At the fame time a Talb attends upon her, to converfe with her relative to the folemn engagement on which fhe is about to enter; on thefe occafions he commonly accompanies his admonitions with finging a pious hymn, which is adapted to the folemnity.   The bride alfo with her near relations go through the ceremony of being painted afrefh; the nature of which cuftom I fhall defcribe when I fpeak of the harem.

During this procefs the bridegroom on the other hand receives vifits from his male friends in the morning, and in the evening rides through the town accompanied by them, fome playing on hautboys and drums, while others are employed in firing volleys of mufquetry.   In all their feftivals the difcharge of mufquetry indeed forms a principal part of the entertainment. 'Contrary to the European mode, which particularly aims at firing with exactnefs, the Moors difcharge their pieces as irregularly as poffible, fo as to have a continual fuccefion of reports for a few minutes.

On the day of marriage, the bride in the evening is put into a fquare or octagonal cage, about twelve feet in circumference, which is covered with fine white linen, and fometimes with gauzes and filks of various colours.   In this vehicle which is placed on a mule, fhe is paraded
round

round the ftreets accompanied by her relations
and friends, fome carrying lighted torches, others
playing on hautboys, and a third party again firing
vollies of mufquetry.

In this manner fhe is carried to the houfe of her
intended hufband, who returns about the fame
time from performing fimilar ceremonies. On her
arrival fhe is placed in an apartment by herfelf,
and her hufband is introduced to her alone for
the firft time, who finds her fitting on a filk or
velvet cufhion, fuppofing her to be a perfon of
confequence, with a fmall table before her, upon
which are two wax candles lighted. Her fhift,
or more properly fhirt, hangs down like a train
behind her, and over it is a filk or velvet robe
with clofe fleeves, which at the breaft and wrifts
is embroidered with gold; this drefs reaches
fomething lower than the calf of the leg. Round
her head is tied a black filk fcarf, which hangs
behind as low as the ground. Thus attired, the
bride fits with her hands over her eyes, when
her hufband appears and receives her as his wife,
without any further ceremony *: for the agree-
ment made by the friends before the Cadi is the
only fpecific contract which is thought neceffary.

If the hufband fhould have any reafon to fufpect
that his wife has not been ftrictly virtuous, he
is at liberty to divorce her and take another. For
fome time after marriage the family and friends

---

* Interim duæ miniftræ negræ exfpectant foris, ut no-
titiam habeant confummationis; quod cum pro certo cog-
noverint cantus buccinarum, & bombardarum emiffio fac-
tum annunciant.

are

are engaged in much feasting and a variety of
amusements, which last a longer or shorter time,
according to the circumstances of the parties.   It
is usually customary for the man to remain at
home eight days, and the woman eight months
after they are first married; and the woman is at
liberty to divorce herself from her husband if she
can prove that he does not provide her with a
proper subsistence.   If he curses her, the law
obliges him to pay her, for the first offence,
eight ducats, for the second, a rich dress of still
greater value; and the third time she may leave
him entirely.   He is then at liberty to marry again
in two months.

At the birth of a child, it is customary for the
parents to grieve eight days, at the expiration of
which they sacrifice a goat or a sheep, and invite their friends and acquaintance to partake of
the feast.   Women suffer but little inconvenience
in this country from child-bearing; they are frequently up the next day, and go through all the
duties of the house with the infant on their backs.
They do not adopt the method of teaching their
children to walk which is customary in Europe,
but when they are twelve months old they put
them on the floor, where from first crawling they
naturally in a short time acquire the habit of walking, and as soon as they can be made in the least
degree useful, they are put to the various kinds of
labour adapted to their age and strength.   Others,
whose parents are in better circumstances, are,
as I before observed, sometimes sent to school;
and those who are intended for the church usually continue their studies till they have nearly

learnt

learnt the Koran by rote. In that cafe they are enrolled among the Talbs or learned men of the law; and upon leaving fchool are paraded round the ftreets on a horfe, accompanied by mufic and a large concourfe of people. The proceffion is conducted in the following manner. Upon the day appointed, one of the moft fhewy horfes in the place is procured for the youth to ride on, who if he is a perfon 'of confequence, is dreft in all the gaiety which filks and brocades can afford, wearing a turban richly ornamented with gold and jewels, and interfperfed with flowers. Thus arrayed, he mounts his horfe, which alfo is not without its decorations, carrying in his hand his prayers pafted on a board, on which he looks with ftedfaft attention; and he proceeds with all the fedatenefs and compofed gravity of old age to the different places appointed for the purpofe, accompanied by mufic, and all his fchool-fellows on horfeback, dreffed according to their circum-ftances. At laft they meet at the houfe of the head boy of the fchool, where they are treated with a collection of fweatmeats. This cuftom, which is evidently adopted with a view of promoting an emulation in their youths, is one of the very few good inftitutions which are obfervable among thefe people.

In celebrating the rite of circumcifion, the child is dreffed very fumptuoufly and carried on a mule, or, if the parents are in poor circumftances, on an afs, accompanied with flags flying and muficians playing on hautboys and beating drums. In this manner they proceed to the mofque, where the ceremony is performed.

When

When any perfon dies, a certain number of women are hired for the purpofe of lamentation (for the men are feldom obferved to weep for the lofs of a friend) in the performance of which nothing can be more grating to the ear, or more unpleafant, than their frightful moans or rather howlings: at the fame time thefe mercenary mourners beat their heads and breafts, and tear their cheeks with their nails. The bodies are ufually buried a few hours after death. Previous to interment the corpfe is wafhed very clean, and fewed up in a fhroud compofed of feven pieces of fine linen united together, with the right hand under the head, which is pointed towards Mecca; it is carried on a bier fupported upon men's fhoulders to the burying-place, which is always, with great propriety, on the outfide of the town, for they never bury their dead in the mofques or within the bounds of an inhabited place. The bier is accompanied by numbers of people, two a-breaft, who walk very faft, calling upon God and Mahomet, and finging hymns adapted to the occafion.. The grave is made very wide at the bottom, and narrow at the top, and the body is depofited without any other ceremony than finging and praying in the fame manner as on their way to the grave.

They have no tombs in this country, but long and plain ftones; and it is frequently cuftomary for the female friends of the departed to weep over their graves for feveral days after the funeral. The Moors will not allow Chriftians or Jews to pafs over their places of interment; as they have a fuperftitious idea, which is perhaps more pre-

valent

valent among the lower clafs of people, than thofe who are better informed, that the dead fuffer pain from having their graves trodden upon by infidels; and I recollect when at Tangier, I receceived a very fevere rebuke from a Moor, for accidentally having paffed through one of their burying grounds.

When a women lofes her hufband fhe mourns four months and eight days, during which period fhe is to wear no filver or gold; and if fhe happens to be pregnant, fhe is to mourn till fhe is brought to bed. For the above time the relations of her late hufband are obliged to fupport her. I could not learn that any mourning was due from the hufband for the lofs of his wife; but it is cuftomary, particularly among the great people, for a fon to mourn for his father by not fhaving his head or any part of his beard, and by not cutting his nails for a certain period.

When a Jew or a Chriftian is converted to the Mahometan faith, he is immediately dreffed in a Moorifh habit, and paraded round the ftreets on horfeback, acsompanied with mufic and a great concourfe of people. He then chufes himfelf a Moorifh name, and fixes on a perfon who adop's him as a child, and is ever afterwards called his father. This adoption, however, is only nominal, for he is by no means bound to fupport him. The new convert is not allowed to marry any other woman than a negro, or the daughter of a renegado; and his defcendants are not confidered as genuine Moors till the fourth generation.

The

The renegadoes in the empire of Morocco are principally Spaniards, though there are some few of other nations in the country, who have deserted from Ceuta or Spain, to avoid the hand of justice for some capital crime or misdemeanor— ommonly, indeed, murder, I met with many of these people at Morocco, who frankly acknowledged to me that murder had been the cause of their desertion. Though the emperor may for various reasons find it convenient to countenance renegadoes, yet the Moors in general so thoroughly detest them, that they cannot be induced upon any terms to allow them to form a part of their society.

I cannot better conclude this section than by submitting to the reader the following account of the caravans to Mecca and Guinea, which I received from a gentleman resident in Barbary, on whose veracity I could place the utmost confidence.

Seven Months before the feast Aid de Cabier, or the commemoration of the birth of Mahomet, pilgrims from every quarter assemble at Fez, in order to join the caravan which at that season proceeds for Mecca. They are composed of three classes of people.—First, The mountaineers, named Brebes: Secondly, The Moorish merchants: and, Thirdly, Persons in public employments, or who are engaged about the court of the emperor. Thus religion and interest conspire to draw together a large and motely groupe, and to induce them to undertake a journey which is as fatiguing and dangerous as it is expensive.

The

The firſt claſs are not required to aſk permiſſion to join the caravan. The ſecond are obliged to preſent themſelves to their reſpective governors, as well to avoid the inconveniences of debts on their own account, as on that of their families, who might be ſubject to be moleſted by creditors during their abſence. If a merchant has the leaſt connection with the court, it is expected that he will alſo preſent to the emperor, who, as he feels himſelf diſpoſed, grants or refuſes him permiſſion to enter upon the journey. Thoſe of the third claſs muſt have an expreſs permiſſion from the emperor, who never allows any to go whoſe circumſtances will not ſufficiently enable them to defray the expences of the pilgrimage.

As there are two modes of performing this pilgrimage, by ſea and by land, thoſe who prefer the former are ſubjected to an examination by the governor of the port whence they embark, to ſee that they pay the freight of the veſſel, and to inform himſelf whether they have ſufficient means to go and return from this ſacred object of Mahometan devotion, without being under the neceſſity of borrowing, or being ſuſpected of uſing any baſe and diſhonourable means of obtaining a ſubſiſtence. Thoſe who proceed by land are liable to be examined alſo, but not ſo rigorouſly as the others; the Shaik of the caravan having the power to puniſh thoſe who are guilty of any irregularities.

The place whence the caravan ſets out by land, is from Teza, a town in the province of Tedla, ſome diſtance to the Eaſt of the city of Fez, the

latter

latter being the firſt place of rendezvous.   At
Fez, the moſt commercial city in the whole empire,
and abounding with proviſions of every deſcription, each perſon furniſhes himſelf in the beſt manner he is able, accorﬞing to hﬞs rank and circumſtances, with a ſuﬃcient ſuppﬞy to laſt till he
reaches Tripoli or Tunis at leaſt.

This grand caravan is always accompanied by
many others, of which one goes to Algier, another
to Tunis, and a third to grand Cairo, &c. Thoſe
perſons who go to Algiers and Tunis are not
under the neceſſity of aſking permiſſion, as they
are perſons who are accuſtomed to carry on a
trade with thoſe two places; whence they return
with a quantity of their reſpective manufactures.
The caps of Tunis are of great uſe in the empire
of Morocco, and their ſilks alſo ſell at a very
good price, though upon the whole thoſe of Algiers are preferable for the girdles uſed by the
Moors, curtains, women's dreſs, and furniture for
beds and rooms. The manufactures indeed of both
Algiers and Tunis are brought to a greater perfection than thoſe of Morocco.   The merchants who
go upon theſe expeditions carry with them ready
money, Haicks and ſlippers, which are the manufactures of Morocco, and diſpoſe of the two laſt
articles to the Arabs and inhabitants of the towns
in the neighbourhood of Algiers and Tunis, who,
though they do not wear the Haick as a part of
their dreſs, yet make uſe of them for a variety of
other purpoſes.

Some time within the firſt fifteen days of the
month Jumeth 'Tenii, every proper preparation
being previouſly made, the grand caravan ſets off
from

from Teza in the following order:—After having invoked the true and fole God and his prophet Mahomet, to give every benediction to this facred journey, they all meet near the tent of the chief conductor, who is named in Arabic Scheck Rebeck, and commence their devotions to the found of clarinets, tabors, &c. The unloaded camels and mules are then firft put in motion, attended by the cooks, watermen, &c. Next to this party follow thofe who travel on foot, either from devotion or neceffity; to thefe is entrufted the care of the loaded mules and camels. And the rear is brought up by thofe who are mounted either on horfes or mules. The caravan is put in motion at fun-rife, ftops at twelve o'clock at noon to dine, and about four in the afternoon the people encamp in the fame manner as they did at Teza.

The courfe which they take is through the interior parts of the country, leaving Tremecen, Algiers, and Tunis to their left. Some of them, indeed, make excurfions to the two latter places, and afterwards join the caravan. By thefe means they are enabled both to obtain a frefh fupply of provifions for themfelves and beafts, and to fell to the Arabs Haicks, flippers, and old caps, for which they ufually receive a very good price; and the profits enable them frequently to make advantageous purchafes at Mecca, Alexandria, and Cairo.

Upon their arrival, after a journey of two months and a half, at that part of the fea-coaft where the tower of Salines is fituated, and which is about half a days ride from the city of Tripoli, they reft themfelves ten days. At this place all the pilgrims supply themselves with forty or fifty days provisions, which is generally sufficient to support them to Alexandria or Grand Cairo; and on their return they purchase in the neighbourhood of Tunis and Tripoli a large supply of mules, frequently giving only twenty-five hard dollars for what they afterwards sell in Morocco for eighty or an hundred.

From the tower of Salines they continue their route as far as Alexandria and Grand Cairo, where they furnish themselves in the same manner as at Tripoli, with sufficient provisions for the remainder of the journey, which requires altogether near seven months to accomplish. To those who undertake this journey for the purpose of trade, it generally answers extremely well. By purchasing goods at one place, and selling them at another, they contrive to make upon each sale a profit of ten per cent.

The Arabs from Fez as far as Alexandria and Grand Cairo, though a rude class of people, are very warmly attached to their religion, and on that account give the pilgrims a friendly reception, furnishing them with barley, butter, eggs, mutton, beef, &c. From that place, however, to Mecca the route is not so easy, as the Arabs, instead of the benefactors, frequently become the plunderers of these holy travellers. On these occasions they spare nothing, and leave them not so much as the necessaries of life; particularly if they refuse the contributions which they usually demand for permitting the caravan to pass peaceably through the country. Within the last seven or eight years this passage is become more dangerous than ever. The

M   banditti

banditti now affemble in very confiderable bodies in thefe deferts, and at certain paffes the travellers may be affailed with great advantage. In paffing the ifthmus of Suez, for inftance, above Alexandia, the caravan may be defeated by an hundred men. Thefe robbers, therefore, generally endeavour to poft themfelves in fuch a manner as to attack it in this place.

Thofe people who carry on a petty trade endeavour to convert their little ftock into ready money upon their arrival at Mecca; where, with the remainder of the caravan, and other Mahometan pilgrims, they commemorate by a feaft the nativity of the great prophet Mahomet, when every perfon is obliged to facrifice at leaft one fheep. It is computed that on this day, which is the tenth of the moon Dalaja, above two millions of fheep are flaughtered at Mecca.

After the performance of this folemn rite the majority of the travellers employ themfelves in laying out their money to the beft advantage. Some purchafe muflins Levant filks, &c.; others effence of rofes, amber, mufk, Perfian filks, &c. while another part of them fave their money to lay it out at Grand Cairo, where they purchafe a good ftock of raw filk, cottons, and manufactured filks of different kinds. In this city, indeed, every article may be had at nearly the fame price as at Mecca. On the whole, we may affert, at a moderate computation, that the value of the articles contained in one of thefe caravans, joined with the ready money, amounts to two millions of hard dollars.

Thofe

Those persons who proceed by sea join the caravan after difembarking at Alexandria, and paying the freight of the veffel in which they fet fail. On their return alfo, confiderable numbers embark at Alexandria, and land at Tetuan or Tangier, whence they depart for their refpective homes, and fell the commodities they bring with them for perhaps a third more than their original price. Others continue their journey by land, and add to the riches brought from the Levant, the merchandizes of Tunis and Algiers, which are held in great efteem throughout the empire of Morocco. By thefe means they double the capital they provided themfelves with at firft fetting out.

It would be no very difficult matter for a Chriftian to join one of thefe caravans, provided he obtained the recommendation and exprefs permiffion of his Moorifh majefty, or the Shaik of the caravan, who would take him under his protection. This obftacle would be ftill further removed, if the Chriftian would confent to wear the Turkifh habit or drefs himfelf in the manner they are obliged to adopt at Grand Cairo. By thefe means he would obviate every inconvenience to which the European drefs fubjects a traveller, both with refpect to the wild Arabs, and to the weak and illiberal people of the caravan. As the caravan, however, does not go far into the interior parts of the country, the object of difcovery would hardly be fufficient to counterbalance the fatigues and dangers of the expedition.

There are no caravans which go directly into the interior parts of the country. It would, in fact, be as dangerous for a Mahometan as for a Chriftian to penetrate an hundred leagues beyond

the inhabitants of thefe parts are favage, avaricious, and capable of committing any crime for a very trifling emolument. A fatal proof the cruelty of thefe Arabs occurred in 1786, when forty pilgrims on their return from Mecca, were maffacred. Thefe people demanded hofpitality from the mountaineers of Zamor near Mequinez, for only one night; but as they brought fome valuable goods with them, it is fuppofed that it was owing to that circumftance, that they were all put to death.

The country beyond the mountains of Atlas, about fix days journey to the Eaft of Morocco, is not even known though it is probable it might be penetrated with fafety, provided the fame means were ufed as are employed by the caravans which go to the South; that is, a fmall proportion of force, and a fmall proportion of generofity.

There is no particular caravan fo confiderable for the South as that which goes to Mecca. As thefe indeed are intended merely for the purpofes of commerce, they feldom confift of more than one hundred and fifty, or perhaps two, or at moft three hundred perfons, including the muleteers, camel-drivers, and other fervants. Some of thefe caravans fet out from Morocco, while others go from Tarudant, Fez, and Tetuan. The firft pafs by way of Domnet, while the others meet at Tafilet, and thence purfue their journey towards the defert. Thefe caravans go no further than Tombut, where there are fome merchants of Morocco, eftablifhed for the purpofe of carrying on a trade with the inland parts of Guinea, where they traffick for flaves, ivory, gold duft, &c. The merchandizes which the caravans carry from

Morocco,

Morocco, Tarudant, &c. confift of Haicks and blue cloths for which they find a good fale throughout the country of the Mohafres and at Thouat.

The city of Thouat is in the interior parts of the country, about thirty days journey from Tafilet. From Thouat the caravans proceed directly to Tombut. There is much greater danger in paffing the two deferts between Tafilet and Thouat, than between the latter place and Tombut. As the Arabs of the deferts are much addicted to rapine, the caravans are obliged to make them trifling prefents, to enable them to travel without being molefted. The other Arabs, who purchafe merchandize, fuch as blue cloths, fmall daggers, looking-glaffes, &c. pay generally in return oftrich-feathers; and this traffick is attended with very tolerable profits.

The articles which the caravans carry immediately to Tombut are tobacco and falt. It is neceffary to pay attention to what camels may be wanted for the purpofes of carrying water through the deferts, as in fome parts they travel four, and in others nine days, without meeting with a drop of water. It is in a great meafure on this account that the camel becomes fo ufeful an animal in hot climates. Their ftomachs, it is well known, are fo conftructed as to allow them to pafs many days without food or drink. In the inner coats of their ftomachs there are a number of little cells, in which they retain a large proportion of water for a length of time, nature having provided them with a method of regurgitating it when thirfty. From the fize of the ftomach it alfo admits of a

 large

large portion of food to be taken in at a time, to which they have recourse by rumination when their appetite calls for a supply of nourishment. Their owners, therefore, have only to give them plenty of barley and water at the entrance of the deserts, and that proves sufficient to laſt them till a freſh supply can be conveniently procured.

Theſe extraordinary animals are able to carry a very great weight in proportion to their ſize, and to perform very long journeys without much apparent fatigue. They are uſed both for the purpoſes of riding and carrying burdens. Their ſteps are very long and ſlow, and they are tractable and eaſily managed. They are taught to kneel down when they are loaded; and when uſed for the ſaddle are entirely managed by a ſhort and thick ſtick, which both ſerves the purpoſes of bridle and whip. It is not uncommon in Barbary to ſee three perſons, with furniture in proportion, mounted upon one camel.

Upon the arrival of the caravans at Tombut, they exchange their tobacco and ſalt for ſlaves, gold duſt, and ivory, which are brought thither from Guinea. Four thouſand ſlaves are ſuppoſed to be annually carried from Tombut, great part of whom are ſent to Maſcar, Algiers, and Tunis. —It but ſeldom happens that any eunuchs are brought away, unleſs by a particular commiſſion from the emperor or ſome of the princes, no other perſon in the country being permitted to keep them. It is indeed extremely difficult to procure them at all. The place whence they are uſually brought is the kingdom of Bambara. In Muley Iſhmael's reign the number of eunuch's in the empire

pire of Morocco was fuppofed to amount to feven hundred; but they are now fo reduced, that one hundred is the utmoft that could be muftered in the whole empire.

Thofe perfons who have been concerned in the trade to Tombut for the laft twenty years, compute the value of the merchandizes tranfported annually thither from the empire of Morocco to amount to at leaft a million of hard dollars; and the commodities received in return, fuch as oftrich-feathers, ivory, gold duft, amber, and Guinea flaves, to ten millions; two thirds of which are carried to Algiers, Tunis, &c. The flaves are purchafed near Tombut, at a very cheap rate, there having been inftances of a fine Negro boy being bought for fix pounds of falt.

As a proof that Chriftians may proceed along the fhore by land from Guinea to Morocco, two French men, in the year 1781, came from Senegal to Morocco, and brought intelligence of fome forts having been taken from the Englifh on that river. It is, however, proper to remark, that they were provided with efcorts from one place to another.

M 4   C H A P.

C H A P. XII.

Summons to appear before the Emperor—Admission into the Royal HAREM. *Attendance on* LALLA ZARA.— *Introduction to* LALLA BATOOM, *the chief Sultana.— Introduction to* LALLA DOUYAW, *the favourite wife of the Emperor—her History.——Description of the* HAREM—*its Economy.——Concubines of the Emperor. ——Adventure and Altercation with one of those Ladies. —Dress of the Ladies in the* HAREM.—*Opinion of the Moors concerning the Female Sex.—Emperor's Children.—Dress, Manners, and Situation of the Female Sex in Barbary.*

FROM the unsuccessful efforts which I had made for the purpose of procuring my dispatches, I had begun to reconcile myself to the idea of remaining a prisoner at Morocco, when, to my great surprize, at the expiration of a month from the time of the prince's departure, his Moorish majesty sent to me in particular haste to repair to the palace.

Upon receiving this message my best hopes were excited. I naturally expected an immediate emancipation, as it is necessary that every stranger should see the emperor previous to his departure; and I flew to the palace with all the alacrity which such an expectation was certain to inspire. What then was my astonishment, when, upon my arrival at the palace, a messenger brought orders from the emperor, the purport of which was, that I should immediately examine one of his sultanas who was indisposed, and in the afternnoon return

with

with proper medicines, and at the same time report my opinion of her case to his majesty.

It is difficult to say whether disappointment or surprize were the predominant emotion in my mind on receiving this order. After the prejudices which from his dislike to the English, and his ignorance of the effects of internal medicines, the emperor was known to have entertained against me, and after having detained me at Morocco for such a length of time, with no apparent view but that of manifesting his contempt of me as an Englishman, it appeared unaccountable that he should give orders for my admission into the Harem, where in addition to the former objections, there were also some still stronger in the eyes of the Moors; as the admission of one of our sex into that sacred depository of female charms, was almost unprecedented, and I believe totally so with respect to the Harem of the emperor.

Whatever might be the motives with his imperial majesty for the violation of Moorish decorum in this instance, I did not conceive I had much reason to rejoice at the event. I had already experienced too much ingratitude from the prince, as well as too much ungenerous treatment from the emperor, to encourage me to undertake any future engagement of the kind in this country; and the difficulties and prejudices which from experience I knew I had to encounter, when employed in my professional line by the Moors, united to the uncertainty of removing the lady's complaint, rendered it altogether not very safe to administer my advice under such disadvantageous circumstances; and even that curiosity which would naturally be ex-

M 5   cited

cited in moſt perſons on ſuch an occaſion, was not ſufficient to reconcile me to this new employment.

Unfortunately in this dilemma I had very little time allowed me to determine, ſince the meſſenger was waiting to conduct me to the gate of the Harem. My embarraſſment, however, continued only for a ſhort period; for I ſoon recollected that it was in vain to oppoſe the emperor's order. I therefore deferred giving a deciſive anſwer till I had ſeen my patient, and made myſelf fully acquainted with the nature of her complaint.

The public and uſual entrance to the Harem is through a very large arched door-way, guarded on the outſide by ten body guards, which leads to a lofty hall, where the captain or Alcaide, with a guard of ſeventeen eunuchs, are poſted. No perſon is admitted into this hall, but thoſe who are known to have buſineſs in the Harem.

The emperor's order being delivered on the outſide of the door to the Alcaide, I was immediately, with my interpreter, conducted into the Harem by one of the Negro eunuchs. Upon entering the court into which the women's apartments open, I diſcovered a motley group of concubines, domeſtics, and negro ſlaves, who were variouſly employed. Thoſe of the firſt deſcription had formed themſelves into circles, ſeated on the ground in the open court, and were apparently engaged in convefation.—The domeſtics and ſlaves were partly employed in needle-work, and partly in preparing their cuſcoſoo. My appearance in the court, however, ſoon attracted their attention, and a conſiderable number of them upon obſerving me, unacquainted with the means by which I had

been

been admitted into the Harem, retreated with the utmoſt precipitancy into their apartments; while others more courageous approached, and enquired of my black attendant who I was, and by whoſe orders he had brought me thither.

The moment it was known that I was of the medical profeſſion, parties of them were detached to inform thoſe who had fled, that I was ſent in by order of the emperor to attend Lalla Zara, my intended patient's name, and requeſting of them to come back and look at the Chriſtian. Seranio Tibib! Chriſtian Doctor! reſounded from one end of the Harem to the other; and in the courſe of a few minutes I was ſo completely ſurrounded by women and children, that I was unable to move a ſingle ſtep.

Every one of them appeared ſolicitous to find out ſome complaint on which ſhe might conſult me, and thoſe who had not ingenuity enough to invent one, obliged me to feel their pulſe; and were highly diſpleaſed if I did not evince my excellence in my profeſſion by the diſcovery of ſome ailment or other. All of them ſeemed ſo urgent to be attended to at the ſame time, that while I was feeling the pulſe of one, others were behind, pulling my coat and entreating me to examine their complaints, while a third party were upbraiding me for not paying them the ſame attention. Their ideas of delicacy did not at all correſpond with thoſe of our European ladies, for they exhibited the beauties of their limbs and form with a degree of freedom that in any other country would have been thought indecent; and their converſation was equally unreſtrained.

This

This apparent laxity of conduct in the Moorish ladies does not proceed from a depravity in principle. As the female sex in this country are not entrusted with the guardianship of their own honour, there is no virtue in reserve. A depraved education even serves to corrupt instead of to restrain them. They are not regarded as rational or moral agents; they are only considered as beings created entirely to besubservient to the pleasure of man. To excite the passions, and to do and say every thing which may inflame a licentious imagination, become therefore necessary accomplishments in the female sex, and their manners and conduct naturally assume a cast totally different from those women in a more refined and more liberal state of society. In those instances to which I refer, they were not conscious of trespassing the limits of decency; and in others they manifested a singular attention to what they conceived to be decorum. When I requested to see the tongues of some patients who complained of feverish symptoms, they refused to comply, considering it as inconsistent with their modesty and virtue; some of them indeed laughed at the singularity of the request, and attributed it either to an impertinent curiosity, or an inclination to impose on their understandings.

As the number of my patients continued to increase rather than to diminish, there appeared but little prospect of an introduction to the sultana Lalla Zara, whom I was first directed to attend, in any reasonable time. The eunuch, however, wearied out with waiting, exerted all the vigour of authority which his natural effeminacy would

admit

admit of in obliging them to difperfe, and which was fo far effectual at leaft as to allow me room to pafs, though this female croud ftill followed me till I had nearly reached the lady's apartment.

From the firft court into which I had been introduced, I paffed through two or three fimilar, till I at length arrived at the chamber of my intended patient. I was here detained a little time in the court, till my patient and her apartment were ready to receive me.—Upon my entrance I found the lady fitting crofs-legged on a mattrefs placed upon the floor, and covered with fine linen, with twelve white and negro attendants, feated on the floor alfo, in different parts of the chamber. A round cufhion was placed for me next to the lady, on which I was defired to be feated. I fhould have remarked, that, contrary to my expectations, I found that none of the emperor's women difguifed their faces in the manner which I had experienced in the prince's Harem, but I faw them all with the fame familiarity as if I had been introduced into the houfe of an European.

Lalla Zara*, who was of Moorifh parents, was about eight years ago remarkable for her beauty and accomplifhments; on which account fhe was then in every refpect the favourite wife of the emperor. So dangerous a pre-eminence could not be enjoyed, without exciting the jealoufy of thofe females whofe charms were lefs confpicuous; and who, befides the mortification of having a lefs

---

Lalla, fignifies lady or miftrefs, but is only applied in this country to the fultanas.

fhare

share of beauty, experienced alfo the difgrace of being deferted by their lord.

Determined to effect her ruin, they contrived to mix fome poifon (moft probably arfenic) in her food, and conducted the deteftable plot with fuch art and addrefs, that it was not perceived until the deleterious drug had began its baneful operations. She was feized with moft violent fpafms, and a continual vomiting; and had fhe not been poffeffed of an uncommonly ftrong conftitution, fhe muft immediately have fallen a victim to the machinations of her rivals. After a fevere ftruggle, however, between life and death, the effects of the poifon in fome degree abated; but it left the unhappy lady in a ftate of dreadful debility and irritation, and particularly in the ftomach, from which it was not perhaps in the power of medicine to extricate her. Her beauty too, the fatal caufe of her misfortune, was completely deftroyed, and her enemies, though difappointed in their aim of deftroying her life, yet enjoyed the malignant triumph of feeing thofe charms which had excited their uneafinefs, reduced below the ftandard of ordinary women.

When I faw her, fhe had fuch a weaknefs of digeftion, that every fpecies of food which fhe took, after remaining a few hours on her ftomach, was returned perfectly crude and undigefted. As fhe did not receive proper nourifhment, her body had wafted away to a fhadow, and her frame was in fo a weak a ftate, as not to allow her to walk without affiftance. Her complexion was entirely altered. Her fkin, from being naturally clear and fair, as I was informed, was changed to a

fickly

sickly brown, which, joined to a ruined set of
teeth, and a ghastly countenance, had effaced
every trace of that beauty, which she before
might have possessed.   Upon my first entering her apartment, though from my profession
accustomed to behold objects of distress and misery
yet I was so forcibly struck with her unhappy situation and wretched appearance, that I was obliged
to exert all the fortitude of which I was master, to
avoid the discovery of my feelings.

Lalla Zara was at this time about six-and-thirty
years of age, and though in so weak a state, had
two beautiful young children; the first was in its
sixth year, and the youngest, which was then
under the care of a wet-nurse, was very little
more than a twelve-month old.   I was quite asto-
nished to observe such strong and apparently heal-
thy children, the offspring of a mother whose constitution was so dreadfully impaired.   It was certainly, however, a very fortunate circumstance
for Lalla Zara that she had these children; since
by the Mahometan law a man cannot divorce his
wife provided she bear him children; so that though
the emperor took very little notice of this poor
lady, yet he was, for the above reason, obliged to
maintain both herself and her offspring.

From the wretched situation in which I have
described this unfortunate female, it is easy to conceive that her spirits must revive at the most distant
prospect of procuring relief in her disagreeable
complaint.   Such, indeed was the the case.   She
received me with all that satisfaction which hope,
united with some degree of confidence, most naturally inspires.

Under

Under these circumstances the predicament in which I felt myself was, I must confess, most truly embarrassing. It was one of those unpleasant situations, in which duty and interest are completely in opposition to each other, or rather when the sympathetic feelings stand opposed to personal safety. Humanity pointed out to me that it was my duty to relieve her if possible; on the other hand, self-preservation no less strongly dictated, that it was absolutely necessary to my safety and happiness to embrace the first opportunity of leaving a country where I existed in the most critical and most disagreeable situation. Both these sentiments for some time pressed equally on my mind, and left me at a loss how to determine. I at length, however, fixed on a middle plan of conduct, which appeared likely to affect the safety of the lady, without endangering my own. This was, to give a proper course of medicines a fair trial for a fortnight; and then, if the least prospect of amendment should appear in consequence of them, I could leave her more, with such directions as might enable her to use them without medical attendance.

This plan I conceived it most prudent not to communicate immediately to my patient: I therefore, without affording her any very flattering hopes of a cure, assured her, that I would use every means with which I was acquainted for the restoration of her constitution. Contrary to most other Moorish females, I found Lalla Zara in every respect affable and polite; though deprived of her health, she retained her natural vivacity, and with the ravages of her inveterate malady, she still remained a pleasing and an interesting character.

I was

I was upon the point of taking my leave of Lalla Zara, when a female meſſenger appeared to re-queſt my attendance upon Lalla Batoom, who, from the priority of her marriage, is called the firſt wife of the emperor, and is more properly en-titled to the denomination of ſultana than any of the others.

As the emperor had given directions for my ad-miſſion to Lalla Zara only, and as I ſoon perceived that the eunuch regarded me with the moſt jealous eye, I muſt confeſs that, however my curioſity might be excited, yet when ſolicited to viſit the other ladies, I could not help feeling ſome ap-prehenſions of the danger which I incurred by tranſgreſſing the emperor's order.   On the other hand, I reflected, that both the eunuch and the women would be equally involved in the conſe-quences of a diſcovery; the firſt for conducting me, and the others for admitting me into their apartments; and therefore that it was as much their intereſt as mine to be cautious, as well in pre-venting the circumſtance from reaching the empe-ror's ears, as in not receiving me in their apart-ments at a time when he was likely to enter the Harem.   All theſe arguments, united to the deſire which I felt to avail myſelf of ſo favourable an opportunity of ſeeing a place where no European had ever before been admitted, had ſo much weight, that my objections were ſpeedily removed.

I found Lalla Batoom to be a perfect Mooriſh beauty; ſhe was moſt immoderately fat, about forty years of age, with round and prominent cheeks, which were painted a deep red, ſmall black eyes, and a viſage completely guiltleſs of expreſſion.

She

She was fitting upon a mattrafs on the floor, which, as ufual, was covered with fine white linen, and fhe was furrounded with a large party of concubines, whom I was informed fhe had invited to be her vifitors on the occafion. Her room bore a much greater appearance of grandeur than that of Lalla Zara, and fhe was indulged with a whole fquare to herfelf.

As foon as I entered her apartment, Lalla Batoom requefted of me to be feated clofe by her fide, and to feel her pulfe. Her complaint was a flight cold, of which an unconquerable defire of feeing me had moft probably been the occafion. As foon as I had felt her pulfe, and pronounced my opinion, I was employed in going through the fame ceremony with all the other ladies in the room, who defired I would acquaint them with all their complaints without any farther enquiries. From the great experience which I had acquired in this kind of practice while at Tarudant, and from the knowledge which I had attained of their complaints, which in general proceeded from too violent an attack upon the cufcofoo, I was enabled to make no defpicable figure in this myfterious art, and was very fuccefsful in my opinions.

From the fubject of their own health, the converfation prefently changed to criticifms upon my drefs. There was not a fingle part of it which was not examined, and commented on with their ufual loquacity. My interpreter was then afked if I was a married man, and if fo, whether I had brought my wife with me, with a variety of equally important queftions. In the midft of this converfation, tea was introduced, though at eleven

o'clock

o'clock in the morning.   A fmall tea-board with four very fhort feet, fupplied the place of a table, and held the tea equipage.   The cups were about the fize of large walnut-fhells, of the very beft Indian china, and of which a very confiderable number was drank.

After I had concluded my vifit to the queen of the Harem, I was next conducted to Lalla Douyaw, the favourite wife of the emperor, whom I found to be what would be termed in Europe a very fine and beautiful woman.   She is a native of Genoa, and was, with her mother fhipwrecked on the coaft of Barbary, whence they became the emperor's captives.   At that period, though but eight years of age, her perfonal charms were fo very promifing and attractive, that they induced the emperor to order her to be taken forcibly from her mother, and placed in his Harem, where, though at fo early a period of life every means were in vain employed to entice her to change her religion, till at length the emperor threatened to pull up every hair of her head by the roots, if fhe defifted any longer; and fhe then found herfelf obliged to fubmit to his inclinations.

After remaining fome time in the character of a concubine, the emperor married her; and from her great great beauty, addrefs, and fuperior mental accomplifhments, fhe foon gained his beft affections, which fhe ever after poffeffed.   She had, indeed, fo much influence over him, that though he was naturally of a very ftubborn difpofition, fhe was never known to fail in any favour fhe folicited, provided fhe perfevered in her requeft.

When

When I faw her fhe was about thirty years of age; in her perfon rather corpulent, and her face was diftinguifhed by that expreffive beauty which is almoft peculiar to the Italian women. Her addrefs was pleafing, and her behaviour polite and attentive. In the Harem, from her accomplifhments in reading and writing well the Arabic language, fhe was confidered by the other females as a fuperior being.

From the circumftance of being taken fo young into the Harem, fhe had nearly forgotten her native language, and could only converfe fluently in Arabic, having but a diftant recollection of the events which firft brought her into her prefent fituation. She, however, informed me that we were brother and fifter (a common phrafe ufed by the Moors to exprefs the affinity which Chriftians bear to each other in a religious fenfe) and had difcernment enough to obferve that fhe was among a very uncouth and ignorant people. She added, that her mother, whom I had afterwards an opportunity of feeing at a Venetian merchant's houfe at Mamora, was ftill a Chriftian, though fhe herfelf was no longer fuch, and that fhe hoped I would vifit her every time I came to the Harem.

Her complaint was a fcorbutic affection of the gums, which threatened the lofs of fome of her front teeth. This circumftance gave her the greateft uneafinefs, as fhe was fearful it might disfigure her other features, and by that means caufe an abatement in the affection of the emperor. On this account fhe was extremely anxious to have my advice, though when I was in her apartment fhe always experienced the ftrongeft apprehenfion;

left

k? my attendance on her fhould come to the emperor's knowledge, which might be attended with the moft ferious confequences to us both.

Lalla Zara, owing to her bad ftate of health, and the confequent ruin of her perfonal charms, had long been neglected by the emperor, who, moft probably, admitted of my attendance on her more for the fake of exonerating himfelf from her conftant importunities to fee me (for it was a confiderable time before fhe could gain his confent) than from any great anxiety on his part for her recovery. With refpect to a perfon of fuch a defcription, it was perhaps a matter of indifference to the emperor by whom fhe was feen or known, and therefore there was no ground for that jealoufy to which the Moors in general are fo notorioufly addicted.

Lalla Douyaw was very differently fituated. She was in the bloom of health and beauty, with all thofe exterior accomplifhments which were likely to excite the moft ardent paffion; and indeed the emperor's attachment to her was unexampled.— Under thefe circumftances, when we confider with what caution the Moors in general endeavour to prevent any foreign intercourfe with their women, it could not be fuppofed that the emperor would relifh the idea of an European in particular being admitted frequently, and almoft alone, to this firft object of his deareft affections.

Lalla Douyaw, however, to prevent the poffibility of detection, enjoined her female flaves to be particularly affiduous to inform her when there was the fmalleft reafon for an alarm; while, on the other hand fhe was continually making prefents

fents to the eunuch who attended me, cautioning him at the fame time not to intimate to any perfon out of the Harem that I had been admitted into her apartment. She fo far gained an afcendancy over him, that I frequently remained with her for an hour at a time, converfing upon European cuftoms; and though fhe knew but little of them, yet the fubject always feemed to afford her the higheft pleafure. As foon as fhe thought it would be imprudent for me to remain any longer, fhe requefted of me to go, but with a promife to call upon her the next time I vifited the Harem. Her apprehenfion of a difcovery was not confined to the chance of an alarm from the emperor, or from the perfidy of the eunuch; it was likewife extended to the jealoufy of the other women in the Harem, who might probably rejoice in an opportunity of effecting her ruin. It was, however, perhaps a fortunate circumftance for us both, that by moft of them admitting me into their apartments, it was equally their intereft to be filent, fince a difcovery of the one would inevitably lead to the detection of the others.

The fourth wife, who is daughter to an Englifh renegado, and mother to the reigning emperor, being at Fez at the time when I vifited the Harem, I had not an opportuntiy of feeing.

When I waited on the emperor in confequence of my vifit to the Harem, I was honoured with quite a private audience; for he received me in the court clofe to his houfe where no perfon is permitted to be prefent while the emperor is there, but a few pages, and the people who immediately belong to his carriage.

The

4

The fovereign was in an open four-wheeled carriage, hung very low, of a fize juft large enough to admit one perfon, and drawn by the fons of four Spanifh renegadoes. As foon as I was obferved by him, his majefty ordered me with my interpreter to approach, and carry him the medicines, defiring me to tafte them before him, to convince him, I imagine, that there was nothing in them that was improper. He then examined them with great attention, and ordered me to explain to him what they were, and in what manner they were expected to act. When required to give my opinion concerning the cafe of my patient, I informed his majefty, that the fultana's complaint was of fuch a nature as to require a very long courfe of medicines, but which I apprehended it would not be neceffary to change; that therefore I propofed to attend her for a fortnight, and then leave her a proper fupply, with fuch directions as might enable her to take them almoft with the fame advantage as if I was prefent. I added, that I had received orders from the governor of Gibraltar to return to the garrifon immediately, which if I difobeyed I fhould certainly lofe a very good employment; and that, as I was convinced of the emperor's kind intentions towards me, by the promifes which he had made at my firft audience, I was perfuaded his majefty would not detain me a day longer than the period I mentioned. In reply, the emperor faid, that he only wifhed me to attend the fultana for about ten days, at the expiration of which, if the medicines proved likely to be ufeful, I fhould then leave her a proper fupply, and he would fend me

home

home (to use his expreſſion) upon a fine horſe. He then gave orders to his prime miniſter to pay me ten hard dollars as a preſent; and commanded that free admittance ſhould be granted me into the royal Harem, whenever I thought it neceſſary.

The Harem, as I before obſerved, forms a part of the palace or ſeraglio, without any other immediate communication with it than a private door, uſed only by the emperor himſelf.

The apartments, which are all on the ground floor, are ſquare, very lofty, and four of them encloſe a ſpacious ſquare court into which they open by means of large folding-doors. Theſe, as in other Mooriſh houſes, which in general have no windows, ſerve the purpoſe of admitting light into the apartments. In the centre of theſe courts, which are floored with blue and white checquered tiling, is a fountain, ſupplied by pipes from a large reſervoir on the outſide of the palace, which ſerves for the frequent ablutions recommended by the Mahometan religion, as well as for other purpoſes.

The whole of the Harem conſiſts of about twelve of theſe ſquare courts communicating with each other by narrow paſſages, which afford a free acceſs from one part of it to another, and of which all the women are allowed to avail themſelves.

The apartments are ornamented externally with beautiful carved wood, much ſuperior to any I have ever ſeen in Europe, as well for the difficulty of the workmanſhip, as for the taſte with which it is finiſhed. In the inſide moſt of the rooms are hung with rich damaſk of various colours; the floors are covered with beautiful carpets, and there

are

are mattreſſes difpofed at different diſtances for the purpoſes of fitting and ſleeping.

Befides theſe, the apartments are furniſhed at each extremity with an elegant European mahogany beadſted, hung with damaſk, having on it ſeveral mattreſſes placed one over the other, which are covered with various coloured ſilks; but theſe beds are merely placed there to ornament the room. In all the apartments without exception, the ceiling is wood, carved and painted. The principal ornaments in ſome, were large and valuable looking-glaſſes, hung on different parts of the walls. In others, clocks and watches of different ſizes, in glaſs caſes, were difpofed in the ſame manner. In ſome of the apartments I obſerved a projection from the wall, which reached about half way to the ceiling, on which were placed ſeveral mattreſſes over each other, and each covered with ſilks of different colours. Above and below this projection the wall was hung with pieces of ſattin, velvet, and damaſk, of different colours, ornamented on each edge with a broad ſtripe of black velvet, which was embroidered in its centre with gold.

The whole Harem was under the management of the principal ſultana, Lalla Batoom: that is in general, ſhe was diſtinguiſhed by the title of miſtreſs of the Harem, without having any particular controul over the women. This lady and Lalla Douyaw, the favourite, were indulged with a whole ſquare to themſelves; but Lalla Zara, and all the concubines, were only allowed each a ſingle room.

N   Each

Each female had a separate daily allowance from the emperor, proportioned to the estimation in which they were held by him. Out of this they were expected to furnish themselves with every article of which they might be in want; the Harem is therefore to be considered as a place where so many distinct lodgers have apartments without paying for them, and the principal sultana is the mistress of the whole.

The daily allowance which each woman received from the emperor for her subsistence was very trifling indeed. Lalla Douyaw, the favourite sultana, had very little more than half-a-crown English *per diem*, and the others less in proportion. It must be allowed, that the emperor made them occasional presents of money, dress, and trinkets; but this could never be sufficient to support the number of domestics and other expences they must incur. Their greatest dependence, therefore, was on the presents they received from those Europeans and Moors who visited the court, and who employed their influence in obtaining some particular favour from the emperor. Nor had the monarch sufficient delicacy to discourage this mode of negociation. He well knew that if his women had not obtained supplies by other means, they must have had recourse to his purse; and as he had taken too good precautions to allow any mischief to arise from this custom, he was always well pleased to have business transacted through that channel. Ambassadors, consuls, and merchants indeed, who were acquainted with the nature of the court, perfectly knew that this was always the most successful mode that could be adopted. As an illustration

of

of this affertion, when I was at Morocco, a Jew, defirous of obtaining a very advantageous favour from the emperor, for which he had been a long time unfuccefsfully foliciting, fent to all the principal ladies of the Harem prefents of pearls to a very confiderable amount; the confequence was, that they all went in a body to the emperor, and immediately obtained the wifhed-for conceffion.

The ladies feparately furnifh their own rooms, hire their own domeftics, and, in fact, do what they pleafe in the Harem, but are not permitted to go out without an exprefs order from the emperor, who very feldom grants them that favour, except when they are to be removed from one palace to another. In that cafe a party of foldiers is difpatched a little diftance before them, to difperfe the male paffengers in particular, and to prevent the poffibility of their being feen. This previous ftep being taken, a piece of linen cloth is tied round the lower part of the face, and afterwards thefe miferable females cover themfelves entirely with their Haicks, and either mount mules which they ride like men, or, what is more ufual, are put into a fquare carriage or litter, conftructed for this purpofe, which by its lattice-work allows them to fee without being feen. In this manner they fet off under the charge of a guard of black eunuchs. This journey, and fometimes a walk within the bounds of the palace, with which they are, however, feldom indulged, is the only exercife they are permitted to take.

The emperor's Harem confifted of between fixty and a hundred females, befides their domeftics and flaves, which were very numerous. The four

N 2

wives

wives which I have already noted are by no means
to be confidered as the firft fet of which the emperor was poffeffed, fince fome died and others
were repudiated*.   So that it is a difficult matter
to determine what was the precife number of Sidi
Mahomet's wives.

Many of the concubines were Moorifh women,
who had been prefented to the emperor, as the
Moors confider it an honour to have their daughters
in the Harem; feveral were European flaves, who
had been either made captives or purchafed by
the emperor, and fome were Negroes.

In this groupe the Europeans, or their defcendants, had by far the greateft claim to the
character of handfome.   There was one in particular, who was a native of Spain, and taken into
the Harem at about the fame age as Lalla Douyaw,
who was indeed a perfect beauty.   Nor was this
lady quite fingular in that refpect, for many others
were almoft equally handfome.

The Moorifh women have in general an inex-
preffive countenance, and a ruftic fimplicity of
manners.   Their perfons are below the middle
ftature, of a remarkably fat and fquare make,
with very large hands and feet.   Their complexions are either a clear brown, or, what is
more ufual, of a fallow caft.   Their faces are
round, and their eyes in general black; the nofe
and mouth very fmall, and the latter is ufually accompanied with a good fet of teeth.

* The Mahometan law allows a man to divorce his
wife, provided fhe does not produce him any children,
and he returns her the portion which was agreed upon
when the marriage firft took place.

Am rg

Among my patients in the Harem, was one of the Moorish concubines, who with a handsome set of features had united an intolerable share of pride and affectation, the effects of which I experienced in the most difgusting degree. I was defired to adminifter to her a remedy for a flight complaint of the ftomach, with which she had been affected for a few days. The medicine was to be of fo gentle a nature as not to create the flighteft degree of pain, or any inconvenience whatever. Determined that she should have no reafon to complain on that account, I prepared her a powder, which, had she given it to a new-born infant, would have proved as inoffenfive as to herfelf.

'The lady, however, ftill apprehenfive of its bad effects, obliged her younger fifter, who was likewife a concubine in the Harem, to take it by way of trial; and then, if it agreed, it was her intention to have had another dofe for herfelf. Unfortunately for me, the young lady, at the idea of being compelled to take a medicine of which she was not in want, foon after she had fwallowed it became very fick, which fo alarmed her fifter, that she immediately fent for me, and upbraided me in the fevereft language, for fending a medicine which had nearly deftroyed the young lady, who had been in the moft violent agonies the whole day; adding, that had she not been poffeffed of a very ftrong conftitution, she muft inevitably have perifhed. She tauntingly obferved, that she had formed a better opinion of the Chriftians than she now found they deferved; and afked me imperioufly, whether I was a proper perfon to un-

dertake

dertake the cure of the fultana? As it was impoffible that I could be pleafed with thefe ignorant and unmerited reproaches, and as I was well aware that fince I had no directions to attend any perfon but Lalla Zara, it was entirely a matter of favour in me to comply at all with their requeft, I embraced the opportunity of at once filencing her ill-timed loquacity, and effectually putting a ftop to fimilar impertinence from any other quarter. I explained to her, in the firft place, that fo far from the medicines having the tendency of which fhe accufed them, that they in reality were of much too mild a nature for a perfon of her conftitution. I added, that fince fhe entertained fuch fufpicions of them from the firft, how could fhe be fo deftitute of affection and feeling as to compel her fifter to take what fhe would not venture upon herfelf, without regard to the difference of her age, or to the ftate of the health? That her ungrateful behaviour would operate as a difcouragement to me, and would perhaps prevent my affording affiftance to many of the other ladies, whofe complaints might require much more attention than hers did; and that in future fhe could not expect to receive from me, if it fhould even be neceffary, the fmalleft affiftance. She now began to relent, and acknowledged that fhe had been rather too warm, adding many apologies, and concluded with wifhing me a happy return to my country and friends.

I could adduce many other anecdotes to illuftrate the ignorance and pride of thefe unfortunate women; but this I think will be fufficiently convincing to anfwer the purpofe. It may not be improper

proper to add, that this little āltercation proved afterwards of great fervice to me in the Harem, by convincing the ignorant part of it that I paid very little attention to their caprice.

Obferving that the eunuchs kept a very clofe and watchful eye over me when I vifited the Harem, I always took care that my deportment in their prefence fhould be fuch as to give them no reafon for any complaint againft me. When in the apartments of my patients I fometimes fo far forgot myfelf, as to enter into a pretty long converfation; but I found that the eunuch was always difpofed to interrupt our entertainment, by hinting that I had already ftaid too long, and muft therefore depart. With Lalla Douyaw, however, they feemed to have lefs influence; and though fhe thought it prudent to make them occafional prefents, yet fhe never would fuffer me to leave the room till by her own requeft.

In one of my vifits I obferved a proceffion, which upon inquiry I found was intended as an invocation to God and Mahomet for rain, of which there had been a fcarcity for feveral preceeding months. The proceffion was commenced by the youngeft children in the Harem, who were barely able to walk, two a-breaft, and thefe were followed by the next in age, till a length a great part of the women fell into the groupe, making altogether upwards of a hundred perfons. They carried on their heads their prayers written on paper, pafted on a fquare board, and proceeded through all the courts finging hymns, the purport of which was adapted to the folemn occafion. I was informed that they had continued this cere-

N 4

mony

money every day during the whole of the dry weather, and were to repeat it till their prayers were attended with fuccefs.

Though the emperor occafionally came into the Harem, yet it was more ufual for him to give notice to thofe ladies whofe company he wifhed, to attend in his apartment; when they made a point of fetting off their charms to the beft advantage. When in his prefence they paid him eve:y attention which a common flave would fhew to his mafter, and never ventured to offer their opinion, except by his approbation.—But to return to the Moorifh ladies.

From the idea which is fo prevalent with this people, that corpulency is the moft infallible mark of beauty, the women ufe a grain which they name Ellhouba, for the purpofe of acquiring that degree of perfonal excellence at which they afpire: this they powder and eat with their Cufcofoo. They likewife take, with the fame intention, large quantities of pafte, heated by the fteam of boiling water, which they fwallow in the form of bolufes. It is certainly true, that the number of corpulent women in this country is very confiderable, but it is probable that this circumftance arifes as much from their very confined and inactive mode of life, as from any of the particular means which they employ to produce that effect.

The drefs of the ladies confifts of a fhirt, with remarkably full and loofe fleeves, hanging almoft to the ground, the neck and breaft of which are left open, and their edges are neatly embroidered with gold. They wear linen drawers, and over the fhirt a Caftan, which is a drefs fomething

fimilar

similar in form to a loose great coat without
sleeves, hanging nearly to the feet, and is made
either of silk and cotton or gold tissue. A sash of
fine linen or cotton folded is tied gracefully round
the waist and its extremities fall below the knees.
To this sash two broad straps are annexed, and
passing over each arm over the shoulders form a
cross on the breast, and to that part of it which
passes between the breast and shoulder of each arm
is fixed a gold tortoise, carelessly suspending in front
a gold chain. Over the whole dress is extended
a broad silk band of the Fez manufacture, which
surrounds the waist, and completes the dress, except when they go abroad, and then they invest
themselves in a careless manner with the Haick.

The hair is plaited from the front of the head
backwards in different folds, which hang loose
behind, and at the bottom are all fixed together
with twisted silk. Over the heads they wear a
long piece of silk about half a yard wide, which
they tie close to their head, and suffer the long
ends, which are edged with twisted silk, to hang
behind in an easy manner nearly to the ground.
The remainder of the head-dress is completed by
a common silk handkerchief which surrounds the
head like a woman's close cap, differing from it
only by being fixed in a full bow behind instead
of in front. At the upper part of each ear hangs
a small gold ring half open, which has at one end
a cluster of precious stones, sufficient nearly to
fill up the vacancy occasioned by the opening of
the ring. At the tip, or lower part of the ear, is
likewise suspended a broad and solid gold ring,
which is so large that it reaches as low as the

N 5

neck,

neck, and which, as well as the other, has a cluf-
ter of precious ftones, in proportion to the fize of
the ring. The ladies wear on their fingers feveral
fmall gold rings, fet with diamonds or other precious ftones, and on the wrifts broad and folid
gold bracelets, fometimes alfo fet with precious
ftones. Their necks are ornamented with a great
variety of bead and pearl necklaces. Below thefe
a gold chain furrounds the neck, and fufpends in
front a gold ornament.

Like the men, the Moorifh women wear no
ftockings, but ufe red flippers, curioufly embroidered with gold which they take off when they
enter their rooms. Immediately above the ankle,
each leg is furrounded with a large folid gold
ring, which is narrow in front, but very broad
behind.

The ladies paint their cheeks of a deep red,
and ftain their eye-lids and eye-brows with a black
powder which I apprehend to be antimony. It is
a branch of artificial beauty in this country, to
produce a long black mark on the forehead,
another on the tip of the nofe, and feveral others
on each cheek. The chin is ftained of a deep red,
and thence down to the throat runs a long black
ftripe. The infide of the hands, and the nails,
are ftained of a deep red, fo deep indeed, that in
moft lights it borders on black; and the back of
the hands have feveral fancy marks of the fame
colour. The feet are painted in a fimilar manner
with the hands.

I feldom obferved in the Harem the women at
any employment but that of forming themfelves
into different circles for the purpofe of converfation,

tion, fometimes in the open courts, at others in the different apartments. As they are not permitted to enter the mofques, they pray at the appointed times in their own chambers. The Moors, indeed, entertain the prejudice which is commonly attributed to the Muffulmen in general, that the female fex are altogether an inferior fpecies of animals, merely formed to be flaves to the pleafures of men, whofe falvation is confequently not of fo much importance; and with this fentiment the conduct of the men towards them in every inftance correfponds. The Moors likewife affign other reafons for not permitting their females to enter their places of worfhip: they affert that it would be not only contrary to the cuftom which prevails in the country, of not allowing the fexes to meet together in any particular fpot, but it might alfo, by creating loofe and improper ideas, draw off the attention from their devotion.

The women have their Talbas as well as the men their Talbs. Thefe perfons who are either wives or concubines, juft as it happens, and whofe principal qualifications appear to be reading or writing, teach the younger part of the Harem to repeat their prayers, and the older females they inftruct in the laws and principles of their religion.

All the emperor's daughters, and the children of his concubines, as foon as they were of a proper age, were fent to Tafilet, where they finifhed their education, and by intermarrying with the defcendants of his anceftors they ferved to people that extraordinary city—extraordinary on this account, that the inhabitants of it are all Sharifs, or the fuppofed lineal defcendants of Mahomet, and

are

are moſt of them collaterally or otherwiſe related to the preſent royal family of Morocco. Muley Iſhmael, who, as I before obſerved, was grandfather to the late emperor, had three hundred children at Tafilet, and their deſcendants are now ſuppoſed to amount to nine thouſand who all live in the ſame place.

The ſons of the emperor's wives are conſidered as princes, who have each an equal claim to the empire, and as ſuch are always reſpected. If they have not diſobliged their father, they are generally appointed to the government of ſome of the provinces, where, in the capacity of Baſhaws, their principal object is the accumulation of riches.

The reader will have obſerved, that I reſerved my obſervations on the female part of ſociety in this country, till I had given ſuch a general account of the Harem as might ſerve for a proper introduction to that part of my ſubject. By this arrangement I have relieved myſelf from the tedi-ouſneſs of repetition, and my readers from that obſcurity which naturally enſues when information is imparted in a disjointed ſtate. A few obſervations will ſerve to complete the deſcription.

The Mooriſh women may be divided into two claſſes; the black or negro women, and the white.

The firſt are either ſlaves or have been ſo formerly; and from their ſervices, or through the favour of their proprietors have obtained their freedom. Theſe women have all the characters, both with reſpect to diſpoſition, features, and complexion, peculiar to the country from which they are brought. Many of them are in the ſituation of concubines, and others in that of domeſtics. Their male children are all brought up to

ſerve

ferve in the army of the emperor.—To this clafs may be added the mulattoes, both male and female, who are the production of a Moor and a Negro woman, and are confequently very numerous in this empire; but as they differ but little in character from the Negroes, and are only diftinguifhed from them being indulged with their freedom, I fhall pafs them over without any further obfervations.

Thofe of the female fex who may be properly confidered as natives of the country, are of a white, or rather a fallow complexion. From the very limited fphere in which they are allowed to act, and the contempt in which they are held as members of fociety, their characters admit of very little of that variety which diftinguifhes the European women. Happy, perhaps, it is for them, that the fun of knowledge has never beamed upon their gloomy prifons, fince it could only ferve to enlighten them to a fenfe of their own mifery, difgrace, and fervitude! Happy is that accommodating power, which providence has vouchfafed to human-kind, which adapts them to their feveral fituations! and happy it is that the information of mankind is generally fuch as fuits the fphere in which they are deftined to act!

Educated with no other view than for the fenfual purpofes of their mafter, or hufband, the chief object of the female fex of this country is to adminifter to his pleafure, and by the moft abject fubmiffion to alleviate the rigours of that fervitude to which they are doomed. When in the prefence of their defpot, both wives and concubines are obliged to manifeft the fame refpect as his com-

common

mon flaves; and though all are not confined clofely to their houfes as is cuftomary in the emperor's Harem, yet when they do go out they are obliged to be extremely circumfpect in concealing their faces, and cautious in every part of their de-meanour. Women of diftinction, however, are very feldom allowed to go abroad; it is only thofe of the loweft clafs which are ufually feen in the ftreets, and even thefe are fo difguifed and wrapped up in their Haicks, that they appear more like a bale of cloth put in motion, than a human form.

If they happen to meet an European in the country, at a time when no Moor is in fight, they feldom mifs the opportunity of difplaying their features, by throwing the Haick on one fide, and even to laugh and converfe with him, though always with the utmoft rifk, as the eye of jealoufy, it is well known, never flumbers.

If an European or a Jew fhould be caught in a clandeftine connection with a Moorifh woman, he is obliged to become a convert to the Mahometan faith, or his life would be forfeit; and the woman, I was informed, is punifhed either by burning or drowning, though I cannot fay I ever knew an inftance of that dreadful fentence being put in execution. A man indeed muft have uncommon addrefs, and no fmall fhare of caution, to carry on an intrigue of that kind, though on the part of the women of this country he will feldom want for encouragement.

It muft, however, be allowed, that the means which the Moors employ for the prevention of intrigues, very often tend to the encouragement of
them.

them. By dreffing themfelves in the female habit, men may very eafily pafs the ftreets unobferved, as they may reft affured they will not be addreffed or even looked at by the Moors; and if they contrive to call at the houfe when the mafter is from home, they need be under no apprehenfions of being detected when he returns. If he fees a ftrange woman's flippers at the doors of his Harem, he concludes it is a female neighbour, and never approaches the room till the flippers are removed.

The drefs of the opulent females among the Moors, is fimilar to that of the emperor's ladies, differing only in the value of the materials. Thofe of the inferior clafs wear linen drawers, and over them a coarfe woollen frock, tied round the waift with a band. They plait the hair in two folds, from the upper part of the head all the way down behind, wearing over it a common handkerchief tied clofe to the head, and when they go out they wear the Haick.

CHAP.

CHAP. XIII.

Duplicity of the Emperor.—Plan of the Author to effect his Emancipation—unsuccessful.—Application through another Channel.—Curious Present from the Emperor. —Striking Instance of Tyranny.—Personal Application to the Emperor.—Traits of Despotism.—The Emperor's Dispatches obtained.—Commissions from the Ladies in the Harem.—Anecdotes of an English Mulatto. —Journey to BULUANE—Description of that Fortress. —Singular Mode of passing the River.—Arrival at SALLEE—at TANGIER.—Present from the Emperor. —Return to Gibraltar.

TEN days having elapsed since my first attendance on Lalla Zata, the emperor desired my patient to acquaint him what effect the medicines had produced; and being informed that she was apparently in a state of recovery, he sent into the Harem a doubloon piece, wrapped up in one corner of a silk handkerchief, and ordered the lady to present me with it as a compliment for the service I had already rendered her, accompanied with splendid promises, if I succeeded in restoring her to perfect health.

Little reflection was necessary to convince me, that these manœuvres had an aim and tendency very different from that of fulfilling the emperor's engagements relative to my return. It required, therefore, some consideration to determine, whether it would be most prudent to continue my attendance, or exert myself immediately with redoubled vigour to accomplish my emancipation.

The

The latter mode of conduct I refolved upon, for the following reafons.

In the firft place, I had been abfent from the garrifon much longer than was originally intended by government; it was, therefore, impoffible to fay how far the protraction of my refidence in in Morocco might interfere with the arrangements of my fuperiors, or affect the fervice. Secondly, every European with whom I converfed, or correfponded, advifed me by all means to embrace the firft opportunity of returning; fince, though my patient was for the prefent in a recovering ftate, yet, from the caprice and ignorance of the Moors, there was fome reafon to apprehend that fhe might tire of her medicines; and confidering the matter in the moft favourable point of view, fuppofing fhe could be relieved entirely from her complaint, it was not improbable that the women, who had been the original occafion of her illnefs, upon obferving her recovery, might with the fame diabolical malignity which induced them to adminifter the firft dofe of poifon, be inclined to avail themfelves of my attendance, and injure her conftitution a fecond time; while all the ill confequences would infallibly be attributed to my treatment. The age and infirmities of the emperor alfo rendering my fituation very precarious, determined me to employ the earlieft opportunity in effecting my efcape; and the following was the plan which appeared to promife the moft probable fuccefs.

I told my patient that I had brought with me very little more medicine than was fufficient for the cure of Muley Abfulem; and that thofe which
I had

I had adminiftered to her were the few which had
not been ufed; that as they muft neceffarily foon
be exhaufted, and as my attendance on her without medicines could anfwer no purpofe whatever,
I would recommend her for her own fake, to ad-
vife the emperor to fend me to Gibraltar for a
frefh fupply. " Ah !" exclaimed the lady, " there
" is no occafion for your going, the emperor can
" write to the conful for them." For a reply of this
kind I was not wholly unprepared; and as I had
found it neceffary to act a part on this occafion, I
determined to go through with it, and reluctantly
to play the empiric, by informing my patient that
the compofition of thefe medicines was known to
no perfon but myfelf; and therefore to write for
them would be totally ufelefs. This ftatement appeared unanfwerable, and my plan was fo far
crowned with fuccefs. An application, on my
account, was immediately made to the emperor by
all the principal women, whom Lalla Zara had
engaged in her fervice for that purpofe.

The emperor, however, whofe difcernment had
been excellent in his youth, and whofe intellect
was at intervals as vigorous as ever, was not to
be impofed on. He promifed the women more
than he ever intended to perform, and ten days
more elapfed, when I found myfelf as near returning as on my firft arrival at Morocco.

Thus baffled in my attempt, though my inde-
fatigable female agents repeated their application
not feldomer than twice every day, I applied to
a German renegado, who fpoke the Englifh language, and who, from his fituation at court, had
frequent opportunities of feeing the emperor privately,

vately, and intreated of him to procure me a licence to depart. But all that he was able to obtain in my favour, was a renewal of the same fair promises which had been so frequently made, and made with the same sincerity. I must not omit, however, to relate, that in a few days after this application, I received from the emperor a present of two horses, accompanied with a positive assurance of being dispatched immediately home.

One of the horses was young, but was in so wretched and emaciated a state, that he appeared better calculated to afford food for the canine race, than to prove of any utility to a traveller. The other, it must be confessed, was not in so starved and miserable a condition, but then he was completely superannuated, and consequently quite as useless as his companion. He had been presented to the emperor in the morning by a poor man, who, for some trifling disgrace which he had incurred, had brought this horse as an atonement; the man, however, was committed to prison, and and in the afternoon the horse was presented to me.

Before I could get these unparalleled coursers out of the walls of the palace, I was stopped by the porters of four gates, who each demanded a hard dollar as a perquisite annexed to their places. On my arrival at home, two deputy masters of horse also came to my apartment for a present for themselves, and for their chief; so that the reader may easily judge how far I was a gainer by the emperor's munificence!

After this circumstance, several days having elapsed without any prospect of accomplishing

.my

my wishes, I was advised by an European, who had come from Mogodore to Morocco upon busi-ness, as the sureft means of succeeding, to seize the firft opportunity that offered of the emperor's appearing in public, which he feldom did fo as to be feen by ftrangers, and, trufting no longer to other agents, at once afk his majefty for my dif-patches. Fortunately, as I thought, the emperor afforded me an opportunity of feeing him the fol-lowing day; and, though the foldiers would not allow me to approach him fo near as to enable me to fpeak to him, yet I took care to place myfelf in a confpicuous fituation; but after continuing about half an hour, he retired without taking the leaft notice of me, or even appearing to obferve me.

The emperor, upon this occafion, was in one of his open courts on horfeback, with a large umbrella fufpended over his head by a foldier of the negro infantry, who was ftanding in front of the horfe; while two other attendants were on each fide, and with pieces of filk fixed to a cane, were, by an eafy but conftant motion, guarding off the flies from the emperor's face. The minif-ters of ftate were placed in front, and behind them were about a hundred foot foldiers in dif-ferent divifions, forming altogether a kind of crefcent. Some of thefe troops were armed with mufquets, which they held in a ftiff manner clofe to their bodies, with the muzzles pointed perpen-dicularly, while others had no weapon of defence but thick clubs.

The fovereign being at this moment in a good humour, was converfing with his minifters; and,

as

as my interpreter informed me, he was boasting
to them of the mighty actions which the Moors
had performed against the Christians; remarking,
that his predecessors had deprived them of nearly
all the places they had formerly possessed in Barbary, and that he had the satisfaction of having
taken Mazagan from the Portugueze.   The ministers entered very little further into the conversation
than to repeat at the conclusion of each sentence,
Alla Cormus Sidi! in English, May God preserve
the king! which was communicated to the nearest
party of soldiers, and from those to the next, till
they made the palace echo with their voices.

My ill success upon this occasion did not deter
me from making an experiment upon another
favourable opportunity which offered, after the
lapse of a few days.   I then had influence enough
with the soldiers to allow me to approach so very
near the emperor's person, as rendered it utterly
impossible for him to avoid observing me, though
not sufficiently close to enable me to speak to him.
A messenger was consequently dispatched by the
sovereign to know (using his own expression)
what the the Christian wanted.   I returned for
answer, that I came to thank his majesty for the
honour he had conferred on me, by presenting
me with the two horses, at the same time to remind him of his royal promise to send me immediately home.   In consequence of his attention
on first seeing me, I expected every moment to
be ordered into his immediate presence, but in
that respect I was disappointed; for, after con-
versing near half an hour with his ministers, he
retired

retired, and left me in the same state of suspense which I had a few days before experienced. The emperor was on horseback, and was endeavouring to explain to his auditors the beauties of various parts of the Koran, and laid a particular stress on those passages which teach the followers of Mahomet to detest the Christians.

Such repeated disappointments, after having exerted myself to the utmost in every mode I could devise, it must be allowed were sufficient to induce me to consider my situation as desperate; and I felt myself totally at a loss what further steps could be adopted in this very critical situation. The uneasiness I experienced at this moment was happily not of long continuance, for the day following the German renegado brought me the emperor's letter of dispatch, consisting merely of a few lines addressed to the governor of Tangier, ordering him to permit me to embark, with my two horses, for Gibraltar.

The reader will too easily anticipate the extreme pleasure I felt at the idea of shortly leaving a country where I had experienced such a continued series of ingratitude, disappointment, and uneasiness, to render it at all necessary for me to enlarge upon that topic. It will be sufficient to say, that I lost no time in making the necessary preparations for the journey, and in availing myself of the earliest opportunity to take my leave of the ladies in the Harem, most carefully avoiding to communicate to them the contents of the emperor's letter. Had they known, indeed, that I was not to return, it is probable they would have employed

the

the fame influence for my detention, which they had before exerted before in favour of my liberation, and moft likely with greater fuccefs.

It is humiliating and unpleafant in the higheft degree to ftoop to deception upon any occafion; to be obliged, therefore, in juftice to myfelf, and for my own perfonal fafety, to carry on a fyftematical plan of duplicity, was not the leaft of the hardfhips to which I was compelled to fubmit in this country. I could not, however, now retreat; and, as I knew that Gibraltar furnifhed many articles which were not to be procured in Barbary, I made an offer of my fervices to the ladies; and received the follow commiffions, for the faithful execution of which, on my return from Gibraltar, I was obliged to pledge myfelf.

For Lalla Batoom, the queen of the Harem, a fet of elegant, but very fmall cups and faucers.

For Lalla Douyaw, the emperor's favourite wife, a neat mahogany tea-board, with four fhort feet, to have two drawers, and to be elegantly ornamented with glaffes; a fet of very fmall Indian cups and faucers; a fet of different kinds of perfumed waters.

For Lalla Zara, my patient, nine yards of yellow, the fame of crimfon, and the fame of cochineal coloured damafk; the fame quantities and colours in fatins; one dozen of Indian cups and faucers; one hundred large red beads; one cheft of tea and fugar; a large quantity of coffee and nutmegs.

For one of the concubines, a large portion of different coloured fattins and filks; a variety of handfome pearls; a fet of Indian cups and faucers;

two

two fmall mahogany boxes for cloaths; two japanned tea-boards, the one to be white and the other yellow.

For another concubine, fome perfumed waters; a mahogany beadftead and pofts; a green Dutch box.

For Lalla Talba, a prieftefs, a handfome prefent, which fhe leaves to my tafte and choice.

For the daughter of Muley Hafem, a mahogany cheft with two drawers; a flafk of lavender water.

For Lalla Zara's nurfe, twelve large red beads.

For two of the eunuchs, each a filver watch.

Thefe commiffions may perhaps appear too trifling to deferve infertion; but I have brought them forward to the reader only becaufe thefe little circumftances frequently difplay the peculiar tafte, the manners, the genius of a country, much better than thofe weighty and important tranfactions in which the paffions common to human nature muft be interefted, and in which, of confequence, all people in fimilar circumftances muft act and feel alike.

It would have required no trifling fum of money to purchafe all thefe articles; and even when that obftacle was removed, there would arife one ftill greater from the difficulty of tranfportation in this country. As Morocco is an inland city, I was entirely precluded from the fafeft and eafieft of carriages; and by land, many of the articles were fo cumberfome and weighty, that in the bad roads it would have been impracticable to employ mules. I fhould therefore have been reduced to the neceffity of hiring camels, the expence of which,

joined

I

joined to that of the commiffions, would confequently have been enormous.

Having fupplied Lalla Zara with the few medicines which remained, and taken my final leave
of the Harem, my next object was to find out a
new interpreter, fince the perfon whom I had
procured at Mogodore, had it not in his power
to accompany me to to Tangier. In his place
I fixed upon a mulatto, who was born a Chriftian
in one of the Englifh Weft India Iflands, and upon coming to Mogodore as a feaman in an Englifh
veffel, was immediately on account of his complexion, claimed by the Moors as a countryman.
They committed him immediately to prifon, and,
by the influence of hard ufage, at length compelled
him to become a convert to their religion. This
man, who is between fixty and feventy years of
age, has been in the country about feven years,
and was occafionally employed in the public works
by the late emperor. He can fpeak the Englifh,
French, Spanifh, Italian, and Arabic languages,
but the Englifh is moft familiar to him. .

The horfe prefented to me by Muley Abfulem
I mounted myfelf, and made my interpreter ride
thofe of the emperor alternately, that I might give
them every poffible chance of reaching Tangier
alive, in cafe I could not difpofe of them on the
road. Thefe, with three horfe foldiers allowed
by the emperor, two mules for my baggage, and
a mulcteer to take charge of them, formed the
whole of my fuite on the journey.

We departed from Morocco on the 12th of
February 1790, and in three days arrived at the
caftle of Bulnane, which is a journey of about
O
eighty

eighty miles, confifting of an uninterrupted feries of wild uncultivated heath. This caftle was the firft piece of architecture which offered itfelf to our view fince we left Morocco; the country being very thinly inhabited by only a few Arabs, who live in tents. In thefe Douhars or encampments, I endeavoured, on the fcore of fafety, nightly to pitch my tent.

The caftle is fituated on the fummit of a very high and rugged hill, forming on its Northern fide a fteep precipice, at the bottom of which runs a deep and rapid river, named the Morbeya, which I had previoufly paffed at its termination in the ocean at Azamore. As a piece of architecture, this caftle has no recommendation but the ftrength of its walls : it is inhabited by fome Negroes who were banifhed to this place, at the time when Sidi Mahomet thought proper to difband a confiderable portion of his black troops; intending, by that means, to prevent their raifing a mutiny or rebellion in the country, to which, as I have intimated, they are always inclined. To difpofe of them in this manner, therefore, was found policy, as, though they were out of the way of mifchief for the prefent, they might eafily be embodied upon any preffing emergency.

The eminent fituation of this fortrefs, the fteep and rugged precipice, the depth and rapidity of the river below, with the wildnefs of the neighbouring country, fill the mind with a mixture of admiration and fublime horror. But what attracted my attention more than any other circumftance, was the mode in which they pafs this dangerous river. At Azamore, Sallee, Mamora, Larache,

Larache, &c. where the rivers are too deep to be-forded, the traveller is ferried over; and yet at this part, though at no very great diftance from any of the above places, the people are totally ignorant what kind of a machine a boat is. What is ftill more remarkable, the firft people of the country who are obliged to pafs this river in their way from Morocco to all the Northern provinces, and who are as well acquainted with the ufe of boats as the Europeans, are content to fubmit to the crazy fubftitute which they find here, rather than impart to the inhabitants of the caftle this eafy piece of information.

The mode in which thefe people crofs the river, ferved to remind me of a puerile amufement, in which moft boys at one period or other have taken delight. A raft is formed of eight fheep-fkins, filled with air, and tied together with fmall cords; a few flender poles are laid over them, to which they are faftened, and this is the only means ufed at Buluane to conduct travellers with their baggage over the river.

As foon as the raft is loaded, in other words, as foon as it is charged with as much weight as it will bear without finking, a man ftrips, jumps in-to the water, and fwims with one hand, while he pulls the raft after him with the other; and in the mean time, a fecond places himfelf behind, pufhing and fwimming in a fimilar manner. The current at firft carries the apparatus a confiderable way down the river, but by the activity of the fwimmers it is fpeedily extricated, and its contents as quickly landed. The horfes, mules, &c. having every article removed from their backs, are driven

in a body to the water fide, where the Moors immediately get behind them, and by the violence
of their fhouts fo completely terrify the animals,
that one or two of them fpeedily take to flight, and
fet the example, by fwimming, to the reft, when
they immediately follow.

Four days after leaving this river, we arrived
at Sallee, which is about a hundred and ten miles
from Buluane, and one hundred and ninety from
Morocco, without the occurrence of a circumftance
worth relating; the country proving a continuance
of the fame uncultivated heath as far as Menfooria,
which has been defcribed in a former part of this
Tour.

Sallee being the firft town I had feen fince my
departure from Morocco, which was feven days,
I was happy to avail myfelf of my former introduction to the French conful, and remain with
him a couple of nights.   After this agreeable relaxation, I departed for Tangier, where I arrived
on the 26th of February.

As it was evident that the horfes which had been
prefented to me by the emperor, were not worth
the expence of exportation, and indeed feemed
fcarcely able to encounter the journey, I took
every oportunity that offered on the road to difpofe
of them, but my efforts were not attended with
fuccefs; and by the time I arrived at Mamora, they
were fo completely tired, that they would certainly have died had I ufed them another day. I therefore found it neceffary to leave them in the care
of a Venetian gentleman who refided at Mamora,
with a requeft to difpofe of them in the beft manner he could; and, as I did not like to lofe the
                                    advantage

advantage of the order for embarkation, which is always to be confidered as very valuable, fince no horfes are exported but by an exprefs order of the emperor, under his fign manual, I requefted this gentleman to purchafe for me two of the beft that were to be procured in the province, and to fend them after me to Tangier; but they unfortunately did not arrive in time.

In about a fortnight after my arrival at Tangier, an order came down from the emperor, defiring the governor to purchafe at the expence of his royal treafury, two oxen, ten fheep, ten milch goats with their kids, a hundred fowls, and a large proportion of fruit and vegetables of every defcription. Thefe articles were to be prefented to me as from the emperor, in return for my attendance on Lalla Zara; and I was to be allowed permiffion to embark them free of all duty, for Gibraltar. The fame order brought likewife a requeft from the emperor, that I would engage to fend my patient a frefh fupply of medicines.

On the 27th of March I arrived at Gibraltar. It would be trifling with the reader to defcribe my feelings on the firft view of a fpot, protected by Englifh laws, and decorated by Englifh manners. My fenfations, indeed, may be more eafily conceived than they can be expreffed. Let it fuffice to fay, that no wretch, efcaped from the gloomy horrors of a dungeon, could experience more lively pleafure on firft contemplating the light of day, than I felt on the firft view of an Englifh garrifon.

As

As the communication between the garrifon and Barbary was not open at the time of my arrival, the prefent of the emperor proved more valuable than I at firft conceived it. It is obvious, however, that its amount, and indeed the total of all which I received during my refidence in the country, could fcarcely be more than adequate to my expences; much lefs could it be confidered as a compenfation for the great rifk, the trouble, and the anxiety which I had encountered. I had been under the neceffity of drawing upon the conful for confiderable fums, befides what I received through other channels; fo that I returned from my expedition with my curiofity fatisfied, my mind, I truft, in fome degree enlightened, as far as the obfervation of a different country, and different manners, ferves to improve our ftock of knowledge; but, in a pecuniary view, I certainly returned very little better than I went*.

* It is certainly incumbent on me to add, that my fervices in Barbary have fince been handfomely rewarded in the appointment of Surgeon to the 20th or Jamaica Regiment of Light Dragoons.

C H A P. XIV.

*Return of the Author to Barbary.—*TETUAN.*—Town
and Buildings—Port.—Prefent State of the Empire of*
MOROCCO *under* MULEY YAZID.*—Anecdotes rela-
tive to his acceffion.—*MULEY YAZID *fent to* MECCA
*by his Father—his Return—takes Refuge in a Sanc-
tuary.—State of the late Emperor.—Death of* SIDI
MAHOMET.*—Diffention among the Princes.—*MULEY
HASEM *proclaimed Emperor—retracts his Preten-
tions.—Anecdote relative to* MULEY ABDRAHAMAN
—curious Letter from him to MULEY YAZID.*—His
Submiffion.—Peaceable Eftablifhment of* MULEY YA-
ZID.*—Depredations of the Arabs.—Perfecution of the
Jews.—Death of* ALCAIDE ABBAS.*—Character of*
MULEY YAZID.*—Death of* MULEY YAZID.

SOON after my arrival at Gibraltar, I was prevailed upon to digeft and arrange the notes and
obfervations which I had made during my refidence
in Barbary, and to publifh propofals for a narrative of my Tour. In thefe propofals, having
engaged to relate the particulars of the emperor's
death, and of his fons fucceffion, and being defirous
of procuring every information that could ferve
to complete my account of the empire of Morocco,
I obtained leave of abfence for a fhort time from
the garrifon for the purpofe, and was induced
from that motive to pay a fecond vifit to Tangier.
It would be ufelefs to detain the reader with any
further defcription of that place, I fhall therefore
only obferve, that after diligently collecting all
the information political or otherwife, that I could

O 4   procure,

procure, I availed myself of the opportunity of visiting Tetuan, which the new emperor had once more opened to the resort of Christians; and which I had long, with much earnestness, desired to see.

The city of Tetuan is very pleasantly situated at the opening of the Straits into the Mediterranean; it is built on a rising ground between two ranges of high mountains, one of them forming a part of the lesser Atlas. It lies about ten leagues to the East of Tangier, and commands a very beautiful prospect of the Mediterranean, from which it is distant about five miles; and the valley near which it is situated is variegated with gardens, plantations of olives, and vineyards, and is ornamented with a river, which takes its course directly through its centre.

The barren and gloomy appearance of the lofty mountains, which seem almost to project over each side of the town, contrasted with the beautiful verdure with which it is immediately surrounded, the distant view of the sea, and the serpentine direction of the river, which is navigable for small craft as far as Marteen, afford altogether a scene in the highest degree picturesque and romantic.

The town itself is of very considerable extent, and its walls are flanked in different parts with square forts, on which a few small pieces of ordnance are mounted. This fortification, however, is merely calculated to defend the place against an attack from the Arabs, who, when discontented, are ready to plunder every thing which is exposed to their depredations; but it

could

could by no means refift the exertions of a regular army.   Befides thefe fmall forts, there is a fquare caftle on the fummit of the hill, on which twenty-four pieces of cannon are mounted; though this is alfo but a weak and ill-conftructed piece of fortification, yet from its elevated fituation it commands the town in every direction.

The ftreets of Tetuan are very narrow, filthy, and many of them are nearly arched over by the houfes.   Of the intention of thefe projections I could form no conception, unlefs they are meant, by keeping off the rays of the fun, to render the ftreets cooler in the fummer feafon.   If fo, it muft on the other hand be allowed, that they alfo prevent a free circulation of air, which, in a hot climate, and in ftreets fo narrow and filthy, muft be greatly injurious to the health of the inhabitants.'

Though the houfes have a very mean appearance from the ftreets, yet their apartments in general are roomy, tolerably convenient, and well furnifhed; and, contrary to thofe of Tangier, are built two ftories high.   The Elcaifferia, or fair for the difpofal of goods, is filled with fhops, containing a great variety of very valuable articles, both of European and their own manufacture. From Fez they procure the articles of that place, as well as thofe of Tunis, Algiers, Alexandria, and Guinea.   From Spain and Gibraltar they import thofe of Europe, for which they give in return provifions and fruit of every defcription; of all the towns in the empire, therefore, Tetuan may now be confidered as next to Fez in commercial importance.

O 5

As

As the Moorish inhabitants are principally merchants on a large fcale, they are opulent, much
more polifhed and acceffible to ftrangers than thofe
of moft of the other towns in this empire. Their
complexions are generally fair, and they are altogether a well-looking people.   On our firft arrival,
from the novelty of feeing Chriftians in the town
after an exclufion of nearly twenty years, when
we walked the ftreets the people univerfally ran
out of their houfes to look at us; and a very confiderable body of them for fome time followed us
wherever we went.   They, however, by no means
offered us any kind of infult; on the contrary, indeed, being informed that we were Englifh, they
expreffed every. mark of fatisfaction, and many
of them invited us to their gardens.   The Moors
were always partial to the Englifh in preference
to every other European nation; they even pro-
feffed their attachment at the very time when Sidi
Mahomet was upon fuch ill terms with our court;
and fince Muley Yazid's acceffion, they have given
the moft unlimited fcope to the expreffion of their
partiality.

The Mofques of Tetuan are very large, numerous, and appear to have by far a greater claim
to magnificence, than thofe in the other towns of
the empire.

The Jews in this place, previous to the late
plunder by order of the new emperor, were wealthy; they live by themfelves in a feparate part of
the town, where they are fhut out every night
from the Moors; their women are remarkable for
their clearnefs of complexion, and the beauty of
their features.

The

The port of Tetuan, is situated at about two miles distance from the sea, and is named Marteen; at this place there is, however, only a single house, which is used for the purpose of collecting the customs. As the mouth of the river on which it is situated, is now nearly choaked up with sand, it only admits of small craft; and even these can proceed no further than Marteen, where there are usually a few of the emperor's row-gallies laid up to winter.

The entrance of the river is defended by a high and square tower, on which are mounted twelve pieces of cannon. This fortification might answer the purpose of preventing the approach of small vessels, but it is by no means calculated to oppose any considerable force. The bay, or more properly the road, of Tetuan, is formed by a high point of land which runs out into the sea a considerable distance to the West of the river, and will only shelter vessels in a westerly wind; when it veers round to the Eastward, they are obliged to leave the bay, and retire to some safer port.

During my continuance at Tetuan, I was not inattentive to the main object of this expedition: but, as the information which I could collect there, was not materially different from what I learned at Tangier, I shall blend the different accounts together, and hasten to gratify the reader's curiosity, as far as it lies in my power, concerning the succeeding events which took place in the empire, from the time of my leaving Morocco to the accession and death of the late emperor. The information which I obtained in consequence of my second visit to Barbary, concerning the events that

took

took place in the empire fubfequent to the death of Sidi Mahomet, and which I communicated in my firft edition, were the moft authentic and beft I could, in the fhort time I was in the country, procure; fince my return to Gibraltar, however, feveral new circumftances have arifen, which have obliged me to alter both my original plan and fentiments, and to carry on my narrative up to the death of Muley Yazid, whofe conduct will now appear in a very different light to what it did at the firft view. The difficulty of obtaining an impartial account of the politics of a country in which individuals are cautious to a degree how they exprefs their fentiments, will be deemed, 1 hope, a fufficient apology for my concifenefs on this fubject, as well as for any errors into which I inadvertently may have fallen.

Muley Yazid, whofe mother is the offspring of an Englifh renegado, having incurred, a few years ago, his father's difpleafure, was fent on a pilgrimage to Mecca; the old emperor hoping, that by feeing the world he would, in a maturer age, reform, and be brought to a fenfe of his duty.

Upon his approaching the frontiers, about four years ago, very ftrong and feemingly authentic reports were circulated, that he was on his march with a large army to dethrone his father. Thefe rumours could not fail to affect the old man with confiderable anxiety, which, however, was afterwards removed by the retreat of Muley Yazid to Tunis, without having made any hoftile exertions whatever.

In the fummer of 1789 the prince privately entered the country, and took refuge, as has already been intimated, in a fanctuary named Muley Abfulem. To this facred fpot, which is held in great veneration by the Moors, he retired as a place of fafety, without any intention of attacking his father, but merely to remain there in readinefs to declare himfelf, when the emperors death fhould take place, which, from his great age and infirmities, was evidently an event which could not be very diftant. Here he had no people about him, but three or four faithful attendants, and lived a ftrictly retired life, as far removed as can well be conceived from that ftate and confequence which are ufually affected by princes.

The old emperor, however, confidered his fon's intentions in a far different point of view, and ufed every ftratagem he could invent to draw him out of the fanctuary, but without fuccefs.

At one time he wrote him word, that if he would come to court, he would reinftate him in his affections, and acquiefce in every demand he would make; or, if he chofe to leave the country, he would allow him fufficient to live in Turkey, or at Mecca, refpected as a prince. On another occafion he threatened to attack him, pull down the fanctuary, and take him away by force. To all thefe letters, the prince, by the prudent advice of his mother, with whom he kept up a private correfpondence, always evaded giving a pofitive anfwer. He affured his father of his affection, duty, and the purity of his intentions; and, without refufing to acquiefce in his wifhes, fent fome excufe or other, explaining why he could not for the prefent comply, but promifing that he would foon.

It

It is difficult to conjecture, whether the emperor would have used any violence towards his son, in case he had repaired to court. But it is well known, that the old monarch wished particularly, that Muley Abfulem might be his fucceffor, and that he had a private diflike to Muley Yazid; which were fufficient motives for the prudent conduct of the latter.

The various reports that were circulated through the country, and particularly by the people at court, that Muley Yazid's intentions were hoftile to his father, and the great efteem in which he knew he was held by every individual in the country, made the emperor confider this fon as a very dangerous rival.

I have already fo fully reprefented the ftate in which the emperor was at that period, that it would be only a repetition to expatiate on it at prefent. It will be fufficient to fay, that after three or four months unfuccefsful negociations, the emperor fent down his fon Muley Hafem to Tangier, with an army of fix thoufand Negroes, which were to be reinforced by men drawn from the neighbouring provinces. The prince's directions were, to offer a confiderable reward from the emperor to the perfons who had the care of the fanctuary, if they would furrender or expel Muley Yazid; but if they refufed to comply with this requeft, he was to pull down the fanctuary, to feize Muley Yazid; and put every man, woman, and child, in the neighbourhood, to the fword. This fanguinary edict, however, the Sharifs had fpirit or enthufiafm enough to refift*, and Muley

* See pag 156, where this order of the emperor refpecting

Hafem, not having fecured the confidence of his troops, was afraid to attack his brother. When they were encamped at Tangier, he did not even venture to fleep among them, but at night always retired to the caftle.

Difgufted with this fruitlefs attempt, the emperor called his fon a coward and a trifler; and immediately ordered Alcaide Abbas, the commander in chief of the black army, and the beft officer in his fervice, to fupercede Muley Hafem in the command. Abbas carried a confiderable reinforcement to the army already at Tangier, and was foon after joined by Muley Slemma, the late emperors full brother. Thefe two officers were directed to encamp near the fanctuary, and wait there till joined by the emperor himfelf, with a confiderable army from the fouthward.

For this purpofe the emperor left Morocco on the 29th March 1790, and travelled on horfeback. At the time he was paffing out at the gate of the city, the umbrella, which is always carried before the emperor, and in that country is the diftinctive mark of royalty, fuddenly broke in two, and the head was carried up in the air to a confiderable height before it fell.

That the enfign of royalty fhould be in fo unaccountable a manner broken, at the very moment of his departure on a journey, upon the fuccefs of which the fate of his empire feemed to depend, was an accident which the emperor, who was remarkably fuperftitious, confidered as a

ing Muley Yazid, and the Sharifs reafons for not obeying it, are fully explained.

bad omen, and he was certain portended fome calamity which was to befal him on the road.

In confequence of thefe apprehenfions he became remarkably uneafy, penfive, and indifpofed; and it is not improbable that this trifling circumftance, united to a previous weak ftate of body and mind, contributed materially to haften his death.

From the time of his departure till the fecond of April he made unufually fhort ftages; and on that day he ordered letters to be written to Muley Slemma and Alcaide Abbas, in very ftrong teims arraigning the conduct of Muley Yazid, and directing them to encamp at the bottom of the mountain on which the fanctuary was fituated, and to block it up in fuch a manner, that the prince fhould not find it poffible to make his efcape. Soon after the figning of thefe letters, he complained of a pain in his head and ftomach, and was feized with vomiting. He contined, there-fore, for the fpace of two days, without being able to proceed on his journey. On the 5th of April, as he found himfelf unable to ride on horfe-back, he ordered his people to place him in his litter, and commanded his own phyfician to ac-company him. When he halted on his journey, in the evening, he was vifited by a large body of people, who came to pay their refpects to him. For thefe adventitious vifitors the fovereign ordered a great feaft to be prepared; he tafted of every difh that was fent to them, and foon after complained of a pain in his bowels.

On the following day he proceeded on his journey, and in the evening the pains of his head and ftomach were confiderably increafed, and were

foon.

foon after followed by a vomiting of blood.   He
now began to exprefs a fenfe of his approaching
diffolution; and, it is faid, ordered a letter to be
written to Muley Yazid, telling him, that he
hoped God would forgive him, and blefs him;
but, as the truth of this circumftance is difputed,
I give it as a mere report.

His uneafinefs concerning his fituation did not
prevent him from regularly and devoutly performing every part of his ablutions and prayers, and
fulfilling every ceremony of his religion.   On the
two fucceeding days the emperor took very fhort
journies, and, finding he had no profpect of a
recovery, he defired that his women would have
him carried to Rabat, and buried in a vault which
he had built in his palace for that purpofe.

On the 11th of April, upon entering the town
of Rabat, he expired in his carriage, without
fpeaking a fingle word.   The news of his death
was not made public till the following day, when
he was buried in his palace, agreeably to his orders,
with all the honours ufually paid to fuch per-
fonages.

The death of Sidi Mahomet was certainly a
moft fortunate event for the people of the Northern
provinces, and particularly for thofe who had
manifefted any attachment to Muley Yazid.   His
intention, indeed, was no lefs than the total ex-
tirpation of all the inhabitants; and it is impoffible
to forefee where his cruelties might have terminated. On the other hand, it was not the intention
of Muley Yazid to come to any engagement with
his father; therefore, as the emperor approached,
he

he would have retired, till he had got beyond the boundaries of his fathers dominions.

Sidi Mahomet, when he died, was in the 81ſt year of his age, and the 33d of his reign. His character has already occupied ſo large a portion of theſe pages, that it would be entirely ſuperfluous to make any additions.

It is well known that, a few months previous to his death, he was thoroughly convinced how greatly he had fallen a dupe to Spaniſh intrigues. By bribing the miniſters, and obſcuring the mental eye of the ſovereign by large and repeated pre-ſents, the court of Spain procured leave to export great quantities of corn free of duty, the cuſtoms of which, at a moderate computation, would have brought him in five times the value of the preſents he received. This indeed was not the only incon-venience which the country ſuffered through this imprudent conceſſion; for the drought had been ſo exceſſive, the preceding year, that a ſcarcity of corn had already taken place, and occaſioned an univerſal murmur among the people: ſo that had the exportation of that article been allowed a little time longer, a general famine, and con-ſequently an univerſal rebellion, muſt have taken place. Beſides this, out of pique to the Engliſh, the Spaniards engaged the emperor to refuſe the ſupplying of Gibraltar with proviſions, by which another conſiderable defalcation was made in his revenue. Latterly, however, the monarch was ſo ſenſible of theſe impoſitions, that he raiſed the duties upon thoſe proviſions and corn which the Spaniards exported, to ſo immoderate a height,

that

that they were obliged to fend home their veffels empty.

Had he lived to this time, it is a matter of doubt, whether affairs with Spain would have ended only by increafing the duties; for he was fo entirely irritated by their conduct, that it is not improbable that a rupture between the two courts would have been the confequence. On the other hand, his differences with England, from the fame circum-ftances, would have been moft probably adjufted and fettled, perfectly to the fatisfaction of our court. Indeed he had given directions for that purpofe two days previous to his death.

I have already mentioned that in this country the fucceffion to the empire, though reftricted to the fame family, is not limited to any particular branch, but depends on the influence each of the princes may have in the country, and particularly on the army. The government may therefore be confidered as partly hereditary, and partly elec-tive*. Wealth, however, is not the only means of obtaining this influence; for Muley Yazid, the late emperor, was the pooreft of the royal brothers.

When the news of the emperor's death reached Muley Slemma and Alcaide Abbas, they certainly fell back with the army towards Sallee; but what-ever they might have in view by fo doing, they

* The Mahometan law particularly directs, and it is well underftood by the more enlightened part of the Moors, that the eldeft fon, is the next heir to the throne; but owing to the influence of the black army, and the ignorance of the majority of the people, this circumftance in the empire of Morocco is but feldom attended to.

could

could meet with no support. At Morocco, the old emperor left his two fons Muley Hafem and Muley Ouffine entrufted with the joint government of that city, ordering the inhabitants to pay to the firft prince the fum of ten thoufand hard dollars, and the latter five. The partiality, however of the monarch, fo greatly irritated Muley Ouffine, that he difcharged a mufquet at his brother upon fome cafual difpute, but miffed him. Muley Hafem, who at Tangier had manifefted a want of refolution, intimidated by this conduct of his brother, retired, fhut himfelf up in the palace, and left Muley Ouffine in full poffeffion of the whole of the money.

As foon as Muley Hafem received intelligence of his father's death, he publifhed it to the people of Morocco, at the fame time prefenting himfelf as the immediate heir of the crown. He was foon after proclaimed by a few mountaineers; but the principal people of the city declaring in favour of Muley Yazid, Muley Hafem was obliged to give up his pretentions, and retire to his late father's houfe.

Muley Ouffine took the firft opportunity of leaving Morocco, and repaired to Muley Abdrahaman, who refided among the Arabs in the moft fouthern part of Suz. His motives for this ftep are differently acccounted for. It is by fome attributed to an apprehenfion of the new emperor's refentment, on account of the robbery he had committed on Muley Hafem; while others allege it was on the fcore of having formerly killed one of Muley Yazid's children.

Muley

Muley Abdrahaman had, during his father's life, amaffed a very confiderable fum of money, by his induftry and attention to commercial affairs, and was at one time in great favour with his father. The old man, however, of whofe immoderate love of riches I have already had occafion to fpeak, foon became jealous of his fon's wealth, and confequently defirous of poffeffing it. To effect his purpofe without oppofition, he diffembled his intentions fo far as to appoint his fon governor of Sallee, a place of no inconfiderable importance; and, in confequence of this appointment, Muley Abdrahaman, having packed up all his money and valuables on mules, in the moft affectionate manner took leave of his father, and proceeded on his journey. He had not, however, long proceeded in peace, before the emperor fent a large detachment of troops after him, with orders to ftrip him of every article in his poffeffion; which they fo effectually accomplifhed, that they left him mafter only of an old rufty piftol. While the prince, naturally irritated by fuch unworthy treatment, made a rafh but moft folemn vow, that he would never fee his father's face again; and he immediately retired to the mountains in Suz, where he has continued ever fince.

The emperor endeavoured to perfuade his fon to return to court, by offering him large prefents of money, and by the moft fplended promifes; but the prince always anfwered, that he never could comply with his father's requeft, as he was convinced his word was not to be trufted. Upon which the old monarch included him in the curfe he had uttered againft Muley Yazid.

When

When the emperor's death came to be known in Suz, forty thousand Arabs immediately tendered their spontaneous services to assist Muley Abdrahaman in ascending the throne, and in resisting the pretentions of Muley Yazid; and it was generally expected that he would have made the attempt, as the following letter was received from him by the new emperor while he resided at Fez. I insert it as a specimen of Moorish composition, and of Moorish politeness.

"I have heard of my father's death, and that "you have left the sanctuary, and call yourself "emperor.—Go to your hole, you rat, or meet "me at Morocco; where I will convince you, that "Fez is not a place for an emperor."

Though this was the only prince, in whose power it was to make any serious opposition to Muley Yazid; yet he since gave up that intention, wrote a letter of congratulation and submission to his brother, and made an offer of his services. Thus amidst so many difficulties, and with so many competitors, all of them considering themselves as equally entitled to the succession, was Muley Yazid seated on the throne without the shedding of a drop of blood, and almost as peaceably as in the best-regulated state in Europe.

If we look back on the changes of masters which this empire had previously experienced, I believe we shall scarcely find an instance where affairs have been settled so successfully and happily as on this occasion. The only disturbances that took place after the old emperor's death, were some predatory incursions of the Arabs into the southern provinces, who, under a pretence of supporting
Muley

Muley Hafem, plundered Morocco, and obliged the Chriftians and Jews to take fhelter in the caftle. Mogodore was faved by being fo well fortified, and by the great exertions of the governor and inhabitants. The country, however, adjacent to thofe places, even as far as Sallee, was in fuch a ftate of confufion that travelling became totally impracticable for a confiderable time.

The town of Dar Beyda, which is garrifoned by about an hundred and fifty Negroes, who on feveral occafions had made themfelves difagreeable to the furrounding Arabs, nearly fhared the fame fate as Morocco. As foon as the emperor's death was made known there, the Arabs bought up all the powder and ball that was in the town, before the inhabitants were aware of their intentions. For balls, which were ufually fold at the price of eight or nine for a blanquil, the Arabs now confented to purchafe at the rate of two blanquils each, and at laft they completely ftripped the town of all its fmall ammunition. Having effected this firft ftep, they affembled in great numbers in the neighbourhood of the town, armed with mufquets.

The governor, alarmed at the appearance of fo confiderable a body of Arabs, went out with fifty foldiers, and demanded of them their intentions in thus tumultuoufly affembling together. They replied, that as the country and town people were both equally fubjects of the empire, it became neceffary that deputations from each party fhould meet in the town, to determine upon the perfon proper to be elected their fovereign.

In return, the governor anfwered, that he had no objection whatever to a few of their principal
people

people coming into the town, for the purpofe they mentioned; but that he could not fee any reafon who fo many perfons fhould on fuch an occafion be collected together, and prefent them-felve in a hoftile ftate againft a city of the empire. To this obfervation the Arabs did not condefcend to reply, but infifted upon being admitted into the town; and were as obftinately refufed. After fome parlying, however, they promifed to difperfe, if the governor would pay them two thoufand dollars. This he refufed, obferving, that in making this demand they were treating the inhabitants of the town like Jews; and that they muft difperfe, or take the confequence. A reply of this nature was calculated to enrage inftead of conciliating the Arabs, and they began to fet the huts on fire, and at the fame time continued to advance towards the town.

Their force at this period was increafing almoft every moment, by numbers who came down from the mountains; and the governor, apprehending immediate danger to the town, privately difpatched a meffenger to the inhabitants, cautioning them to be on their guard againft the Arabs, and at the fame time announcing that he had no opportunity of retiring himfelf.

As the town had been previoufly cleared of its flints, powder, and ball, it is impoffible to de-fcribe the confternation of the people. To add to their diftrefs, fome fmall veffels, which had am-munition on board, had the day before before been unfortunately driven, by bad weather, out of the bay, and the town appeared deftitute of every re-fource. The Spanifh houfe, however, which was

2

fettled

settled at Dar Beyda, and had very confiderable property in the place, advifed the inhabitants to clofe the gates immediately, and to mount on the wall fronting the enemy an old twelve pounder, which was without a carriage, and was the only piece of ordnance in the place. At the fame time they offered three dollars to every man, who would affift in defending the ramparts. Having mounted the gun on the wall, they were ftill at a lofs for one of the moft material articles, viz. powder; there was fome in the magazine, but the governor was on the outfide, and had the key in his cuftody. The Spaniards advifed them by all means, upon fuch a preffing emergency, to break open the door of the magazine, which they immediately did, and with powder only fired off their piece of cannon among the Arabs.

An attack fo unexpected upon the Arabs, who had flattered themfelves that there was neither a gun or powder in the place, put them for fome time into the utmoft confternation, and they began to difperfe. But upon finding that no perfon was wounded, they foon affembled again, with a full determination to attack the town. The Spaniards now advifed the people to load the piece with a ball, which they by accident found, and fire it directly among them. This manœuvre was attended with the moft brilliant fuccefs. The Arabs immediately difperfed, and gave the governor time to re-enter the town with his troops; and at length, being fenfible that they could effect nothing by a regular attack, they next attempted to take the place by ftratagem. For this purpofe, they divided themfelves into two parties; one was posted on the right side of the town, and the other on the left. The party on the right side sent in a deputation to the governor, informing him that they were friends, and requesting that they might be let into the town, to assist him in conquering those on the left, who were enemies, from whom they had deserted. This proposal, however, was obstinately refused on the part of the governor, who desired them to keep at a distance, or take the consequence; upon this the two parties again united, and endeavoured to surprise the town on the water side.

The vessels, which had been driven out the day before, returning about this time, powder, balls, and a few small pieces of cannon were taken out of them; and when the Arabs made their last attack, by night, the town took the alarm, fired on them, and obliged them to retire. The following day the pieces of cannon were mounted in different parts on the walls of the town, which had the desired effect; for the Arabs, finding they had no chance of success, dispersed totally, and went to their different homes. For some time after this circumstance, not one of them was permitted to enter the town, but upon condition that he should first leave his musquet and sword on the outside of the gate.

The Spanish house, during this petty siege, supplied the late emperor's women, who happened to be in the town, on this occasion, with money and other necessaries, and out of their own stores furnished corn to the inhabitants. The new sovereign was so pleased with the conduct of the Spaniards, that he sent them a letter of thanks,

as

as well for their zeal in defending the town, as for the support they afforded to his father's women. Not satisfied, however, with the barren return of thanks, he ordered them also to be repaid the whole of their expences, and sent them a present of two lions.

These were the principal disturbances which took place, in consequence of the emperor's death. By degrees the spirit for plunder, on the part of the Arabs, was less general, and the country became in a state of perfect peace and tranquility.

The news of the emperor's death reached Tangier on the 15th of April; upon which the governor repaired to the great mosque, made a short prayer for Sidi Mahomet, and proclaimed Muley Yazid his successor. After this ceremony, the public crier was placed in a conspicuous situation, where he publicly proclaimed Muley Yazid; in his name denouncing the severest punishment against any person, who should dare to oppose the new sovereign.

As Muley Yazid had been proclaimed both in the church and in the town, the consuls all agreed to write him a letter, condoling with him on his father's decease, and congratulating him upon his accession to the throne. I should have observed, that the only ceremony attending a new emperor's accession to the throne, is a public proclamation in the streets and mosques. When the proclamation takes place in the presence of the emperor, which by the law ought to be performed publicly, at least in the three capitals of the empire, it is customary for all the chief priests and doctors of

P 2

law

law to affemble, with the other great people of the town, and for the Mufti or Cadi to read aloud to the emperor, a fhort recapitulation of fome of the laws of the Koran; which direct, that he fhall preferve the empire, adminifter fpeedy juftice, protect the innocent, deftroy the wicked, and fo far from countenancing and keeping near his facred perfon any adulterer, that he fhall punifh adultery, prevent the exportation of corn and provifions to the prejudice of the people, tax provifions according to their plenty or fcarcity, and forbid ufury to be exercifed towards the poor, which is an abomination before God. He is told, that if he breaks thefe articles, he fhall be punifhed, as he ought to punifh others under a fimilar circumftance.

The fame ceremony is performed before all Bafhaws, Alcaides, and Shaiks, upon their firft receiving their appointment. How far thefe few but excellent admonitions are attended to, either by the emperor or the officers under his command, I have already fufficiently explained in a former part of the narrative.

On the fucceeding day, which was the Moorifh fabbath, all the great people of the town affembled at the mofques, and, with greater ceremony than the day before; prayed for the foul of the deceafed fovereign, and proclaimed Muley Yazid his fucceffor. On the fame day all the Jeweffes of Tangier were ordered by the governor to repair to the caftle, and lament Sidi Mahomet's death; which they performed by loud fhrieks and lamentations.

On

On the 17th, the bashaw communicated to the consuls a letter, which he had received from Muley Yazid at the sanctuary, wherein he ordered the bashaw to conduct all the consuls to him with their presents, under a guard of fifteen soldiers. On the same day a salute of twenty-one guns was fired from the battery, in consequence of an order having arrived for a general release and pardon to all prisoners.

Seven poor sharifs or petty princes, who brought this order, delivered at the same time directions to the consuls to clothe them from head to foot at their own expence. In consequence of this, the consuls furnished each of them with cloth for a caftan, with two britannias, and twenty dollars; to this, as it was not sufficient to satisfy them, they were obliged to add a still further supply of money. On the following day the consuls set off on their journey with the bashaw, and the principal people of the town both, Moors and Jews. In the evening, Reis Mufti Galli, with two other sea captains, arrived at the consul's camp with a letter from the new emperor, inviting them to repair to him at Tetuan, and promising to renew the ancient treaties of peace and commerce with their nations. The captains related, that Muley Yazid had left the sanctuary, and had made his public entrance into Tetuan the day before.

On the 19th of April the consuls arrived in the evening at Tetuan, where upon entering the gates, they were met by a messenger, who informed them that the emperor would give them audience immediately, whilst upon their horses; upon which their baggage was all sent away, and the consuls

all

all ranged themselves in a regular form. After waiting, however, a short time, another messenger came to acquaint them, that the emperor would see them the next day. On the following day, at twelve o'clock at noon, the consuls were sent for to the emperor's camp, where they found the sovereign on horseback, in a very rich Turkish dress, and his horse ornamented with Turkish furniture.

After having asked their respective names and titles, the emperor told the consuls he was at peace with the English and Ragousi, but at war with all the other nations; whose consuls he allowed only four months to retire from his dominions with their property, and ordered them to send him back every thing which belonged to his subjects. On the 22d of April, the consuls had their second audience, at which each of them brought their separate presents.

The emperor now told them, he would remain at peace with all their nations on the same footing as before, requiring of the Spaniards only an ambassador within four months. At this audience he promised the consuls letters to their respective courts, expressive of the same sentiments; and assured them that the bashaw at Tangier should make them out, in terms most agreeable to the consuls. The succeding day the consuls received orders to return to Tangier, at which place the emperor was to deliver to them the papers he had promised.

On the 25th of the same month, the emperor arrived at Tangier, and the day following was waited upon by all the consuls, to congratulate

him

him on his fafe arrival.   The emperor continued at
Tangier till the 29th, during which time he gave
private audiences to thofe confuls who afked them.
He was every day fully employed by people who
came from the different provinces to pay their
homage to him.   Thefe were fuppofed to amount
to no lefs than twenty thoufand.   The bafhaw of
Tangier, who had the commiffion to write out the
letters which the confuls were to fend home to
their refpective courts, behaved in the moft arbitrary and infolent manner towards thofe gentlemen.
He demanded of fome no lefs than two thoufand,
of others fifteen hundred dollars, for the trouble
he had taken, by interfering in their favour with
the new fovereign; at the fame time pofitively refufing to make out or deliver the letters till they
had either paid the fum he exacted, or given him
fecurity for it.

After the confuls had endeavoured to fatisfy
the bafhaw in the beft manner they were able, they
at laft did not receive the letters till the day after
the emperor's departure from Tangier, when they
were brought to them by the bafhaw's fecretary,
and another of his attendants, who not only demanded a prefent for themfelves, but alfo obliged
them to pay an exorbitant price for the feal on
each paper, which the bafhaw pretended he had
paid to the keeper of the feals.

The emperor arrived on the 10th of May at
Mequinez, whence, after fome little ftay, he went
to Fez, and there kept the feaft of the Ramadam.
About this period, in confequence of the emperor's
not having appeared in public for feveral days, a
falfe report was circulated, that he had been killed

by

by his brother Muley Haffem, who had juft before arrived at Fez from Morocco.

Having conducted the emperor to Mequinez, it will be only neceffary to take a fhort general view of his fubfequent conduct, during the fhort time that elapfed between his acceffion to the throne, and arrival at that city; and thence go on to thofe circumftances which led to the caufe of his death. After the caprice, pufillanimity, and avarice which had diftinguifhed the reign of his predeceffor, Muley Yazid appeared to poffefs many qualities well calculated to render him a very popular prince in the eyes of the Moors. To a tall, elegant, and majeftic perfon, were united a handfome and expreffive countenance, which, with a fpecious and perfuafive addrefs, a generous and difintcrefted but determined conduct, a great activity of body, and an uncommon agility in horfemanfhip, were requifites which were certain of impreffing on the minds of his fubjects a very favourable opinion of their new fovereign; and it is certain that Muley Yazid fuccecded to the throne by the voluntary choice of the majority of the people. Happy it had been, if he had poffeffed fufficient virtue or policy to have preferved this good opinion which they had formed; but his ungovernable propenfity to cruelty and drunkennefs, which he had artfully concealed in his minority, he had not refolution fufficient to command when he fuccceded to the throne; and in the whole hiftory of Morocco, we do not meet with a tyrant who exercifed greater barbarities than this monfter was guilty of.

His

His firſt ſtep after leaving the ſanctuary, was to repair to Tetuan, where he immediately ordered a general plunder of the Jews to be put in execution by his black troops, in conſequence of an inſult he had received from that people upon a former occaſion. In purſuance of this edict, their houſes were inſtantly ranſacked, the furniture which could not be carried off, was deſtroyed and thrown into the ſtreets, ſome of the owners were put to death, and others were ſeverely beaten; and the perſons of the wives and daughters violated by the outrageous ſoldiery, who indiſcriminately ſtripped them even of their clothes, and turned them naked into the ſtreets. It is not poſſible to paint in juſt colours, the diſtreſs and hardſhip that unfortunate race experienced for ſeveral days, till a concluſion was put to their perſecutions by an order from the emperor, who, in conſequence of a pardon to the Jews, threatened death to every perſon who ſhould in any degree further moleſt them.

There were two perſons of this nation, of ſome conſequence, whom Muley Yazid marked out as particular objects of his revenge. The firſt was a Jew, who, in the character of Spaniſh vice conſul, had committed ſome act during the reign of Sidi Mahomet, which the new emperor conſid red as having been inimical to his intereſts. For this real or imaginary crime, the culprit was ſuſpended by a cord paſſed through the tendons of the lower part of the legs, with his head downwards; in which ſituation, without any ſuſtenance, he continued alive for near four days, when the emperor ordered his head to be taken off, by way of relieving

lieving him from his misery. The other person was Jacob Attal, who in a former part of the work has already been noticed as the favourite of Sidi Mahomet. There is great reason to believe that this young man, who possessed considerable abilities, was accessary to his own unhappy fate, by his too busy interference in politics, which occasioned him many enemies at court, who were now glad of seizing the oportunity of gratifying their revenge, by persuading the emperor that he was one of those who, in the court of Sidi Mahomet, had been particularly inimical to him. Attal conscious of his danger, put himself under the protection of the English consul, with an intention of accompanying that gentleman to Tetuan, in hopes that a considerable present of money, might induce the emperor to treat him with some lenity. Unfortunately, before this plan could be put in execution, an order for seizing Attal met the party on the road, upon which the unfortunate Jew was forced off his mule, stripped of his dress, and in an old Moorish frock, and with a cord about his neck, was driven on foot with whips to Tetuan. Upon his arrival, he was immediately conducted to the emperor, who ordered both his hands to be cut off, in which state he continued three days in the greatest misery, and then he was decapitated.

These are by no means the only instances of cruelty that were exercised upon the Jews. Those of most of the towns of the empire, were either plundered or obliged to pay the emperor a very heavy fine; and at Mequinez, and some other places, several were put to cruel deaths; and
their

their wives and daughter left to the mercy of the black troops, who treated them with the greateſt indecencies.

A third objeċt of the emperor's perſonal revenge was Alcaide Abbas, his father's black general: with reſpeċt to this officer, the emperor had two motives for puniſhing him. In the firſt place, he was the commander of that very army which was intended for his own deſtruċtion; and, in the ſecond, upon his father's deceaſe, inſtead of ſurrendering the army to Muley Yazid, he withdrew it to the Southward, and, it was ſuppoſed with an intention of ſupporting Muley Slemma.

Notwithſtanding, however, this conduċt on the part of Abbas, the emperor certainly would not have put him to death, had it not been at the particular requeſt of his black army, whom at that time he did not wiſh to offend. Abbas, fully conſcious how much he was diſliked by his troops, attempted to make his eſcape to a ſanċtuary upon a very ſwift horſe; but his horſe falling he was unluckily ſeized, and immediately carried before the emperor, with very heavy charges on the part of his ſoldiers. After a hearing of the charges, the emperor ſignified to the culprit that he might yet partake of his royal mercy, provided he would confine himſelf for two months to the ſanċtuary of Muley Abſulem. For this purpoſe he ſet off; but he was again ſeized by the ſoldiers, who brought him back to the emperor with ſtill heavier charges; and the emperor, finding that the ſoliers were determined on his deſtruċtion, with his own hands, by one blow of his ſabre, divided his head in two, and he immediately expired.

Abbas

Abbas was the beſt officer in the emperor's ſervice, and never manifeſted the ſlighteſt token of timidity, or condeſcended to aſk his life; on the contrary, when the emperor lifted up his ſabre, he in a ſtern and undaunted manner looked his ſovereign in the face, and died with the countenance and the tranquility of a hero. As his body had not received the emperor's pardon, it remained on the ground unburied, to the great nuiſance of every perſon who paſſed that way. For ſuch is the barbarous cuſtom of the country, that when a man is put to death by the emperor, or his order, his body cannot be buried without its firſt receiving a formal pardon from the emperor.

Muley Yazid, long before his father's death, had threatened the life of the Effendi. He had been a principal agent in exciting the father's hatred and prejudice againſt his ſon. A further cauſe of the emperor's reſentment, was the great impoſition practiſed on his father by the Effendi reſpecting the corn buſineſs with the Spaniards, by which he had amaſſed a very conſiderable ſum of money in bribes and preſents.

Upon the emperor's death, the Effendi took refuge in a ſanctuary, and, had he been wiſe, he would not have ventured abroad; but Muley Yazid having poſitively promiſed to pardon him, he was induced to forſake his aſylum. For ſome time the new ſovereign diſſembled his intentions, and waited for a favourable oportunity to ſeize him. As ſoon as he was taken, he offered the emperor two hundred thouſand dollars to ſpare his life; but the monarch haughtily replied, that he wanted not his money, and that he would not condeſcend to accept a bribe from a traitor. He then ordered his two hands to be cut off, in which state he suffered him to remain for some days, and then commanded him to be beheaded. One of his hands was placed on the walls of Fez, and the other sent down to Tangier, and ordered to be nailed on the door of the Spanish conful, to convince that nation in what manner the emperor was difpofed to treat all the friends of the Spaniards.

The emperor always, indeed, manifefted an exclufive preference to the Englifh beyond all European nations, and on many other occafions, evinced an inveterate diflike to the Spaniards. From the moment of his acceffion to the throne, he expreffed a difapprobation of the Spanifh meafures, during his father's reign; and threatened to revenge himfelf very fhortly on that country. The Spaniards, who have more reafon to wifh for peace, from their ports being fo contiguous to the emperor's, as well as from the immenfe fupplies which they procure from his dominions, than any other nation, endeavoured to ward off the threatening ftorm, by very large and repeated prefents of money, and other valuable articles, to the emperor and his minifters. But this plan, which had been fo fuccefsful in the former reign, effected nothing in the prefent. Muley Yazid had, from his youth, been difregardful of money; and, indeed, in his contempt of wealth, had even exceeded the boundaries of prudence; he had alfo conceived a very ftrong and very early predilection in favour of the Englifh. Notwithftanding thefe circumftances, the Spaniards ftill continued to en-

Q

tertain

tertain hopes of fuccefs in their negociations, till they heard of the death of the Effendi, their great friend and patron, and of the infult offered to their court, by the Effendi's hand being nailed on their conful's door. Such an affront was fufficient to convince them, that war was inevitable; but they efteemed it moft prudent to get their conful, and friars, out of the country, before they commenced hoftilities; and a frigate for this purpofe was difpatched to Tangier. When they arrived there, they informed the governor, that they had on board a very valuable prefent for the emperor, and defired that he would fend proper perfons to receive it. The conful and friars took this opportunity of coming on board; and the frigate, having fent off the Moors with the prefent, fet fail, and the next day captured two Moorifh gallies off Larache, in fight of the emperor, who was walking upon his terrace at the very moment. The valuable prefent which they carried, proved nothing more than huge bales of rags.

Thefe repeated infults were not calculated to conciliate the emperor; he confequently made immediate preparations for the attack on Ceuta, and foon after befieged it. But this garrifon proved too ftrongly fortified, both by nature and art, to render it poffible for the Moors to be fuccefsful, unlefs affifted by a naval power; and the emperor, after a fruitlefs fiege for feveral months with a very confiderable army, was obliged to retire. The infults offered by the Spaniards in the deception they employed to procure the releafe of their conful and friars, and afterwads in the capture of the two Moorifh veffels, made fuch an impreffion

I

on the emperor, that he threatened to put the town of Tangier to the fword, for fo flagrant a piece of neglect.   In their juftification, the people informed their fovereign, that the error muft be imputed to the governor, who alone was refponfible for every circumftance which happened within his diftrict. This officer, who at the rifk of his life had fupported Muley Yazid in his minority with money, and afterwards placed him on the throne, for which the emperor took a folemn oath that he would never do him or his family the fmalleft injury, was now thrown into irons, and immediately ordered into the royal prefence.   The unfortunate man, forefeeing his fate, requefted the emperor would do juftice to God and Mahomet; to which he replied, "I mean to do juftice to my country by punifhing a traitor;" and he immediately difpatched him with a mufquet.

The numberlefs cruelties which were perpetrated by Muley Yazid, I have not fufficient authentic information to authorife me to detail, nor am I fufficiently informed of the actual circumftances of his reign, to be able to offer to the public a perfect narrative of it. Thus far I can venture to affert with truth, that he in a fhort time devoted himfelf entirely to the drinking of ftrong *liquors*, which for the greateft part of the day rendered him unfit for bufinefs, and excited him to the moft favage cruelties; and, what was moft diftreffing, where they were the leaft deferved; with fome he amufed himfelf by galloping up with great violence and fpearing them, others were buried alive, while a third party were cut to pieces with fwords.

Q 2

It

It is almoft unneceffary to add, that the neglect of public bufinefs, and the total infecurity of their perfons from the tyranny of the monarch, deftroyed in time intirely the confidence which the people had at firft placed in their fovereign, and encouraged Muley Hafem, towards the latter part of the year 1791, to put himfelf at the head of an army in oppofition to his brother. This prince, who poffeffed moft of the bad, without any of the good qualities of the emperor, and who commanded againft him during the life of Sidi Mahomet, was further induced to this meafure in confequence of a fupply of ftores, and confiderable fums of money, which he received from the Spaniards, who had great reafon to wifh a change of government. The emperor, who ftill had many friends, foon collected a confiderable army, with which he marched to the Southward to diflodge his brother, who had taken poffeffion of the city of Morocco and its vicinity. Muley Hafem, upon this occafion, difcovered his ufual pufillanimity, by refigning his command to one of his generals; who, however, was an active and enterprizing officer. When the two armies met, a dreadful engagement enfued. The emperor difcovered an uncommon fhare of perfonal courage, intermixing with the enemy and fighting like a private foldier. After a fevere conflict, he totally routed the enemy and took poffeffion of Morocco; but not before he had received feveral wounds, which in a few days proved mortal. During the fhort period of life which remained to him, his whole attention was occupied in punifhing the people of Morocco for their attachment

ment to his brother. Between two and three thoufand of the inhabitants, without regard to age or fex, were maffacred in cold blood; while fome of them he ordered to be nailed alive to the walls, he tore out the eyes of others with his own fpurs, and, in his dying moments, paffed an edict that fixty people of Mogodore, among whom were moft of the European merchants, fhould be decapitated for the affiftance which he fuppofed they had afforded to his brother. Fortunately for them, he died foon after iffuing the order, and it was not forwarded.

Muley Yazid, who only reigned two years, and at his death was in the forty-third year of his age, was poffeffed of many qualities, which, if they had been properly improved, would have rendered him a very ufeful monarch in a country where the fovereign poffeffes fo much influence over his fubjects; naturally quick of apprehenfion, determined in his conduct, and not eafily biaffed by the perfuafion of others, poffeffing a great fhare of perfonal courage, and a total contempt of wealth; had thefe endowments of nature been meliorated by an enlightened education, they might have enabled him to have accomplifhed fome reformation in his fubjects, and perhaps led the way to fome further impovement. Unfortunately this prince too eafily gave way to the dictate of his paffions, which foon totally incapacitated him from carrying on even the common bufinefs of government; and rendered him as great a monfter as ever filled the throne of Morocco.

Since

Since the death of Muley Yazid, the country has been in a very unfettled ftate; the people being now rendered extremely cautious how they elect another monarch. To the Southward of Sallee, Muley Hafem, from poffeffing the army, is obeyed as the fovereign; while on the Northern fide of the empire, Muley Solyman, who from his exemplary conduct has gained the efteem of the people, is confidered as emperor. It now refts for time to determine which is to be the fuccefsful candidate.

FINIS.